A Practical Guide to Avoiding Japanglish

WHEN ENGLISH
—— ISN'T ——
ENGLISH

Japanglish を避けるための実用ガイド

LAUREN GREEN IMAI

Translations by Tamaki Tiballi

英語なのに英語じゃない

LAUREN'S LANGUAGE LESSONS

Library of Congress Number: 2025916000

First paperback edition August 2025

ISBN 979-8-9899078-7-8 (Paperback)
ISBN 979-8-9899078-9-2 (Hardcover)
ISBN 979-8-9996509-1-7 (eBook)

Lauren's Language Lessons, LLC
Houston, Texas, USA
www.LaurensLanguageLessons.com

TABLE OF CONTENTS

24 WORK, OFFICE, JOBS

INTRODUCTION: WHY I WROTE THIS BOOK
はじめに──本書を執筆したわけ

One of my earliest students from Japan once told me that Japanese people love Kentucky at Christmas. For months, I thought that visiting the state of Kentucky at Christmas time was popular for Japanese expats and tourists. Still, I was baffled. I didn't know Kentucky was so popular in Japan; many Americans haven't even been there. Maybe there was a special Christmas exhibit that had become famous among Japanese tourists. "Have many Japanese people visited there?" I eventually asked, curious. "Oh yes, many people eat Kentucky every Christmas," she answered. Obviously Kentucky did not mean the same thing to Japanese people as it did to me. Something had been lost in translation.

　私が教師として最初に教えた日本人の生徒の一人が、「日本人はクリスマスのケンタッキーが大好きなんです」と言っていました。私は何か月も、クリスマスにケンタッキー州を訪れることが、日本人駐在員や観光客の間で人気があるのだろうと思っていました。しかし、どうにも不思議でなりませんでした。ケンタッキー州が日本でそんなに人気があるとは知りませんでした。なぜかというと、アメリカ人でも多くの人は行ったことすらないのですから。もしかしたら、日本人観光客の間で有名になった特別なクリスマス展があったのかもしれないと思いました。私は、「たくさん日本人はそこを訪れたことがあるの？」と興味津々で尋ねました。「そうそう。毎年クリスマスには、ケンタッキーを食べるんですよ」と彼女は答えました。明らかに、日本人が言う"ケンタッキー"は、私が思っていたものとは意味が異なっていたのです。翻訳の過程で何かが失われていたのでした。まさに、言葉が、文化の背景とともにすれ違った瞬間でした。

During my early years of teaching English to Japanese students, I noticed that students would often say English words that didn't fit into the context of our conversation and didn't make sense. "I don't want earrings; I want pierce." I'd feel confused and try to ask clarifying questions to understand their meanings. "You want pierced ears but you don't want to wear earrings? I don't understand." Students would feel frustrated, wondering why I didn't understand the English they were speaking, but in reality, they were speaking Japanglish.

　日本人の生徒に英語を教え始めた初期の頃から、私は、生徒の皆さんが、しばしば会話の文脈に合わない、意味のわからない英単語で話すのに気づきました。「イヤリングじゃなくてピアスが欲しいです」。私は困惑し、その意味を理解するために確認の質問をしました。「ピアスが欲しいのにイヤリングはつけたくないの？ちょっとよく分からないわ」。生徒さんたちは、なぜ先生は私たちが話す英語を理解できないのだろうとフラストレーションを感じたと思

いますが、実は生徒さんたちが話していたのは「ジャパングリッシュ」だったのです。

Japanglish, as you may already know, includes many borrowed words (gairaigo) with similar meanings and sometimes just slightly different pronunciations (*cake*). However, Japanglish also includes hundreds of Japanese-made English (wasei eigo) with completely different meanings than their English counterparts. Sometimes, there are even words that are neither Japanese nor English and come from an entirely different language (*Pierrot*). There are many others that are technically English but in practicality don't exist at all (*food fighter*) while others are creative abbreviations of English words that are unrecognizable outside of Japan (*appo*).

　ジャパングリッシュには、似たような意味を持ち、時には発音が少し違うだけの借用語（外来語）がたくさん含まれていることは、皆さんもすでにご存知だと思います。（例えば、cakeなどがそれに該当します）。しかし、ジャパングリッシュには、英語とは全く異なる意味を持つ数百に及ぶ和製英語も含まれています。時には、日本語でも英語でもない、全く別の言語から入ってきた言葉さえあります。（例えば、ピエロはフランス語が語源です）。また、厳密には英語ですが、実際には英語圏には全く存在しない言葉（例えば、フードファイター）や、日本で作られ、日本国外では認識されない略語（例えば、アポイントメントの略のアポ）もあります。

In many ways, Japanglish reflects the special history that Japan has shared with the English-speaking world and serves as a fascinating and evolving example of the ever-changing world of language and our ever-growing global connectedness. However, outside of Japanese communities themselves, the Japanese version of English gets lost in translation, and misunderstandings abound.

　多くの点で、ジャパングリッシュは、日本が英語圏の世界と共有してきた特別な歴史を反映しています。そして、常に変化し続ける言語の世界と私たちの拡大し続ける世界的なつながりを示す興味深い事例となっています。しかし、日本語独自の英語表現は、日本人コミュニティ以外では翻訳の際に意味が正しく伝わりづらく、誤解を招きやすくなります。

The purpose of this book is to serve as a guide for Japanese people learning English and to help avoid some of the miscommunications that are often encountered from using certain Japanglish words that don't mean the same thing in English.

　本書の目的は、英語を学ぶ日本人のための手引書で、また、英語と異なる意味をもつジャパングリッシュの単語によって生じがちな誤解を避ける助けとなることです。

In this book, you will learn what many Japanglish words actually mean to native English speakers and what you should say instead in order to be properly understood. You will also find a few words that aren't true Japanglish but are common confusing mistakes that Japanese speakers often make when speaking English. My hope is that this book will help you speak English more like a native speaker and avoid some of the miscommunications and frustrations I've seen some of my students experience when speaking English!

本書では、多くのジャパングリッシュの単語が、英語ネイティブスピーカーにとって実際にどのように理解されるのかを解説し、伝わる英語に言い換える方法をご紹介しています。そして正しく伝えるためには、代わりに何と言うべきなのかを学ぶことができます。また、厳密にはジャパングリッシュではないものの、日本人が英語を話す際に誤解されやすい表現や、混乱を招きやすい言葉についてもいくつか取り上げています。

本書が、英語を学ぶ皆さまにとって、より自然なコミュニケーションの手助けとなり、ネイティブスピーカーのように英語を話し、かつて私の生徒さんたちが経験したような誤解や戸惑いを減らす一助となることを願っています。

If you would like to introduce your English-speaking friends to Japanglish, please check out *Hang with Japanglish: Understanding Wasei-eigo and other Japanese-made English*. It's made for foreigners who are interested in Japan, Japanese, Japanglish, and Japanese culture!

また、英語話者の友人にジャパングリッシュを紹介されたい場合は、姉妹書である『Hang with Japanglish: Understanding Wasei-eigo and other Japanese-made English』もぜひお読みいただければ幸いです。これは、英語圏読者向けに、日本や日本語、ジャパングリッシュ、そして日本文化への理解を深める内容になっています。

Special Note:

注意事項:

Language is constantly changing! Even in the years of writing and putting together this book, new Japanglish words have been adopted; older Japanglish words have become outdated; and some previously obscure words have become mainstream and commonly used even in English circles.

言葉は絶えず変化しています！本書を執筆・編集している数年の間にも、新しいジャパングリッシュが生まれたり、古いジャパングリッシュが使われなくなったり、以前はあまり知られていなかった単語が主流になり、英語圏で普通に使われるようになった単語もあります。

It's also important to keep in mind that English itself is extremely diverse. This book focuses on American English and does its best to include British English. It does not address the differences that may be found between Japanglish and other varieties of English. Differences between American English and British English are well-known, but even within just the United States, there can be regional differences in certain word choices as well as differences based on one's age, generation, socioeconomics, life experiences, subculture, ethnic background, field of work, and much more.

　また、英語そのものが極めて多様であることを念頭に置いていただくことも重要な視点です。本書は主にアメリカ英語に焦点を当て構成しています。イギリス英語についても可能な限り取り上げています。しかし、ジャパングリッシュと他の英語圏の表現の違いについては、本書では詳しくは扱っておりません。アメリカ英語とイギリス英語の違いはよく知られていますが、アメリカ国内だけをとっても、地域による単語の選び方の違いや、年齢層、世代、社会的背景、人生経験、サブカルチャー、民族的アイデンティティ、専門分野などによる違いがでてきます。

For example, people in the UK tend to say "trainers" while people in the South and West of the United States are more likely to say "tennis shoes" while those in the Northeastern United States are more likely to say "sneakers." Similarly, those under the age of 25 are more likely to use the newly abbreviated term "sus" to describe someone or something "suspicious."

　例えば、イギリスで「トレーナー」と言う言葉が一般的に使われますが、アメリカ南部や西部では「テニスシューズ」、アメリカ北東部では「スニーカー」と言われる傾向があります。最近では、25歳以下の若い世代が"sus"という略語を、「怪しい」という意味で使う傾向も見受けられるようになっています。

For some terms, there are far too many meanings and nuances to include every single use case. Since this book is not meant to serve as a complete dictionary, I have just included the most common, useful, or relevant information. With those caveats, I have done my best to make this book as extensive as possible, knowing that because of the diversity of English and the ever-changing nature of language, it will never be completely possible for it to be truly all-inclusive.

　このように、単語によっては、非常に多くの意味や用法が存在するため、すべてのケースを網羅することはできません。本書は辞書ではなく、英語を学ぶ方々にとって、最も一般的で役立ち、重要と思われるものを厳選して掲載しています。そうした点を踏まえ、可能な限り幅広い情報を盛り込むように努めましたが、英語のもつ多様性や言語が常に変化していくという特性を踏まえたうえで、完全に包括することは難しいことをご理解いただけますと幸いです。

NOTE ABOUT QR CODES: Scan the QR code located on each chapter title page to hear audio for English pronunciation of the words included in each chapter! For a continuous playlist of all chapters and words included in this book, scan this QR code →

QRコードについてのご案内: 各章のタイトルページに掲載されているQRコードをスキャンしていただくと、その章で登場する英単語の発音を音声でお聞きいただけます。また、本書に登場するすべての単語を連続で音声再生できるプレイリストもご用意しております。こちらのQRコードからご視聴いただけます。

ACADEMICS, SCHOOL, EDUCATION

1

学問・学校・教育

ANKET (ENQUETE)

アンケート

Meaning in English:
英語の意味:

Doesn't exist
英語には該当する単語がない

Say Instead:
適切な英語表現:

Survey, Questionnaire

Example Sentences:
例文:

> The survey researcher came up and asked me, "If you have an extra five minutes, we'd love your help with our _anket_ about cultural differences!"

> The survey researcher came up and said, "If you have five extra minutes, we'd love your help with our **_questionnaire_** about cultural differences!"

街頭アンケート調査の人が私に「もし5分ほどお時間があれば、文化の違いについてのアンケートにご協力いただけると嬉しいです」と声をかけてきた。

BROKEN ENGLISH

ブロークンイングリッシュ

Meaning in English:
英語の意味:

Non-fluent, low-level, grammatically incorrect English
流暢ではない、低レベルの、文法的に正しくない英語

Say Instead:
適切な英語表現:

Conversational English, Casual English, Informal English

Example Sentences:
例文:

I like speaking _broken English_ more than business English.

I like speaking _**conversational/ informal English**_ more than professional business English.

私は、ビジネス英語よりもブロークンイングリッシュの方が好きだ。

This sounds like you enjoy speaking non-fluent English that people can't understand very well!
これは、人があまり理解できないようなたどたどしい英語を話すのを楽しんでいるように聞こえる。

How English Speakers use "broken English":
英語話者は (broken English) をどのように使うか:

S Sarah

I have the cutest little boy in my 1st grade class this year. He speaks **broken English** because he just recently moved here, and today he brought me an apple and said, "Teacher, is apple for you from family."

Aw that's so sweet!

B Benji

I want to introduce you to my friend. She speaks **broken English**, but you can understand her. She's really smart and I think you two have a lot in common and will get along really well!

Ok, is she the one who works at the hospital?

CENTI

セ
ン
チ

Meaning in English:
英語の意味:

Doesn't exist
英語には該当する単語がない

Say Instead:
適切な英語表現:

Centimeter

Example Sentences:
例文:

| My little snake plant is now 10 _centi_! | | My little snake plant is now 10 **_centimeters_**! |

小さなサンセベリアが、今は、10センチになった！

COURSE

コース

Meaning in English:
英語の意味:

1. A class
授業、講座、課程

2. Part of a meal (e.g., main course, 1st course, 2nd course)
食事の一部（例：メインコース、第1コース、第2コースなど）

3. An area for a sporting activity in a few specific sports
(e.g., racecourse, golf course)
特定のスポーツで使用される競技場やコース
（例：競馬場、ゴルフコース）

Say Instead:
適切な英語表現:

Trail, Hiking trail

Example Sentences:
例文:

The national park has a lot of great _courses_.

→ The national park has a lot of great **_hiking trails_**.

その国立公園には、素晴らしいコースがたくさんある。

This sentence sounds like the national park either offers many great classes or maybe has many great obstacle courses or ropes courses. With added context, many people could probably guess that you mean trails, but this sentence would be extremely confusing and unclear.

これは、国立公園が多くの素晴らしい講座を提供しているか、あるいは多くの優れた障害物コースやロープコースがあるように伝わる。文脈によっては、ほとんどの人があなたの意図する『遊歩道やハイキングコースなどのトレイル』を指していると推測できるだろうが、この文章だけでは非常に紛らわしくて、分かりにくい。

DEMERIT

デ
メ
リ
ッ
ト

Meaning in English:
英語の意味:

Usually a *demerit* is some kind of mark or point against someone for an infraction. This is part of a system where a certain number of *demerits* equals a consequence. For example, a school might issue a *demerit* to a student who arrives late to class. After a student has five *demerits*, he might receive a punishment like detention (staying extra time after school) or be required to eat lunch alone (rather than with friends).

通常、違反に対して与えられる警告や減点などの印(ポイント)のことを指す。この制度では、一定のデメリット(減点)が累積すると、罰則が適用される。例:学校では、授業に遅刻した生徒にデメリットを与えることがある。生徒が5つのデメリットを受けると、罰として放課後に居残りを命じられたり、友人とではなく一人で昼食をとるよう指示される場合がある。

Say Instead:
適切な英語表現:

Disadvantage, Con, Negative (point)

Example Sentences:
例文:

One <u>*demerit*</u> of living in Texas is that there aren't many public transportation options.

One <u>*con*</u> of living in Texas is that there aren't many public transportation options.

テキサスに住むデメリットの一つは、
公共交通機関が少ないことだ。

Gym

ジム

Meaning in English:
英語の意味:

1. Gymnasium
   体育館
2. Place to exercise
   ジム

Say Instead:
適切な英語表現:

Gym

Example Sentences:
例文:

Schools in Japan don't have a *gym* ジム with machines to work out, only a *gymnasium* 体育館 for basketball games.

→

Schools in Japan don't have a *gym* with machines to work out, only a *gym* for basketball.

日本の学校には、トレーニング機器があるジムはなく、
バスケットなどをする体育館しかない。

How English Speakers use "gym":
英語話者は(gym)をどのように使うか:

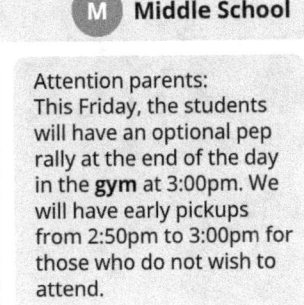

M Middle School

Attention parents:
This Friday, the students will have an optional pep rally at the end of the day in the **gym** at 3:00pm. We will have early pickups from 2:50pm to 3:00pm for those who do not wish to attend.

D Dani

What time do you want to meet up for dinner?

How about 7? I'd like to go to the **gym** after work first.

HALF

ハーフ

Meaning in English:
英語の意味:

1/2
半分

Say Instead:
適切な英語表現:

Biracial, Multi-racial,
Multi-ethnic, Mixed race,
Half [Japanese], 1/4 [Japanese],
Part [Japanese]

Example Sentences:
例文:

He's _half_. His mom is Irish,
and his dad is 1/2 Japanese
and 1/2 Malaysian.

He's _Irish, Japanese, and
Malaysian_. He's half Irish, 1/4
Japanese, and 1/4 Malaysian.

彼はハーフだ。母親はアイルランド人で、
父親は日本人とマレーシア人のハーフだ。

How English Speakers use "half":
英語話者は(half)をどのように使うか:

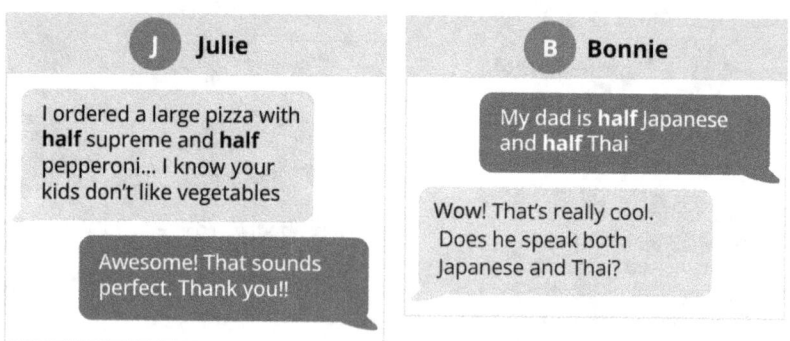

Julie

I ordered a large pizza with **half** supreme and **half** pepperoni... I know your kids don't like vegetables

Awesome! That sounds perfect. Thank you!!

Bonnie

My dad is **half** Japanese and **half** Thai

Wow! That's really cool. Does he speak both Japanese and Thai?

Meaning in English:
英語の意味:

A title or subtitle at the top of a page, document, or presentation

見出し、ページ、文書、プレゼンテーションの上部にあるタイトルまたはサブタイトル

ヘディング

Say Instead:
適切な英語表現:

Header

Example Sentences:
例文:

She scored the last goal in the soccer game with a _heading_.

She scored the last goal in the soccer game with a **_header_**.

サッカーの試合で、彼女はヘディングで最後のゴールを決めた。

MERIT

メ
リ
ッ
ト

Meaning in English:
英語の意味:

1. Deserving of praise or reward
☞ Example: Bonuses will be given out based on *merit*; the employees who did the best work will receive the biggest bonuses.
☞ Example: Is success in life based only on *merit* and hard work; or does luck also play a role?

称賛や報酬に値すること
例:ボーナスは能力や成果に基づいて支給される。
最も良い仕事をした従業員が最高のボーナスを受け取る。
例:人生の成功は能力と努力だけに左右されるのか、
それとも運も関係するのか?

2. A good quality
☞ Example: I'd like to discuss the *merits* of the new policy.

優れた点・良い品質
例:新しい方針のメリットについて議論したい。

Say Instead:
適切な英語表現:

Advantage, Pro

Example Sentences:
例文:

| It's important to consider the *merits* and demerits of all the options before making our final decision. | | It's important to consider the **pros** and cons of all the options before making our final decision. |

最終決定をする前に、すべての選択肢のメリットとデメリットを
考慮することが重要だ。

MINUS

マイナス

Meaning in English:
英語の意味：

1. Subtract (e.g, 5-1=4)
引く（減算する）
2. Con/negative
短所、欠点、マイナス面

$3-1 = 2$

$4-2 =$

$2-1 =$

Say Instead:
適切な英語表現：

Disadvantage, Con, Negative (point)

Example Sentences:
例文：

One _minus_ of living in Texas is that there aren't many public transportation options.

One **_disadvantage_** of living in Texas is that there aren't many public transportation options.

テキサスでの生活には、
公共交通の不便さといったマイナス面も存在する。

How English Speakers use "minus":
英語話者は（minus）をどのように使うか：

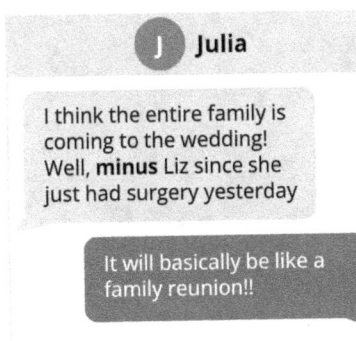

J Julia

I think the entire family is coming to the wedding! Well, **minus** Liz since she just had surgery yesterday

It will basically be like a family reunion!!

R Rachel

How are you both doing with the new baby?

We are great! Everything is going really well so far **minus** the lack of sleep!

NATIVE

ネイティブ

Meaning in English:
英語の意味:

1. Related to where someone or something is originally from
☞ Example: He's a *native* Californian, born and raised there.
☞ Example: Cherry-blossoms are *native* to Japan.
人や物がもともと属している場所に関連する
例:彼は生まれも育ちもカリフォルニアで生粋のカリフォルニア人だ。
例:桜は日本原産の植物だ。

2. Indigenous; the first people to live/settle in an area
☞ Example: The *native* inhabitants of the island have their own unique customs.
先住民:ある地域に最初に住んだ／定住した人々
例:その島の先住民は独自の風習を持っている。

Say Instead:
適切な英語表現:

Native [language] speaker

Example Sentences:
例文:

I want to learn English from her; she's a _native_! I want to learn English from her; she's ***a native speaker*** / English is ***her first language***!

彼女から英語を習いたい。ネイティブだからね!

NIGHTER

ナイター

Meaning in English:
英語の意味:

Doesn't exist, but an *all-nighter* means staying up all night
英語には、「ナイター」に相当する単語はないが、"all-nighter"は、
一晩中起きていること、つまり徹夜をすることを意味する

Say Instead:
適切な英語表現:

Night game, Game at night

Example Sentences:
例文:

I can't meet you for dinner today because our team has a _nighter_.

I can't meet you for dinner today because our baseball team has a **_night game_**.

今日は、チームのナイター試合があるから、
夕食を一緒にできない。

How English Speakers use "all-nighter":
英語話者は(all-nighter)をどのように使うか:

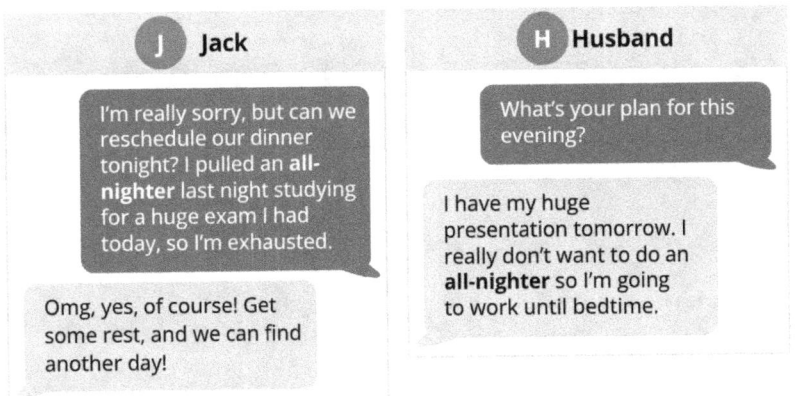

Jack

I'm really sorry, but can we reschedule our dinner tonight? I pulled an **all-nighter** last night studying for a huge exam I had today, so I'm exhausted.

Omg, yes, of course! Get some rest, and we can find another day!

Husband

What's your plan for this evening?

I have my huge presentation tomorrow. I really don't want to do an **all-nighter** so I'm going to work until bedtime.

ZEMI

ゼミ

Meaning in English:
英語の意味:

Doesn't exist

英語には該当する単語がない

Say Instead:
適切な英語表現:

Seminar

Example Sentences:
例文:

I belong Dr. Sakamoto's *zemi*. I'm part of Dr. Sakamoto's ***seminar***.

私は、坂本先生のゼミに所属している。

ACCESSORIES

2

アクセサリー

Scan for Audio

ACCESSORY

アクセサリー

Meaning in English:
英語の意味:

1. Any additional items to pair with your outfit, clothing, or attire (including but not limited to jewelry, scarves, belts, bags, etc.)

服装や衣装と合わせるための追加のアイテム（ジュエリーを含むがそれだけに限らない：スカーフ、ベルト、バッグなど）

2. Accessories for smartphones, computers, and other machines (earphones, covers, keyboards, mice, power banks, etc.)

スマホやパソコンなどの機械類の付属品（イヤホン、カバー、キーボード、マウス、モバイルバッテリーなど）

Say Instead:
適切な英語表現:

Jewelry

Example Sentences:
例文:

All of these *accessories* are handmade.

All of this *jewelry* is handmade.

このアクセサリーは全部手づくりだ。

This sentence sounds really unclear. The handmade accessories could include anything from jewelry, bags, hair clips, clothing items like belts or scarves, phone accessories, and more!

この文は非常に分かりにくく感じられる。ハンドメイドのアクセサリーには、ジュエリー、バッグ、ヘアクリップ、ベルトやスカーフなどの衣類、スマホ関連の小物など、実に多種多様なアイテムが含まれる。

Bag

Meaning in English:
英語の意味:

Bag is a general word for something you carry that includes everything from a disposable plastic or paper bag to a luxury brand purse and everything in between.

「Bag（バッグ）」とは、使い捨ての ビニール袋、紙袋から、高級ブラン ドのハンドバッグまで、あらゆる種 類の袋を含む一般的な語である。

Say Instead:
適切な英語表現:

Purse (US), Handbag (UK)

Example Sentences:
例文:

I don't like putting my groceries in a _bag_.

I don't like putting my groceries in a **_purse_**.

私は買った食料品をバッグに入れるのが好きじゃない。

This sounds like you don't use any kind of bag at all. Maybe you just carry your groceries bagless in your hands!

まるで買い物袋を使わずに、全部手で持っているみたいに 聞こえる!

CHACK

チャック

Meaning in English:
英語の意味:

Doesn't exist
英語には該当する単語がない

Say Instead:
適切な英語表現:

Zipper (US), Zip (UK)

Example Sentences:
例文:

My _chack_ is broken. My _zipper_ is broken.

チャックが壊れた。

FASTENER

ファスナー

Meaning in English:
英語の意味:

A general word for something that joins two things together, usually non-permanently (e.g., a button, a clasp, a hook, a zipper)
一般的に、2つのものを一時的に接合するためのものを指す語（例：ボタン、留め具、フック、ジッパー）

Say Instead:
適切な英語表現:

Zipper (US), Zip (UK)

Example Sentences:
例文:

My _fastener_ is broken. My _zipper_ is broken.

ファスナーが壊れた。

DIA

ダイヤ

Meaning in English:
英語の意味:

Doesn't exist
英語には該当する単語がない

Say Instead:
適切な英語表現:

Diamond
Schedule, (Bus/train) timetable

Example Sentences:
例文:

He bought her a huge _dia_. He bought her a huge **_diamond_**.

彼は彼女に大きなダイヤを買った。

Let's look at the _dia_ to see when the next train to Osaka is. Let's look at the train **_schedule_** to see when the next train to Osaka is.

大阪行きの次の電車の時間を、ダイヤ（時刻表）で確認しよう。

Due to the _dia_ revision, the number of bus services has decreased, making the bus inconvenient. Due to the bus **_schedule_** / **_timetable_** revision, the number of buses throughout the day has decreased, making the bus an inconvenient option.

ダイヤ改正により、バスの運行本数が減ったので、不便だ。

EARRINGS

イヤリング

Meaning in English:
英語の意味:

Any kind of earrings including clip-on earrings and earrings for pierced ears
ピアス・イヤリング

Say Instead:
適切な英語表現:

Clip-on earrings

Example Sentences:
例文:

> These are pierce, but I need _earrings_.

> These are regular earrings, but I need **_clip-on earrings_**.

これは、ピアスだけど、イヤリングがいるのよ。

⚠ This sentence sounds like someone gave you earrings; however, your ears aren't pierced, so you can't wear them!
この文は、イヤリングをもらったものの、耳に穴が開いていないため身につけることができない、という状況を示しているようだ。

How English Speakers use "earrings":
英語話者は(earrings)をどのように使うか:

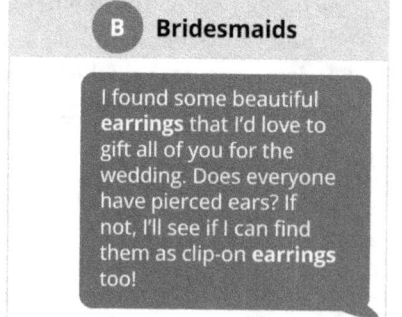

B Bridesmaids

I found some beautiful **earrings** that I'd love to gift all of you for the wedding. Does everyone have pierced ears? If not, I'll see if I can find them as clip-on **earrings** too!

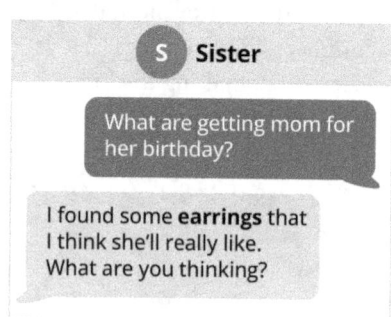

S Sister

What are getting mom for her birthday?

I found some **earrings** that I think she'll really like. What are you thinking?

GOM

Meaning in English:
英語の意味:

Doesn't exist
英語には該当する単語がない

Say Instead:
適切な英語表現:

Rubber (US), Natural rubber (UK); Rubber band (US), Elastic band (UK)

Example Sentences:
例文:

Southeast Asia has a lot of
gom trees. ➤ Southeast Asia has a lot of
rubber trees.

東南アジアにはゴムの木がたくさんある。

HAIR GOM

Meaning in English:
英語の意味:

Doesn't exist
英語には該当する単語がない

Say Instead:
適切な英語表現:

Hair band, Hair tie, Ponytail

Example Sentences:
例文:

My cat always steals my
hair gom from my
nightstand at night! ➤ My cat always steals my
hair band from my
nightstand at night!

私の猫は毎晩、
ナイトスタンド(ベッドのサイドテーブル)からヘアゴムを盗んでいく!

HAIR BAND

Meaning in English:
英語の意味:

Hair tie
ヘアゴム
(UK) Same as in Japanese
(英) ヘアバンド

Say Instead:
適切な英語表現:

Headband (US), Hairband (UK)

Example Sentences:
例文:

I want to buy that _hair band_. ➜ I want to buy that **_headband_**.

あのヘアーバンドを買いたい。

How English Speakers use "hair band":
英語話者は(**hair band**)をどのように使うか:

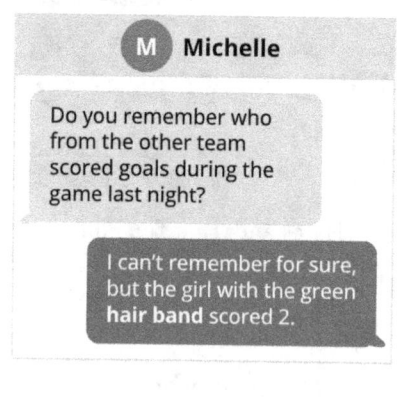

M Michelle

Do you remember who from the other team scored goals during the game last night?

I can't remember for sure, but the girl with the green **hair band** scored 2.

J Jessica

The cat has stolen my **hair band** from my dresser every night this week. I have no idea what she's doing with them or where she's taking them.

Hahaha! My cat does the same thing! So crazy!

HAIR PIN

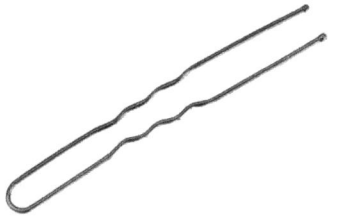

Meaning in English:
英語の意味:

A bobby pin for your hair or one specifically for hairstyling
髪を留めるためのヘアピン、またはヘアスタイリング専用のピン

Say Instead:
適切な英語表現:

Clip
Bobby pin
Barrette

Example Sentences:
例文:

Your _hair pin_ is so cool. Your **_hair clip_** is so cool.

あなたの ヘアピン 、すごく素敵だね。

How English Speakers use "hair pin":
英語話者は（hair pin）をどのように使うか:

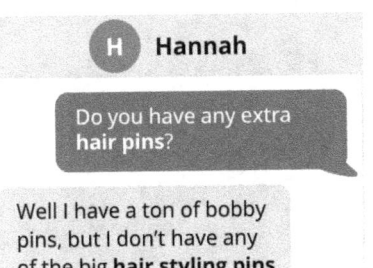

H **Hair Stylist**

I'll see you tomorrow at 10am! I'll bring everything we need, including extra **hair pins** for the updo

Thank you so much!

H **Hannah**

Do you have any extra **hair pins**?

Well I have a ton of bobby pins, but I don't have any of the big **hair styling pins**

39

JEWELRY

Meaning in English:
英語の意味:

Earrings, Rings, Necklaces, Bracelets, etc., of any kind including "*accessories*"
ピアス、指輪、ネックレス、ブレスレット
などを含むアクセサリー

Say Instead:
適切な英語表現:

Expensive jewelry, Diamond jewelry

Example Sentences:
例文:

> My husband never buys me <u>*jewelry*</u>, only accessories.

> My husband never buys me ***expensive diamond jewelry***, only fashion jewelry.

夫はジュエリーを買ってくれない。
アクセサリーしか買ってくれない。

How English Speakers use "jewelry":
英語話者は(jewelry)をどのように使うか:

> **H** Hair Stylist
>
> They have a lot of great **jewelry**! But it depends on your style... they have a lot of bohemian and beaded **jewelry** but not a lot of diamond **jewelry**
>
> Ok, I'd love to check it out!

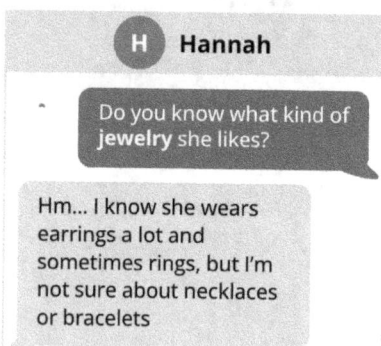

> **H** Hannah
>
> Do you know what kind of **jewelry** she likes?
>
> Hm... I know she wears earrings a lot and sometimes rings, but I'm not sure about necklaces or bracelets

NECKTIE PIN

ネクタイピン

Meaning in English:
英語の意味:

Doesn't exist
英語には該当する単語がない

Say Instead:
適切な英語表現:

Tie clip

Example Sentences:
例文:

My husband said he wanted a new *necktie pin* for his birthday.

My husband said he wanted a new *tie clip* for his birthday.

夫が誕生日に新しいネクタイピンが欲しいって言ってた。

PIERCE

ピアス

Meaning in English:
英語の意味:

To make a hole in something or go through it using a sharp object
鋭い先端や物を使って、何かに穴を開けたり、突き通したりすること

Say Instead:
適切な英語表現:

Earrings

Example Sentences:
例文:

I think I'll buy her some *pierce* for her birthday!

I think I'll buy her some *earrings* for her birthday!

彼女の誕生日にピアスを買おうと思っている!

PURSE

Meaning in English:
英語の意味:

(US) Handbag
(米) バッグ

(UK) Same as in Japanese
(英) パース

Say Instead:
適切な英語表現:

Wallet (US), Purse (UK)

Example Sentences:
例文:

I'm only going to bring my _purse_, not a bag.	I'm only going to bring my **_wallet_**, not a purse.

バッグじゃなくて、財布だけ持っていくつもり。

How English Speakers use "purse":
英語話者は(purse)をどのように使うか:

Olivia

Hey, I think I left my **purse** at your house. Do you mind checking if I left it in your kitchen... maybe near that green chair?

Yes! Do you want me to bring it to you later today?

Stephanie

I need to get a new **purse**. Mine is sooo dirty!

I read recently that leather or vinyl **purses** are cleaner than cloth and that people with kids have dirtier **purses** haha

YES! My kids are the reason my **purse** is dirty!

RIBBON

Meaning in English:
英語の意味:

A long, narrow strip of fabric or material that is used to tie or make a bow or used for decoration

細長い帯状の布や素材で、結んだり装飾に使ったりするもの

Say Instead:
適切な英語表現:

Bow, Hair bow
Bow tie

Example Sentences:
例文:

The pink _ribbon_ in the baby's hair is so cute. → The pink **_bow_** in the baby's hair is so cute.

赤ちゃんの髪につけたピンクのリボン、すごくかわいい。

The men looked sharp in their _ribbons_ at the wedding. → The men looked sharp in their **_bow ties_** at the wedding.

男性は、結婚式に蝶ネクタイでびしっと決めていた。

SHOE CREAM

シュークリーム

Meaning in English:
英語の意味:

Shoe polish
靴磨き

Say Instead:
適切な英語表現:

Cream puff, Profiterole

Example Sentences:
例文:

Let's get some _shoe cream_ for dessert!

Let's get some **_cream puffs_** for dessert.

デザートにシュークリームを買おう。

! This sentence sounds like you are going to eat some kind of cream for shoes!
靴用のクリームを食べようとしていると聞こえる。

How English Speakers use "shoe cream":
英語話者は(**shoe cream**)をどのように使うか:

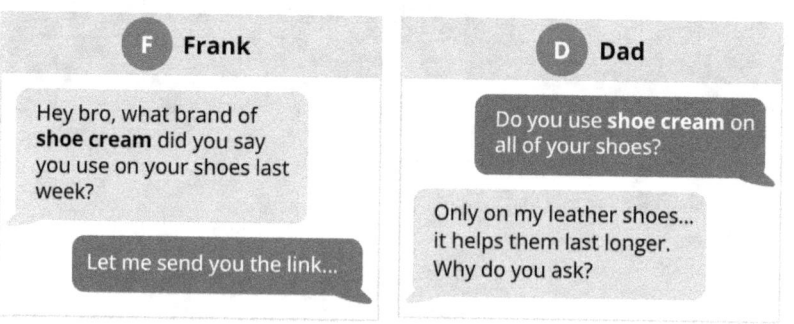

F Frank

Hey bro, what brand of **shoe cream** did you say you use on your shoes last week?

Let me send you the link...

D Dad

Do you use **shoe cream** on all of your shoes?

Only on my leather shoes... it helps them last longer. Why do you ask?

Business, Government, Economics

3

ビジネス・政府・経済

Scan for Audio

APPO

Meaning in English:
英語の意味:

Doesn't exist
英語には該当する単語がない

Say Instead:
適切な英語表現:

Appointment

Example Sentences:
例文:

> I have an *appo* tomorrow at 2 p.m.

> I have an ***appointment*** tomorrow at 2 p.m.

明日、私は2時にアポが入っている。

APPOINT

Meaning in English:
英語の意味:

(Verb) To choose someone for a job, role, or task
(動詞)仕事、役割、任務のために誰かを選ぶこと、任命すること

Say Instead:
適切な英語表現:

Appointment

Example Sentences:
例文:

> I have an *appoint* tomorrow at 2 p.m.

> I have an ***appointment*** tomorrow at 2 p.m.

明日、私は2時にアポイントが入っている。

CAMPAIGN

キャンペーン

Meaning in English:
英語の意味:

1. Marketing campaign in business (not used to mean a sale)
マーケティングキャンペーン(販売という意味ではない)
2. Political campaign
政治運動/選挙戦/選挙活動
3. Military campaign
軍事作戦/戦役/攻勢/作戦行動

Say Instead:
適切な英語表現:

Promotion, Sale

Example Sentences:
例文:

We appreciate our valued members and are offering an exclusive half-price *campaign* just for you. This *campaign* includes products from popular manufacturers, so please don't miss this chance to make a purchase!

We appreciate your continued patronage and are offering a half-price ***special offer*** exclusively for members. This ***promotion*** includes products from popular manufacturers, so please take advantage of this limited opportunity!

日頃のご愛顧に感謝し、会員様限定の半額キャンペーンを実施いたします。人気メーカーの商品も対象です。ぜひこの機会にお買い求めください。

Their new *business marketing campaign* innovatively uses old photos and video clips from successful *political campaigns* 政治活動 and military campaigns 軍事作戦.

Their new ***business marketing campaign*** innovatively uses old photos and video clips from successful ***political campaigns*** and ***military campaigns***.

彼らの新しいビジネス・マーケティング・キャンペーンでは、過去の政治活動や軍事作戦で成功を収めた際に撮影された写真や映像クリップを斬新な形でビジネスに応用している。

CLAIM

クレーム

Meaning in English:
英語の意味:

1. (Verb) To say something is true but without evidence
☞ Example: He *claimed* he was a foreign prince.
（動詞）証拠もないのにそれが真実だと主張する
例：彼は自分が「外国の王子だ」と主張した。

2. (Noun) A statement said as true but without evidence
☞ Example: I doubted his *claim* that he was a foreign prince.
（名詞）証拠ものないのに真実だと述べられた主張
例：私は彼の「外国の王子だ」という主張を疑った。

3. (Verb) To formally attest that something belongs to you
☞ Example: Please *claim* your lost items at customer service.
（動詞）正式に自分のものだと申し立てる
例：「紛失した持ち物はカスタマーサービスで受け取ってください」

4. (Noun) A formal demand or application for what is owed by insurance
☞ Example: We filed a *claim* with our car insurance after the accident.
（名詞）保険で支払われるべき金額を請求すること
例：私たちは事故後、車両保険の請求をだした。

Say Instead:
適切な英語表現:

Complain; Complaint, Demand

Example Sentences:
例文:

We got a *claim* about our new website.		We got a ***complaint*** about our new website.

新しいウェブサイトについてクレームが来たよ。

Oh no, Karen is here again. She always *claims* to the manager.		Oh no, Karen is here again. She always ***complains*** to the manager.

ええ、またカレンか。彼女は、
いつもマネージャーにクレームを言うんだよなあ。

CLAIMER

クレーマー

Meaning in English:
英語の意味:

Doesn't exist
英語には該当する単語がない

Say Instead:
適切な英語表現:

Demanding customer, Customer who complains a lot, A "Karen"

Example Sentences:
例文:

Oh no, Karen is in the store again today. She's a _claimer_! Tell her the manager isn't here today.

→

Oh no, Karen is in the store again today. She's a **_demanding customer_** who complains a lot! Tell her the manager isn't here today.

うわあ。カレンがまた店に来てるよ。クレーマーだ!
今日マネージャーは居ないって言って。

DEFLE

デ
フ
レ

Meaning in English:
英語の意味:

Doesn't exist
英語には該当する単語がない

Say Instead:
適切な英語表現:

Deflation

Example Sentences:
例文:

Defla is less common than infla in most modern economies.

**Deflation** is less common than inflation in most modern economies.

デフレは、
ほとんどの現代経済においてインフレほど一般的ではない。

DEMO

Meaning in English:
英語の意味:

1. In British English, *demo* has the same meaning as in Japanese. However, in American English, *demo* only refers to a demonstration of a product and its capabilities, or an example of a way of doing something.

イギリス英語では「デモ」は日本語と同じ意味を持つ。しかし、アメリカ英語では、「デモ」は製品の実演やその機能の紹介、または何かのやり方を示す例としてのみ使われる。

2. *Demo* can also mean "demolition," especially in construction
"Demo"は、特に建設の分野では「解体」を意味することもある。

Say Instead:
適切な英語表現:

Protest (US), Demonstration, Demo (UK)

Example Sentences:
例文:

| They had a big <u>demo</u> because of the politician's illegal actions. | | They had a big ***protest*** because of the politician's illegal actions. |

政治家の行動に抗議して、大規模なデモが行われた。

51

Food Loss

フードロス

Meaning in English:
英語の意味:

Food loss usually means losing edible food before consumers are able to eat it, usually because the food is unintentionally damaged or destroyed. ☞ Example: After the hurricane, our city lost power for more than one week and many people experienced *food loss* due to lack of electricity for their refrigerators.

フードロスとは、消費者が食べる前に、食べ物が意図せず傷んだり廃棄されたりして失われることを指す。
例:ハリケーンの後、私たちの街では1週間以上停電が続き、冷蔵庫が使えず、食べ物が傷んでしまったことで多くの人がフードロスを経験した。

Food waste usually means good food that is thrown out or spoiled food ☞ Example: We are trying to reduce *food waste* in our home by planning our meals more carefully and only buying what we know we will be able to eat.

一方、食品廃棄は、食べられるはずの食べ物が捨てられたり、食べずに腐ってしまったりすることを意味する。
例:私たちは食品廃棄を減らすために、献立をたてて、食べきれる分だけを購入するようにしている。

Say Instead:
適切な英語表現:

Food waste (noun), Waste food (verb)

Example Sentences:
例文:

| We need to protect the earth, so we shouldn't make _food loss_. | We need to protect the earth, so we shouldn't **_waste food_**. |

地球を守るために、フードロスをなくすべきだ。

| Developed countries have a lot of _food loss_, so our non-profit is devoted to helping people and communities reduce their _food loss_. | Developed countries **_waste a lot of food_**, so our non-profit is devoted to helping people and communities reduce their **_food waste_**. |

先進国にはフードロスが多いようなので、私たちのNPOは人々や地域がフードロスを減らせるよう支援している。

IMAGE UP

イメージアップ

Meaning in English:
英語の意味:

Doesn't exist
英語には該当する単語がない

Say Instead:
適切な英語表現:

Improve one's image/reputation

Example Sentences:
例文:

The company is trying to _image up_ after all the bad publicity it got last year.

The company is trying to **_improve its image_** after all the bad publicity it got last year.

その会社は、
昨年の悪い評判を挽回しようとイメージアップを図っている。

INFLA

インフレ

Meaning in English:
英語の意味:

Doesn't exist
英語には該当する単語がない

Say Instead:
適切な英語表現:

Inflation

Example Sentences:
例文:

If _infla_ is bad, people can't afford to buy what they need. → If **_inflation_** is bad, people can't afford to buy what they need.

インフレがひどいと、人々は必要なものを買う余裕がなくなる。

INFRA

インフラ

Meaning in English:
英語の意味:

Doesn't exist
英語には該当する単語がない

Say Instead:
適切な英語表現:

Infrastructure

Example Sentences:
例文:

The politician said he wants to improve the country's _infra_. The politician said he wants to improve our country's **_infrastructure_**.

その政治家は、国のインフラを改善したいと言った。

LONG SELLER

Meaning in English:
英語の意味:

Doesn't exist
英語には該当する単語がない

Say Instead:
適切な英語表現:

Long-standing best seller, All-time best seller

Example Sentences:
例文:

ロングセラー

The author was so successful and had several *long sellers*.

→ The author was so successful and had several ***long-standing best sellers***.

その著者は大きな成功を収め、
いくつものロングセラーを生み出した。

MINUS IMAGE

マイナスイメージ

Meaning in English:
英語の意味:

Doesn't exist
英語には該当する単語がない

Say Instead:
適切な英語表現:

Bad reputation, Negative public image

Example Sentences:
例文:

The company got a _minus image_ after all three of its latest products were recalled for catching on fire.

The company developed a **_bad reputation_** after all three of its latest products were recalled for catching on fire.

その会社は、最新の3つの製品が発火によるリコールとなり、マイナスイメージを持たれるようになった。

MODEL CHANGE

Meaning in English:
英語の意味:

Doesn't exist
英語には該当する単語がない

Say Instead:
適切な英語表現:

Release a new/updated model

Example Sentences:
例文:

モデルチェンジ

That company does *model change* every year. It's kind of hard to keep up with all of its new products. → That company ***releases a new updated model*** every year. It's kind of hard to keep up with all its new products.

その会社は毎年モデルチェンジをしている。
すべての製品についていくのは少し大変だ。

NAME VALUE

ネームバリュー

Meaning in English:
英語の意味:

Name-value pair is a specific way of organizing information and data on a computer or web forms

Name-value　pair（ネームバリューペア）とは、コンピューターやウェブフォームなどで情報やデータを整理・表現するためのしくみである。

Say Instead:
適切な英語表現:

Well-known, Highly-respected, (Good) reputation
Not well-known / obscure, Not well-respected, (Bad) reputation

Example Sentences:
例文:

> Many people think it's important to go to a university with a good _name value_.

> Many people think it's important to go to a **_well-known_** university with a **_good reputation_**.

多くの人が「ネームバリューのある(名前の通った)大学」に行くことが大切だと考えている。

NEGO

Meaning in English:
英語の意味:

Doesn't exist
英語には該当する単語がない

Say Instead:
適切な英語表現:

Negotiation

Example Sentences:
例文:

Work is so busy right now; we're in the middle of a huge _nego_.

→

Work is so busy right now; we're in the middle of a huge **_negotiation_**.

今、仕事がめちゃくちゃ忙しい。
大きなネゴ（交渉）の真っ最中なんだ。

OUTPUT

アウトプット

Meaning in English:
英語の意味:

1. Most commonly, the amount of goods or items produced by a business, factory, machine, country, etc.
☞ Example: Because of an increase in demand for our product, we need to increase *output* by 10% this month.

主に、企業・工場・機械・国などが生み出す商品や製品の量
(※「国」は、国内の産業全体を指すことが多い)
例:当社製品の需要が増えたため、今月は生産量を10%増やす必要がある。

2. The power a computer or electronic equipment produces
☞ Example: The battery has a maximum total *output* of 800 watts.

機器が出力するもの、または生成する電力や信号
例:このバッテリーの最大出力は800ワットだ。

3. The place on a piece of equipment where power or sound exits
☞ Example: Unfortunately, this computer does not have an audio *output* jack. You'll have to use wireless headphones or use the sound directly from the computer.

電力や音声などが外部に送られる端子や出力部分
例:「残念ながら、このコンピューターにはオーディオ出力端子がありません。ワイヤレスヘッドホンを使うか、コンピューター本体のスピーカーを使用してください」。

Say Instead:
適切な英語表現:

Speaking, Writing, Producing language

Example Sentences:
例文:

Many students are bad at doing *output* but are great at input.

Many students are bad at ***speaking and writing*** but are great at reading and listening.

多くの学生はアウトプットが苦手だが、インプットは得意だ。

Paper Company

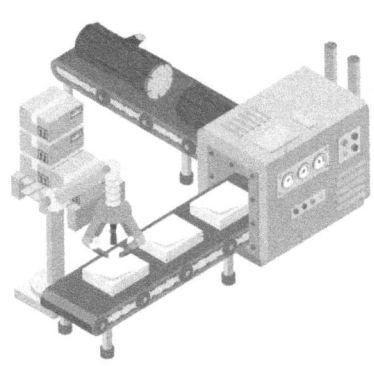

Meaning in English:
英語の意味:

A company that produces or sells paper

紙を製造または販売する会社

Say Instead:
適切な英語表現:

Shell company

Example Sentences:
例文:

It's difficult to tell who really owns the company becuase it seems to be a *paper company*.

It's difficult to tell who really owns the company because it seems to be a **_shell company_**.

そこがペーパーカンパニーみたいで、
実際のオーナーが誰なのか分からない。

This sentence sounds like the company produces or sells paper!
その会社は紙を製造している、あるいは販売している
ように聞こえる。

How English Speakers use "paper company":
英語話者は(paper company)をどのように使うか:

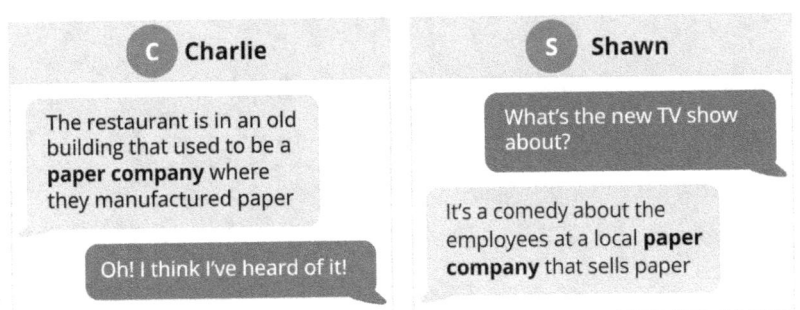

Charlie

The restaurant is in an old building that used to be a **paper company** where they manufactured paper

Oh! I think I've heard of it!

Shawn

What's the new TV show about?

It's a comedy about the employees at a local **paper company** that sells paper

RECALL

リコール

Meaning in English:
英語の意味:

1. To call back a product, often because of a dangerous or harmful defect
危険または有害な欠陥があるために製品を回収すること

2. To remember something
何かを思い出すこと

3. To remove someone from office before their term finishes
任期満了前に誰かを解任・罷免すること

Say Instead:
適切な英語表現:

Recall

Example Sentences:
例文:

> The mayor was _recalled_ リコール after he lied publicly about the company that was forced to _recall_ 解任された all of its products that kept catching on fire.

> The mayor was **_recalled_** after he lied publicly about the company that was forced to **_recall_** all of its products that kept catching on fire.

製品の発火が相次いだため、
全製品をリコールせざるを得なかった企業について、
市長は、公共の場で虚偽の発言をしたことで、解任された。

REFORM

リフォーム

1. (Verb) To make an improvement in a person
☞ Example: Some modern-thinking prison systems hope to *reform* criminals rather than just punish them.

(動詞)人を改善・更生させる
例:近代的な考え方を取り入れた一部の刑務所制度では、犯罪者を単に罰するのではなく、更生させることを重視している。

2. (Adjective) An improved person
☞ Example: He's a *reformed* criminal.

(形容詞)更生した/改心した人
例:彼は更生した(あるいは改心した)犯罪者だ。

3. (Verb) To make an improvement or change in a system
☞ Example: Some people believe the tax system needs *reform*.

(動詞)制度を改善・改革する
例:税制改革が必要だと考える人もいる。

4. (Noun) An improvement or change in a system
☞ Example: The education *reforms* have really benefited our country.

(名詞)制度の改善・改革
例:教育改革は我が国に大きな恩恵をもたらした。

Say Instead:
適切な英語表現:

Remodel, Redo, Renovate, Redocorate, Rearrange

Example Sentences:
例文:

They just did <u>*reform*</u> in their kitchen, and it looks amazing! ↗ They just ***<u>remodeled</u>*** their kitchen, and it looks amazing!

彼らは、キッチンをリフォームしたばかりで、
すごく素敵になってるね。

SALES POINT

セールスポイント

Meaning in English:
英語の意味:

Doesn't exist
英語には該当する単語がない

Say Instead:
適切な英語表現:

Selling point

Example Sentences:
例文:

I asked the sales manager, "What is the _sales point_ of your company's new product?" ➔ I asked the sales manager, "What is the **_main selling point_** of your company's new product?"

「御社の新製品のセールスポイントは何ですか?」
とセールスマネージャーに聞いた。

St / Suto

Meaning in English:
英語の意味:

Doesn't exist
英語には該当する単語がない

Say Instead:
適切な英語表現:

Strike

Example Sentences:
例文:

St is not very common in Japan.

Workers' strikes are not very common in Japan.

日本では、あまりストを見かけない。

SUPPORTER

サポーター

Meaning in English:
英語の意味:

1. Anyone who supports, encourages, and helps another person
☞ Example: My grandma was always my biggest *supporter*.
他人を支えたり、励ましたり、助けたりする人
例:「祖母はいつも私のいちばんの応援者だった」

2. People who support an idea or movement
考えや運動を支持する人々

3. People who support a specific leader, often in politics
特定の政治的リーダーを支持する人々

4. (UK) sports fans
(英) 英国では「スポーツファン」の意味でも使われる

Say Instead:
適切な英語表現:

Brace
Fan

Example Sentences:
例文:

She had to wear a *supporter* for four weeks after she injured her elbow.	She had to wear a ***brace*** for four weeks after she injured her elbow.

彼女は、肘をケガしてから、
4週間サポーターをつけないといけなかった。

The soccer team has some really enthusiastic *supporters*! They even help clean up after the game!	The soccer team has some really enthusiastic ***fans***! They even help clean up after the game!

そのサッカーチームにはとても熱心なサポーターがいる。
試合後の片付けまで手伝ってくれる!

CARS & TRANSPORTATION

4

車・交通

ACCEL

アクセル

Meaning in English:
英語の意味:

Doesn't exist, but sounds close to "excel" and "Excel"
英語には、該当する単語はないが、エクセル（秀でる、優れる）かマイクロソフトのエクセルに聞こえる。

Say Instead:
適切な英語表現:

Accelerator, Gas pedal

Example Sentences:
例文:

There is a problem with my car. When I press the _accel_, my car doesn't move.

There's a problem with my car. When I press the **_accelerator_**, my car doesn't move.

車の調子がおかしいよ。アクセルを踏んでも動かないんだ。

How English Speakers use "excel":
英語話者は（**excel**）をどのように使うか:

If you want to _excel_ at learning a new language, NEVER be afraid of making mistakes!

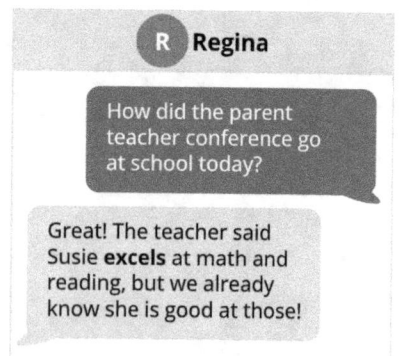

R Regina

How did the parent teacher conference go at school today?

Great! The teacher said Susie **excels** at math and reading, but we already know she is good at those!

ALL RAI

オーライ

Meaning in English:
英語の意味:

Doesn't exist
英語には該当する単語がない

Say Instead:
適切な英語表現:

All right, Back, More, Keep going

Example Sentences:
例文:

Can you please help me back up my car? Of course. Back. Backu, _All rai_. _All rai_.

→

Can you please help me back up my car? Of course.
Back, back, more. Keep going.

車をバックさせるのを手伝ってもらえるかな。もちろん。
バック、バック、バックオーライ。

AUTOBI

オートバイ

Meaning in English:
英語の意味:

Doesn't exist
英語には該当する単語がない

Say Instead:
適切な英語表現:

Motorcycle (US), Motorbike (UK)

Example Sentences:
例文:

It's fun to ride an _autobi_. → It's fun to ride a **_motorcycle_**.

オートバイに乗るのは楽しい。

AUTOMA

オートマ

Meaning in English:
英語の意味:

Doesn't exist
英語には該当する単語がない

Say Instead:
適切な英語表現:

Automatic transmission

Example Sentences:
例文:

Most cars in Japan nowadays are _automa_. → Most cars in Japan nowadays have **_automatic transmissions_**.

今の日本では、ほとんどの車がオートマ車だ。

Back Mirror

Meaning in English:
英語の意味:

Doesn't exist
英語には該当する単語がない

Say Instead:
適切な英語表現:

Rearview mirror

Example Sentences:
例文:

I looked at my kids in the _back mirror_.

I looked at my kids in the **_rearview mirror_**.

私は、バックミラー越しに子どもたちを見た。

バックミラー

Back Monitor

Meaning in English:
英語の意味:

Doesn't exist
英語には該当する単語がない

Say Instead:
適切な英語表現:

Backup camera

Example Sentences:
例文:

Does your car have a _back monitor_?

Does your car have a **_backup camera_**?

あなたの車にはバックモニターが付いてる?

バックモニター

BIKE

バイク

Meaning in English:
英語の意味:

1. Bicycle
自転車

2. Motorcycle
モーターサイクル(二輪車)
オートバイ/バイク

Say Instead:
適切な英語表現:

Motorcycle (US), Motorbike (UK)

Example Sentences:
例文:

I love to ride my _bike_ in the countryside.

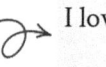

I love to ride my **_motorcycle_** in the countryside.

私は、田舎をバイクで走るのが大好きだ。

 Without other context, this sounds like you enjoy riding your bicycle in the countryside.
他の文脈がなければ、「田舎で自転車に乗るのを楽しんでいる」と受け取られる可能性がある。

CAMPING CAR

キャンピングカー

Meaning in English:
英語の意味:

Doesn't exist
英語には該当する単語がない

Say Instead:
適切な英語表現:

Camper, RV, Small carstay van, Motorhome, Caravan (UK)

Example Sentences:
例文:

Let's go camping in our new _camping car_! → Let's go camping in our new **_RV_**!

新しいキャンピングカーでキャンプに行こう!

CLAXON / KLAXON

クラクション

Meaning in English:
英語の意味:

Doesn't exist
英語には該当する単語がない

Say Instead:
適切な英語表現:

Horn

Example Sentences:
例文:

I hate driving here because people always use the _claxon_. I hate driving here because people always honk the **_horn_**.

ここで運転するのは、嫌だなあ。
いつでも皆がクラクションを鳴らすから。

DRIVER

ド
ラ
イ
バ
ー

Meaning in English:
英語の意味:

1. A person who drives
(e.g., a bus driver)
運転する人（例：バスの運転手）

2. A type of golf club
ゴルフクラブの一種

Say Instead:
適切な英語表現:

Screwdriver

Example Sentences:
例文:

He bought a _driver_ at L's Hardware.

He bought a **_screwdriver_** at L's Hardware store.

彼はL's Hardwareでドライバーを買った。

 This sounds like he went to a hardware store that sells sports equipment and bought a golf club, or he hired a driver there to drive him around!

彼がスポーツ用品も売っているホームセンターに行ってゴルフクラブを買ったか、あるいは運転手（driver）を雇ったように聞こえる。

How English speakers use (driver):
英語話者は（driver）をどのように使うか:

 Delivery Service

Your delivery **driver** has arrived and will be dropping off your order momentarily

 Hotel in NYC

The **driver** will wait for you at the passenger exit at the airport with a sign with your name

DUMP CAR

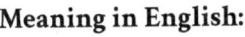

Meaning in English:
英語の意味:

Doesn't really exist but sounds like it could be a junky car that's old and falling apart
英語には実際には存在しない単語だが、古くてボロボロの車のような印象を与える。

Say Instead:
適切な英語表現:

Dump truck (US), Tip lorry (UK)

Example Sentences:
例文:

| My son really likes to play with toy _dump cars_. | | My son really likes to play with toy **_dump trucks_**. |

私の息子は、おもちゃのダンプカーで遊ぶのが好きだ。

| My husband drives a _dump car_ for work. | | My husband drives a **_dump truck_** for work. |

私の夫は、仕事でダンプカーに乗っている。

This sounds like your husband drives an old junky car that is falling apart and near the end of its usefulness!
夫が、そろそろ寿命がきそうな古びた車に乗っているように聞こえる。

FRONT GLASS

フロントガラス

Meaning in English:
英語の意味:

Doesn't exist
英語には該当する単語がない

Say Instead:
適切な英語表現:

Windshield (US), Windscreen (UK)

Example Sentences:
例文:

> A rock hit my *front glass*, and now it has a huge crack.

> A rock hit my *windshield*, and now it has a huge crack.

石がフロントガラスに当たり、現在は大きなひびが入っている。

GASOLINE STAND

ガソリンスタンド

Meaning in English:
英語の意味:

Doesn't exist
英語には該当する単語がない

Say Instead:
適切な英語表現:

Gas station (US), Petrol station (UK)

Example Sentences:
例文:

> We drove for 3 hours and didn't even see 1 *gasoline stand*!

> We drove for 3 hours and didn't even see 1 *gas station*!

テキサスの田舎を3時間走ったのに、
ガソリンスタンドが1軒もなかった！

HANDLE

Meaning in English:
英語の意味:

1. Part of an object to control, carry, or open with your hand
(e.g., bicycle handle, door handle)
手で操作・持ち運び・開閉するためのパーツ
（例：自転車のハンドル、ドアの取っ手）

2. Name used for social media or online accounts
ハンドルネーム

Say Instead:
適切な英語表現:

Steering wheel

Example Sentences:
例文:

I took my car to the auto shop because my _handle_ had a problem.	I took my car to the auto shop because there was a problem with my **_steering wheel_**.

ハンドルに不具合がでたので、車を修理に出した。

This sentence sounds like the door handle has a problem.
この文では、ドアの取っ手に問題があるように聞こえる。

HANDLE KEEPER

ハンドルキーパー

Meaning in English:
英語の意味:

Doesn't exist
英語には該当する単語がない

Say Instead:
適切な英語表現:

Designated driver, DD

Example Sentences:
例文:

I prefer not to drink tonight, so I can be our *handle keeper*! I prefer not to drink tonight, so I can be ***designated driver***!

今夜は飲まないようにするね。ハンドルキーパーになるから。

HELI

ヘリ

Meaning in English:
英語の意味:

Doesn't exist
英語には該当する単語がない

Say Instead:
適切な英語表現:

Helicopter

Example Sentences:
例文:

We saw the biggest *heli* yesterday. We saw the biggest ***helicopter*** yesterday.

私たちは、昨日大きなヘリを見た。

IDLING STOP

An *idling stop, idling stop system,* or *start-stop system* is a system in a car that automatically shuts off the vehicle's engine when it is idling or stopped briefly (like at a stop light).

アイドリングストップ、アイドリングストップシステム、またはスタートストップシステムとは、車が一時的に停止しているとき(例えば信号待ちなど)に、自動的にエンジンを停止するシステムのことである。

Leave your car engine running while stopped

In Japan, it's illegal to do an *idling stop* in some cities.

In Japan, it's illegal to *leave your car engine running while you're stopped* in some cities.

日本では、一部の都市でアイドリングストップは違法だ。

MUFFLER

マフラー

Meaning in English:
英語の意味:

An important part in your car that helps make it more quiet

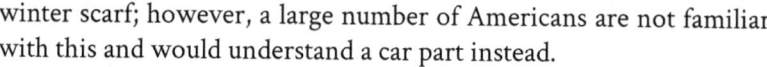

車のマフラー、車の騒音を抑える重要な部品
例:マフラーは車の排気音を減らすのに役立つ。

2. In the UK and some areas of the U.S., *muffler* is also used to mean a winter scarf; however, a large number of Americans are not familiar with this and would understand a car part instead.

イギリスや一部のアメリカ地域では"muffler"は冬用のマフラー（首に巻く防寒具）を指すこともある。しかし、多くのアメリカ人はこの言葉を主に車の部品として認識している。

Say Instead:
適切な英語表現:

(Winter) scarf
(Car) muffler (US), Silencer (UK)

Example Sentences:
例文:

I'm going to give her a *muffler* for her birthday.

I'm going to give her a *scarf* for her birthday.

私は、彼女の誕生日にマフラーをあげるつもりだ。

This sounds like he's going to give her a car part!
まるで彼が車の部品を彼女にプレゼントするみたい。

MY CAR

Meaning in English:
英語の意味:

A car that is mine or in my possession for use
私の車

Say Instead:
適切な英語表現:

My own car

Example Sentences:
例文:

I just got _my car_ last month.

I just got _**my own car**_ last month. / I just _**bought a car**_ last month.

先月、マイカーを買ったんだ。

This sentence sounds like you didn't have any car to use at all until last month!
この文だと、先月まで車を持っていなかったみたいに伝わってしまう。

How English speakers use "my car":
英語話者は(my car)をどのように使うか:

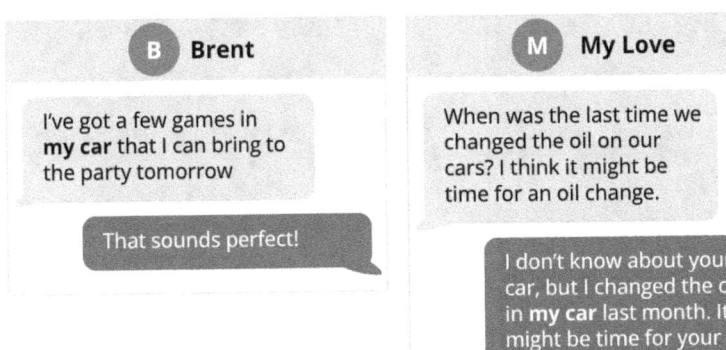

B Brent

I've got a few games in **my car** that I can bring to the party tomorrow

That sounds perfect!

M My Love

When was the last time we changed the oil on our cars? I think it might be time for an oil change.

I don't know about your car, but I changed the oil in **my car** last month. It might be time for your car

81

NUMBER PLATE

ナンバープレート

Meaning in English:
英語の意味:

(US) Doesn't exist
(米) 英語には該当する単語がない

(UK) Same meaning as in Japanese
(英) ナンバープレート (日本語と同様)

Say Instead:
適切な英語表現:

License plate (US), Registration plate (UK), Number plate (UK)

Example Sentences:
例文:

What's our back number? I can't see our _number plate_.

What's our license plate number? I can't see our **_license plate_**.

「うしろのナンバープレートが見えないんだけど、
私たちの車の番号って何だった?」

OPEN CAR

オープンカー

Meaning in English:
英語の意味:

Doesn't exist
英語には該当する単語がない

Say Instead:
適切な英語表現:

Convertible

Example Sentences:
例文:

My dad had an _open car_ when I was a kid.

My dad had a **_convertible_** when I was a kid.

私の父は、私が子どもの時、オープンカーを持っていた。

PAT CAR

パトカー

Meaning in English:
英語の意味:

Doesn't exist
英語には該当する単語がない

Say Instead:
適切な英語表現:

Police car

Example Sentences:
例文:

There were a lot of _pat cars_ outside the building. I wonder what happened.

There were a lot of **_police cars_** outside the building. I wonder what happened.

建物の外にパトカーがたくさん来ていたけれど、何があったのだろう。

PAPER DRIVER

ペーパードライバー

Meaning in English:
英語の意味:

Doesn't exist
英語には該当する単語がない

Say Instead:
適切な英語表現:

Has a license but doesn't drive
Have a license but don't drive

Example Sentences:
例文:

There are many *paper drivers* in big cities like NYC since there are so many good alternative transportation options.

There are many **people who have a driver's license but don't drive** in big cities like NYC since there are so many good alternative transportation options.

ニューヨークのような大都市には、
便利な交通手段が豊富にあるため、
ペーパードライバーが多い。

REVERSE

Meaning in English:
英語の意味:

1. To go backwards (especially in a vehicle)
   (特に乗り物で)逆戻りすること

2. To change the order to its opposite or
   go the opposite direction.
   ☞ Example: Everyone wants to *reverse*
   the aging process.

順序や方向を逆にする／逆行すること
例：「みんな、老化の流れを逆戻りでき
　　たらいいのにと思っているよね。」

Say Instead:
適切な英語表現:

Vomit, Throw up

Example Sentences:
例文:

I drank way too much last night and did <u>*reverse*</u>.	I drank way too much last night and **_threw up_** a lot.

「昨日は、飲み過ぎてリバースしたわ。」

How English speakers use "reverse":
英語話者は(reverse)をどのように使うか:

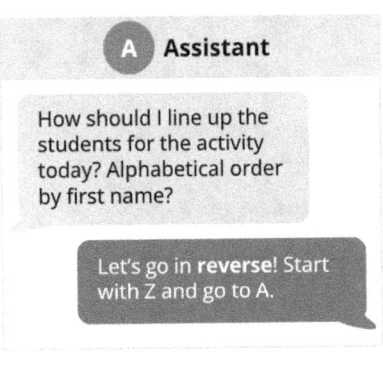

A Assistant

How should I line up the students for the activity today? Alphabetical order by first name?

Let's go in **reverse**! Start with Z and go to A.

L Aunt Lisa

OMG. Grandpa just **reversed** the car into the neighbor's mailbox... What do I do?

Is he ok? Go see if the neighbor is home to talk to them. Our insurance should cover it...

RUSH

ラッシュ

Meaning in English:
英語の意味:

To go or do something quickly
急いで行くこと、
急いで何かをすること

Say Instead:
適切な英語表現:

Rush hour

Example Sentences:
例文:

> I hate driving in *rush*!
> It's the worst!

> I hate driving in ***rush hour***!
> It's the worst!

通勤ラッシュの運転って本当に嫌いだ。最悪だよね。

 This sounds like you hate driving when you're in a hurry!
急いでいるときの運転がすごく嫌なように聞こえる。

How English Speakers use "rush":
英語話者は（rush）をどのように使うか:

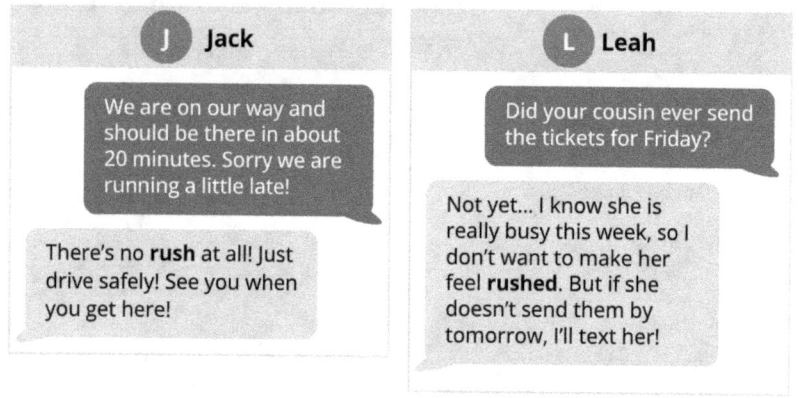

J Jack

We are on our way and should be there in about 20 minutes. Sorry we are running a little late!

There's no **rush** at all! Just drive safely! See you when you get here!

L Leah

Did your cousin ever send the tickets for Friday?

Not yet... I know she is really busy this week, so I don't want to make her feel **rushed**. But if she doesn't send them by tomorrow, I'll text her!

RV

アールブイ

Meaning in English:
英語の意味:

Recreational vehicle
RV（レクリエーションビークル）車

Say Instead:
適切な英語表現:

SUV

Example Sentences:
例文:

What kind of car do you have? I have a small _RV_.

What kind of car do you have? I have a small **_SUV_**.

どんな車に乗ってるんだい。小型のRV だよ。

This sentence sounds like you drive an RV or motorhome as your main vehicle!
普段からキャンピングカーやモーターホームに乗っているように聞こえる。

How English speakers use "RV":
英語話者は（RV）をどのように使うか:

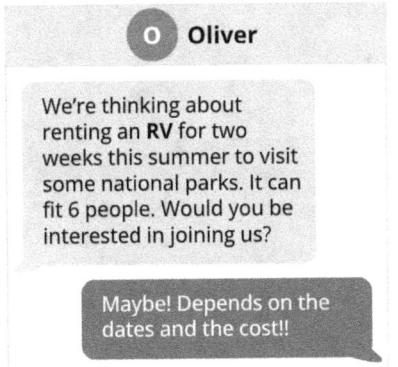

O Oliver

We're thinking about renting an **RV** for two weeks this summer to visit some national parks. It can fit 6 people. Would you be interested in joining us?

Maybe! Depends on the dates and the cost!!

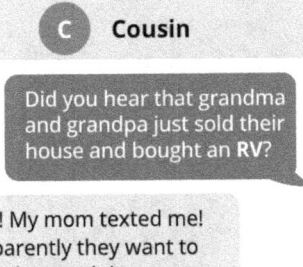

C Cousin

Did you hear that grandma and grandpa just sold their house and bought an **RV**?

Yes! My mom texted me! Apparently they want to travel around the country and thought it would be cheaper that way...

SHORT CUT

Meaning in English:
英語の意味:

A shorter way to go somewhere or do to something
物事をより早く達成したり、どこかへ早く行くための近道や効率的な方法

Say Instead:
適切な英語表現:

Short haircut, Short hairstyle

Example Sentences:
例文:

I saw Yuka this weekend. She got image change, did _short cut_ and hair color, and she looks so much younger now!

I saw Yuka this weekend. She totally changed her look, **_cut her hair short_** and dyed it, and she looks so much younger now!

週末ユカに会ったんだけど、イメチェンして、髪をショートカットにしてカラーもしてて、すごく若返って見えた!

How English Speakers use "short cut":
英語話者は(short cut)をどのように使うか:

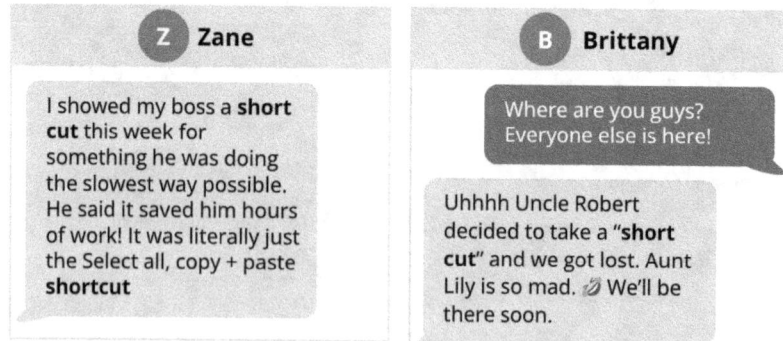

Z Zane

I showed my boss a **short cut** this week for something he was doing the slowest way possible. He said it saved him hours of work! It was literally just the Select all, copy + paste **shortcut**

B Brittany

Where are you guys? Everyone else is here!

Uhhhh Uncle Robert decided to take a **"short cut"** and we got lost. Aunt Lily is so mad. 🤦 We'll be there soon.

SIDE BRAKE

Meaning in English:
英語の意味:

Doesn't exist
英語には該当する単語がない

Say Instead:
適切な英語表現:

Parking brake, Emergency brake

Example Sentences:
例文:

When I park my car,
I use the _side brake_.

When I park my car,
I use the **_parking brake_**.

車を停めるときはサイドブレーキを使う。

SL

Meaning in English:
英語の意味:

Doesn't exist
英語には該当する単語がない

Say Instead:
適切な英語表現:

Steam train, Steam locomotive

Example Sentences:
例文:

My grandfather loves visiting
historical locations with _SL_.

My grandfather loves
visiting historical places with
old **_steam trains_**/**_locomotives_**.

祖父は昔のSL(蒸気機関車)が走っていた史跡を訪れるのが大好きだ。

89

WINKER

ウインカー

Meaning in English:
英語の意味:

Someone who winks often
よくウィンクする人

Say Instead:
適切な英語表現:

Blinker, Turn signal, Indicator (UK)

Example Sentences:
例文:

You should always use your _winker_ when you want to turn. You should always use your **_blinker_** when you want to turn.

曲がるときは、ウインカーをちゃんと使ったほうがいい。

USE
TURN
SIGNAL

CLOTHING & FASHION

5

衣服・ファッション

DRESS

ドレス

Meaning in English:
英語の意味:

The general word for all types of women's dresses including casual dresses

ドレス、ワンピース、カジュアルなドレスを含むあらゆるタイプの女性用ドレスの総称

Say Instead:
適切な英語表現:

Formal dress
Specific name (wedding dress)

Example Sentences:
例文:

You shouldn't wear a _dress_ to a casual restaurant.

You shouldn't wear a **_formal dress_** to a casual restaurant.

カジュアルなレストランにはドレスを着ていかないほうがいいよ。

 This sounds like you're advising that it's inappropriate to wear a dress of any kind including a『ワンピース』to a casual restaurant and sounds like a woman should wear either a skirt, pants, or shorts instead.

カジュアルなレストランにワンピースを含むすべての種類のドレスを着ていくのは不適切で、代わりにスカートやパンツ、ショートパンツを履くべきだとアドバイスしているように聞こえる。

Free Size

Meaning in English:
英語の意味:

Doesn't exist
英語には該当する単語がない

Say Instead:
適切な英語表現:

One size fits all

Example Sentences:
例文:

These one pieces are _free size_. These dresses are
one size fits all.

このワンピースは、フリーサイズだ。

フリーサイズ

G Jan

Meaning in English:
英語の意味:

Doesn't exist
英語には該当する単語がない

Say Instead:
適切な英語表現:

Denim jacket, Jean jacket

Example Sentences:
例文:

I think I'll wear my _G jan_
tonight. It's warm but stylish. I think I'll wear my **_denim jacket_**. It's warm but stylish.

今夜はGジャンを着ようと思う。暖かいし、おしゃれだからね。

ジージャン

G Pan

ジーパン

Meaning in English:
英語の意味:

Doesn't exist
英語には該当する単語がない

Say Instead:
適切な英語表現:

Jeans, Blue jeans, Denim trousers (UK)

Example Sentences:
例文:

| I was surprised that in the U.S. some people wear _G pan_ to their office every day. | | I was surprised that in the U.S. some people wear _**jeans**_ to their office every day. |

アメリカでは毎日ジーパンを履いて出勤する人がいると知って驚いた。

GOWN

ガウン

Meaning in English:
英語の意味:

1. A very nice, formal dress
イブニングドレス、パーティードレスなどのフォーマルドレス

2. A hospital gown for patients
患者用の病院着

3. A night gown
ナイトガウン

Say Instead:
適切な英語表現:

Robe (US), Dressing gown (UK)

Example Sentences:
例文:

The hotel has free *gowns* for guests.

The hotel has free *robes* for guests.

そのホテルでは、宿泊客向けに無料のガウンが用意されている。

This sentence sounds like the hotel may be giving guests free night gowns, free ball gowns, or free hospital gowns.
ホテルが宿泊客に無料のガウン、ボールガウン、あるいは病院用ガウンを配っているように聞こえる。

HIGH NECK

ハイネック

Meaning in English:
英語の意味:

Clothing with a higher neckline than usual, but not a turtleneck
通常よりもネックラインが高いが、タートルネックではない服

Say Instead:
適切な英語表現:

Turtleneck

Example Sentences:
例文:

Some people think *high neck* is fashionable, but others disagree.

Some people think **turtlenecks** are fashionable, but others disagree.

ハイネックはおしゃれだと思う人もいるが、そう思わない人もいる。

⚠ This sounds like maybe people who have long necks are considered beautiful or fashionable.
首が長い人は美しい、またはおしゃれだとみなされているように聞こえる。

96

JACQUE (CHOKKI)

Meaning in English:
英語の意味:

Doesn't exist
英語には該当する単語がない

チョッキ

Say Instead:
適切な英語表現:

Fishing vest
Bulletproof vest
Safety vest
(Suit) vest (US), Waistcoat (UK)

Example Sentences:
例文:

My dad loves wearing *chokki* even though I keep telling him they're old-fashioned.

My dad loves wearing **_vests_** even though I keep telling him they're old-fashioned.

父はチョッキを着るのが大好きだ。
私は何度も「古くさいよ」と言っているのに。

JUMPER

ジャンパー

Meaning in English:

英語の意味:

1. (US) A girls' outfit that is a dress with a shirt underneath

(米) ジャンパースカート

2. (UK) A pullover sweater

(英) プルーオーバータイプのセーター

3. A person who jumps

ジャンプする人

4. Jumper cables to help jump start your car if it breaks down

ジャンプスタート(バッテリーが上がった際の始動)に使用する
ブースターケーブル(英語では jumper cables)

Say Instead:

適切な英語表現:

Jacket, Coat

Example Sentences:

例文:

I really like your _jumper_. Where did you get it?		I really like your _**jacket**_. Where did you get it?

そのジャンパーとても素敵ね。どこで買ったの?

JUMPER SKIRT

ジャンパースカート

Meaning in English:
英語の意味:

Doesn't exist
英語には該当する単語がない

Say Instead:
適切な英語表現:

Jumper (US), Pinafore dress (UK)

Example Sentences:
例文:

She wore a *jumper skirt* to school.

She wore a ***jumper uniform*** to school.

彼女はジャンパースカートを着て学校に行った。

NO SLEEVE

ノースリーブ

Meaning in English:
英語の意味:

Doesn't exist
英語には該当する単語がない

Say Instead:
適切な英語表現:

Sleeveless shirt, Sleeveless top

Example Sentences:
例文:

She wore *no sleeve* to school and got sent home for breaking the dress code.

He wore a ***sleeveless top*** to school and got sent home for breaking the dress code.

彼女は、ノースリーブを着て登校して、校則違反で家に帰された。

ONE PATTERN

Meaning in English:
英語の意味:

Literally, one pattern
文字通り一つのパターン

Say Instead:
適切な英語表現:

Repetitive

Example Sentences:
例文:

> The conference was really _one pattern_. I was hoping there would be more of a variety of topics.

> The conference was really _**repetitive**_. I was hoping there would be more of a variety of topics.

会議はワンパターンだった。
もっといろんな話題が出るかと思ってたんだけどね。

How English Speakers use "one pattern":
英語話者は(one pattern)をどのように使うか:

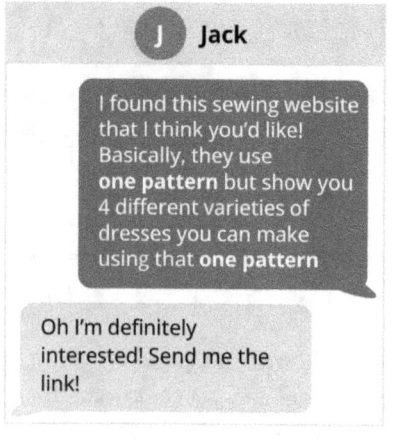

Jack

I found this sewing website that I think you'd like! Basically, they use **one pattern** but show you 4 different varieties of dresses you can make using that **one pattern**

Oh I'm definitely interested! Send me the link!

Leah

Do you have any **patterns** for making shorts?

Hm... I do, but I think I might only have **one pattern** for that!

ONE PIECE

Meaning in English:

英語の意味:

Swimsuit that is all one, not a bikini

ビキニではないつながった形の水着
（ワンピース水着）

Say Instead:

適切な英語表現:

Dress, Casual dress

Example Sentences:

例文:

She's wearing a _one piece_ to the party.

→ She's wearing a **_dress_** to the party.

彼女はパーティーにワンピースを着て行った。

This sentence sounds like she's wearing a bathing suit!

この言い方だと、彼女が水着を着てパーティーに
来たような感じに受け取られる。

How English speakers use "one piece":

英語話者は（one piece）をどのように使うか:

S School

For the school swimming party this year, we'd like to remind all parents that girls must wear **one pieces** (no bikinis or tankinis), and boys must wear swim trunks (no speedos)

E Elizabeth

Looking forward to the beach next week!

Same! I'm not wearing a two piece, but I'll bring a **one piece** and plenty of cover-ups to wear!

ワンピース

Pair Look

ペアルック

Meaning in English:
英語の意味:

Doesn't exist
英語には該当する単語がない

Say Instead:
適切な英語表現:

They match. They are matching. They have matching outfits.

Example Sentences:
例文:

Oh cute! I like their *pair look*! → Oh cute! ***They are matching***!

わあ、かわいい！ふたりのペアルック、いい感じ。

Pants Style

パンツスタイル

Meaning in English:
英語の意味:

Doesn't exist
英語には該当する単語がない

Say Instead:
適切な英語表現:

Wear slacks, Wear a pantsuit (US), Wear a trouser suit (UK)

Example Sentences:
例文:

I am usually *pants style*. I usually wear ***slacks*** / ***a pantsuit*** to the office.

私は、たいていパンツスタイルだ。

PANTS

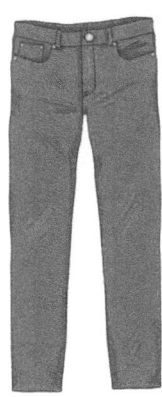

Meaning in English:
英語の意味:

(US) Any kind of pants, including jeans
(米) ズボン・ジーパン

(UK) Underwear for men or women
(英) 下着

Say Instead:
適切な英語表現:

Men's underwear (US), Men's pants (UK)

Example Sentences:
例文:

パ
ン
ツ

> I told my husband to buy his own _pants_. I don't want to choose for him.

> I told my husband to buy his own **_underwear_**. I don't want to choose for him.

私は、夫に自分でパンツを買うように言った。
私が選びたくないから。

In American English, this sounds like you asked your husband to buy his own jeans.
アメリカ英語では、夫にズボン（またはジーンズ）は自分で買ってきて、と言ったように聞こえる。

PARKER

パーカー

Meaning in English:
英語の意味:

Doesn't exist
英語には該当する単語がない

Say Instead:
適切な英語表現:

Hoodie (US), Hooded jumper (UK)

Example Sentences:
例文:

My school doesn't allow _parkers_, but I love wearing them around the house. My school doesn't allow **_hoodies_**, but I love wearing them around my house.

学校ではパーカーは禁止されているが、家ではよく着る。

RECRUIT SUIT

リクルートスーツ

Meaning in English:
英語の意味:

Doesn't exist
英語には該当する単語がない

Say Instead:
適切な英語表現:

Simple, professional suit for job-hunting

Example Sentences:
例文:

The professor advised the graduates to make sure they have a good _recruit suit_ in their closets. The professor advised the graduates to make sure they have a **_good, simple, professional suit_** in their closets.

教授は卒業生たちに、「リクルートスーツを一着はクローゼットに入れておきなさい」と助言した。

S/M/L Size

Meaning in English:
英語の意味:

S, M, L are only used in writing.
In speaking, people say small, medium, and large, respectively.
「S」「M」「L」といった表記は、基本的に書き言葉で使われ、会話
ではそれぞれ Small、Medium、Large と言うのが一般的だ。

Say Instead:
適切な英語表現:

Small, Medium, Large

Example Sentences:
例文:

She wears _S size_. She wears a **_small_**.

彼女はSサイズを着ている。

I need _M size_ for shirts. I need **_medium_** for shirts.

私は、シャツはMサイズが欲しい。

Can you buy _L size_ for my dad? Can you buy a **_large_** for my dad?

私の父にLサイズを買ってくれる?

LL Size

エルエルサイズ

Meaning in English:

英語の意味:

Doesn't exist
英語には該当する単語がない

Say Instead:

適切な英語表現:

Extra large, XL

Example Sentences:

例文:

Do you sell this shirt in _LL size_? → Do you sell this shirt in **_XL_**?

このシャツのLLサイズはありますか?

3L Size

スリーエル

Meaning in English:

英語の意味:

Doesn't exist
英語には該当する単語がない

Say Instead:

適切な英語表現:

Extra extra large, 2XL, XXL

Example Sentences:

例文:

His shirt size is _3L_. His shirt size is **_XXL_**.

彼のシャツのサイズは3Lだ。

SHORT PANTS

ショートパンツ

Meaning in English:

英語の意味:

1. Pants that are too short

短すぎるパンツ

2. An older term for shorts. Most people will probably understand this, and there are certainly people who still use it. However, it sounds unnatural to many people as "shorts" is much more common.

「ショートパンツ」は、古い言い方。今でも意味が通じる人は多く、実際に使っている人もいる。ただ、現在では「shorts（ショーツ）」の方が一般的で、「ショートパンツ」という表現は、多くの人にとってやや不自然に感じられることもある。

Say Instead:

適切な英語表現:

Shorts

Example Sentences:

例文:

You should wear your new _short pants_ to the zoo today. You should wear your new **_shorts_** to the zoo today.

新しいショートパンツで今日の動物園に行くといいよ。

SHORTS

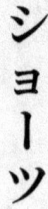

Meaning in English:
英語の意味:

(US) Short pants
(米) ショートパンツ
(UK) Men's underpants
(英) パンツ

Say Instead:
適切な英語表現:

Panties (US), Knickers (UK)

Example Sentences:
例文:

The woman loves her new pink *shorts*.

The woman loves her new pink **_underwear_**.

その女性は新しいピンクのショーツが気に入っている。

 This sounds like she has new pink『ショートパンツ』.
新しいピンクのショートパンツを持っているように聞こえる。

How English Speakers use "shorts":
英語話者は(shorts)をどのように使うか:

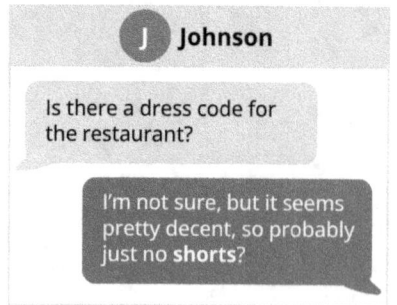

Johnson

Is there a dress code for the restaurant?

I'm not sure, but it seems pretty decent, so probably just no **shorts**?

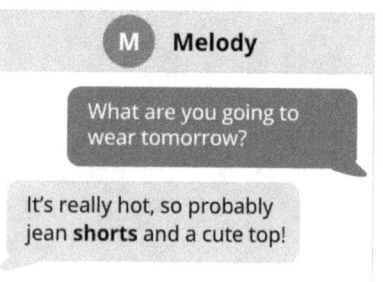

Melody

What are you going to wear tomorrow?

It's really hot, so probably jean **shorts** and a cute top!

SPATS

Meaning in English:
英語の意味:

Doesn't exist
英語には該当する単語がない

Say Instead:
適切な英語表現:

Yoga pants, Exercise pants, Leggings, Workout pants, Tights

Example Sentences:
例文:

スパッツ

I was really surprised when I saw people wearing _spats_ at the store.

I was really surprised when I saw people wearing **_yoga pants_** at the store.

お店でスパッツを履いてる人を見て、すごく驚いた。

STA JAN / STADIUM JUMPER

スタジャン・スタジアムジャンパー

Meaning in English:
英語の意味:

Doesn't exist
英語には該当する単語がない

Say Instead:
適切な英語表現:

Letter jacket

Example Sentences:
例文:

Everyone on our team wore their *sta jan*.		Everyone on our team wore their *letter jackets*.

チームのみんなは、パーティーにスタジャンを着てきた。

Everyone on our team wore their *stadium jumpers*.		Everyone on our team wore their *letter jackets*.

チームのみんなは、パーティーにスタジアムジャンパーを着てきた。

STYLE

Meaning in English:
英語の意味:

1. Fashion-sense
ファッションセンス

2. Design
デザイン

3. Way of doing something
物事のやり方、方法

Say Instead:
適切な英語表現:

Body shape, Figure, Body type, Body structure, Bone structure

Example Sentences:
例文:

If you understand your _style_, then you can learn what kind of fashion looks best on your body.	If you understand your **_body shape/figure/type_**, then you can learn what kind of fashion looks best on your body.

自分のスタイルを理解すると、
自分に合うファッションがわかってくるよ。

How English Speakers use "style":
英語話者は(style)をどのように使うか:

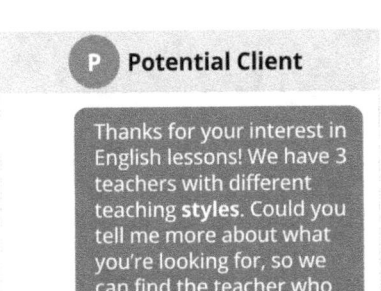

P Potential Client

Thanks for your interest in English lessons! We have 3 teachers with different teaching **styles**. Could you tell me more about what you're looking for, so we can find the teacher who will be the best fit for you?

T TJ

I just signed up for a really cool class! It's called Dance **Styles** Across Time. We will examine different **styles** of dance and learn how popular dance moves have changed over time.

111

THREE SIZE

スリーサイズ

Meaning in English:
英語の意味:

Doesn't exist
英語には該当する単語がない

Say Instead:
適切な英語表現:

Body measurements; Bust, waist, hip measurements

Example Sentences:
例文:

You can choose clothes that suit you by referring to your _three size_.

Referring to your **_body measurements_** will make it easier to choose clothes that fit well.

自分のスリーサイズを知っておくと、
体に合った服を選びやすくなる。

TRAINER

トレーナー

Meaning in English:
英語の意味:

(US) Someone who trains others
（米）トレーニングをする人
訓練・練習を提供する人

(UK) Tennis shoes, sneakers
（英）テニスシューズ

Say Instead:
適切な英語表現:

Sweatshirt (US), Jumper (UK)

Example Sentences:
例文:

| He always wears a _trainer_, even in the summer. | ⟶ | He always wears a **_sweatshirt_**, even in the summer. |

彼は夏でもいつもトレーナーを着ている。

How English Speakers use "trainer":
英語話者は（trainer）をどのように使うか:

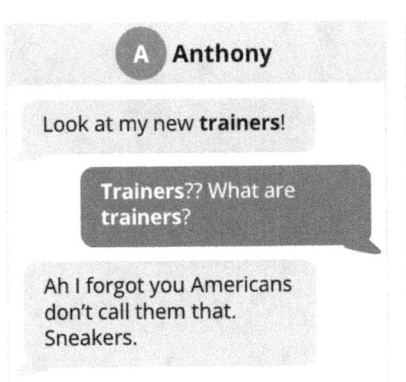

A Anthony

Look at my new **trainers**!

Trainers?? What are **trainers**?

Ah I forgot you Americans don't call them that. Sneakers.

K Kim

Do you know anyone who trains dogs?

Yes! My good friend is a dog **trainer**! She's really good. Want her number?

Y Shirt

ワイシャツ

Meaning in English:
英語の意味:

Doesn't exist
英語には該当する単語がない

Say Instead:
適切な英語表現:

Dress shirt, Button-up shirt, Button-down shirt

Example Sentences:
例文:

I can't find my _Y shirt_. I need it for work tomorrow.

→

I can't find my **_white dress shirt_**. I need it for work tomorrow.

ワイシャツが見つからない...明日仕事なのに。

DESCRIBING PEOPLE

人物描写

6

Scan for Audio

ALL BACK

オールバック

Meaning in English:
英語の意味:

Doesn't exist
英語には該当する単語がない

Say Instead:
適切な英語表現:

Slicked-back hair(style)

Example Sentences:
例文:

He's a famous celebrity who always has _all back_. → He's a famous celebrity who always has **_slicked-back hair_**.

彼は有名なセレブで、いつもオールバックの髪型をしている。

ARO FO

アラフォー

Meaning in English:
英語の意味:

Doesn't exist
英語には該当する単語がない

Say Instead:
適切な英語表現:

Around forty (years old), Forty-ish

Example Sentences:
例文:

He's _aro fo_. He's **_around 40 years old_**.

彼女は、アラフォーだ。

ARO SA

アラサー

Meaning in English:
英語の意味:

Doesn't exist
英語には該当する単語がない

Say Instead:
適切な英語表現:

Around thirty (years old), Thirty-ish

Example Sentences:
例文:

She's _aro sa_.	➚	She's **_around thirty years old_**.

彼女は、アラサーだ。

BARCODE HAIR

バーコードヘア

Meaning in English:
英語の意味:

Doesn't exist
英語には該当する単語がない

Say Instead:
適切な英語表現:

Comb-over (hairstyle)

Example Sentences:
例文:

I met a photographer who photographs old men with _barcode hair_.	➚	I met a photographer who photographs old balding men with **_comb-overs_**.

バーコードヘアのおじさんの写真をとる写真家に会った。

CHARM POINT

Meaning in English:
英語の意味:

Doesn't exist
英語には該当する単語がない

Say Instead:
適切な英語表現:

Attractive, Best (physical) feature/quality/attribute

Example Sentences:
例文:

Her *charm point* is her eyes.  Her eyes are ***really attractive***.
Her eyes are ***her best physical quality***.

彼女のチャームポイントは、目だ。

CHARMING

Meaning in English:
英語の意味:

A charming person is not only physically attractive and appealing, but also usually likeable and good at influencing others or winning their trust.

魅力的で人を惹きつける存在。それは外見だけに限らず、内面の魅力をも含んでいる。チャーミングな人物とは、一般的に好感を持たれやすく、他者に良い影響を与えたり、自然と信頼を得たりすることのできる人を指す。

Say Instead:
適切な英語表現:

Attractive, Good-looking

Example Sentences:
例文:

He is so _charming_!

He's so **_attractive/ good-looking_**!

彼はとてもチャーミングだ。彼はとても魅力的だ。

How English Speakers use "charming":
英語話者は(charming)をどのように使うか:

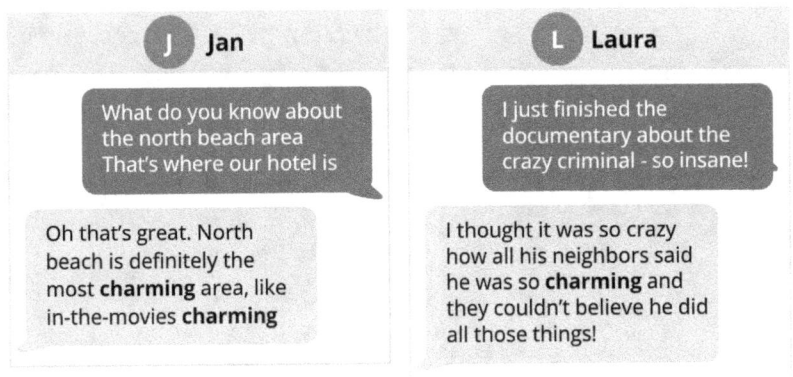

Jan

What do you know about the north beach area That's where our hotel is

Oh that's great. North beach is definitely the most **charming** area, like in-the-movies **charming**

Laura

I just finished the documentary about the crazy criminal - so insane!

I thought it was so crazy how all his neighbors said he was so **charming** and they couldn't believe he did all those things!

CONSERVA

コンサバ

Meaning in English:
英語の意味:

Doesn't exist
英語には該当する単語がない

Say Instead:
適切な英語表現:

Classic, timeless clothing (style)
Classy business casual (style)

Example Sentences:
例文:

She is really _conserva_. She has a really ***classic, timeless style***.

彼女は、本当にコンサバだ。

She wears a lot of _conserva_ clothes. She wears a lot of ***classic, timeless clothing***.

彼女の服装は、いつもコンサバ系だ。

CUNNING

Meaning in English:
英語の意味:

Sly, dishonest, able to trick you in a dishonest but smart way
ずる賢い、狡猾(こうかつ)、悪賢い

Say Instead:
適切な英語表現:

Cheating (on a test), Copying [someone's] answers

Example Sentences:
例文:

I told my teacher, "Sensei, Taro is *cunning* my answer!"	I told my teacher, "Teacher, Taro is ***cheating*** / ***copying my answers***!"

ぼくは、先生に「先生、太郎君が、
ぼくの答えをカンニングしてくる」と言った。

How English Speakers use "cunning":
英語話者は(cunning)をどのように使うか:

to: Parent <Bobbobson@email.com>

subject: Ms. Blane's Kindergarten Class Weekly Update

Dear Parents:

This week, as part of our reading curriculum, we will be studying the story of the **Cunning** Fox. In this story, the fox uses lies and deceit to trick the other animals to get what he wants. In the end, he gets sent away from the village after he loses everyone's trust. We will use this story to learn new vocabulary words like **cunning** and learn the importance of being honest and hard-working rather than using lies and trickery to get what we want.

GLAMOUR

グラマー

Meaning in English:
英語の意味:

Beauty, charm, riches, or fame, often that make a person or place desirable or eye-catching
美しさや魅力、富や名声など、人や場所を魅力的にし、目を引く要素

Say Instead:
適切な英語表現:

Curvy, Voluptuous

Example Sentences:
例文:

| People love _glamour_ women nowadays. | → | People love **_curvy_** women nowadays. |

最近、人々はグラマーな女性を好む。

How English speakers use "glamour":
英語話者は(glamour)をどのように使うか:

P Perla

I just got a job doing investment trading with a big company

Wow! Fancy!

Haha, it's not as **glamorous** as it sounds

D Diana

Here are some of the photos!

Wow! Those photos look so good! They look like **glamour** shots!

GORGEOUS

ゴージャス

Meaning in English:
英語の意味:

Beautiful
美しい、きれいな

Say Instead:
適切な英語表現:

Luxurious

Example Sentences:
例文:

The sheets at the hotel felt so _gorgeous_! The sheets at the hotel felt so **_luxurious_**!

ホテルのシーツは、触り心地がとてもゴージャスだった 。

This sounds like the sheets felt like they looked beautiful!
この言い方だと、シーツが「見た目が美しいように感じた」と言ってるみたいだ。

How English speakers use "gorgeous":
英語話者は(gorgeous)をどのように使うか:

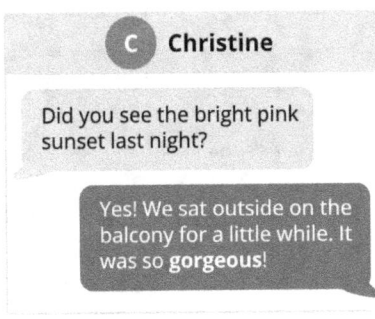

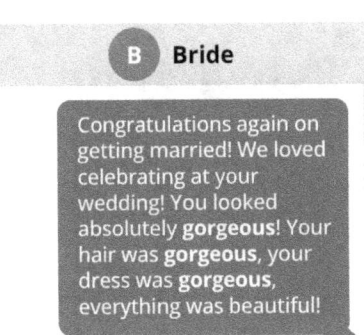

HAIR COLOR

Meaning in English:
英語の意味:

The color of one's hair
髪の色

Say Instead:
適切な英語表現:

Hair dye, Dyed hair, Hair coloring, Color one's hair

Example Sentences:
例文:

She has red _hair color_. She **_dyed her hair_** red.

彼女は髪を赤く染めた。

 This sounds like her hair is red, possibly naturally.
この言い方だと、彼女の髪は赤毛で、それが
染めていない地毛のようにも聞こえる。

How English Speakers use "hair color":
英語話者は(hair color)をどのように使うか:

A Agent

Here's the details of what they're looking in the commercial casting:

Female, under age 30:
Height: 5'2" to 5'9"
Hair color: Red
Language: English with a French accent

B Betty

Here's the advice from my aunt about dying your hair to hide gray hair:

Make sure you choose a color that matches your natural **hair color**... otherwise, it will look strange...

HOSTESS

ホステス

Meaning in English:
英語の意味:

1. A woman who has guests at her home
   自宅にゲストを迎える女性
2. At a restaurant, a lady at the front who takes reservations and often seats customers at their table
   レストランで、予約を受け付けたり、客を席へ案内する女性

The male equivalent of both of these meanings is "host"
これらの意味の男性版の言葉は「ホスト」である

Say Instead:
適切な英語表現:

Hostess

Example Sentences:
例文:

I was surprised when my Canadian friend told me her 16 year old daughter was a '_hostess_.' I thought that was too young for that job.

I was surprised when my Canadian friend told me her 16 year old daughter was a '_hostess_'. I thought that was too young for that job.

カナダ人の友人が、
16歳の娘が『ホステス』だって言うから驚いたの。
そんな仕事にしては若すぎると思って...。

She is such a wonderful _hostess_ and always makes everyone feel so welcome at her house.

She is such a wonderful _hostess_ and always makes everyone feel so welcome at her house.

彼女、本当に素敵な『ホステス』で、
家に来た人みんなを温かく迎えてくれるの。

125

HYSTERIE

ヒステリー

Meaning in English:
英語の意味:

Doesn't exist
英語には該当する単語がない

Say Instead:
適切な英語表現:

Have a bad temper

Example Sentences:
例文:

Some of the girls complained that their new teammate was _hysterie_. → Some of the girls complained that their new teammate **had a bad temper**.

何人かの女子は、
新しいチームメイトがヒステリーを起こしていると文句を言っていた。

INTELLI

インテリ

Meaning in English:
英語の意味:

Doesn't exist
英語には該当する単語がない

Say Instead:
適切な英語表現:

Intelligent

Example Sentences:
例文:

The new boss is extremely _intelli_; I really admire her. → The new boss is extremely **_intelligent_**; I really admire her.

新しい上司はとてもインテリで、私は彼女を尊敬している。

126

IMAGE CHANGE

Meaning in English:
英語の意味:

Doesn't exist
英語には該当する単語がない

Say Instead:
適切な英語表現:

Change your look, Get a new look, Get a makeover

Example Sentences:
例文:

イメチェン

I saw Yuka this weekend. She got _image change_ - did short cut and hair color - and now she looks so much younger!

I saw Yuka this weekend. She **_totally changed her look_** - cut her hair short and dyed it - and looks so much younger now!

今週末ゆかに会ったよ。イメチェンして、
ショートカットにして髪を染めたので、ずっと若く見えるよ!

MASTER

マスター

Meaning in English:
英語の意味:

As a noun, this word has negative connotations in English because its oldest meaning was a person who owned slaves or servants. Some other common meanings in noun form include:

名詞としてのこの単語は、英語では否定的な意味合いを持つ。もともとは奴隷や召使いの所有者を指す言葉だったためである。名詞の形では、以下のような意味も持つ:

1. A person who controls or cares for an animal
☞ Example: Dogs are loyal to their *masters*.

動物を管理・世話する人
例:犬は主人に忠実である。

2. Someone who has control of leadership over something or someone
☞ Example: It is important to be your own *master*; do not let others make choices for you.

誰かや何かを統率・支配する人
例:自分の人生の主(あるじ)となることが重要だ。人に選択を委ねてはいけない。

3. The original copy of something
☞ Example: You should keep the *master* copy of your birth certificate in a safe place.

何かの原本
例:出生証明書のマスターコピーは、安全な場所に保管しておくべきだ。

4. Someone who is highly skilled in a specific area
☞ Example: He is a Kung fu *master*.

特定の分野で卓越した技術を持つ人
例:彼はカンフーの達人である。

5. UK - The head of a school
☞ Example: He's the *Master* of the college.

イギリスでは、学校の長を指すこともある
例:彼はその大学の学長だ。

MASTER

Say Instead:
適切な英語表現:

Manager, Owner

Example Sentences:
例文:

My brother is the _master_ of the new coffee shop.

My brother is the **_owner_** / **_manager_** of the new coffee shop.

私の兄は、新しいコーヒーショップのマスターだ。

How English Speakers use "master":
英語話者は(master)をどのように使うか:

to: Parent <Parent0505@ElementarySchool.com>

subject: 2nd Grade Weekly Update

This week, we will begin our next science unit titled **Masters** of Disguise.

As part of this chapter, we will be studying different animals that disguise themselves, use camouflage, or hide in unique ways to protect themselves in order to thrive in their environments. Each student will be asked to give a presentation on one animal that is a **master** of disguise in his environment. Some examples include: chameleons, walking sticks, some species of owls, snakes, etc.

MISS CON / MISS CONTEST

ミスコン・ミスコンテスト

Meaning in English:
英語の意味:

Doesn't exist
英語には該当する単語がない

Say Instead:
適切な英語表現:

Beauty contest, Beauty pageant

Example Sentences:
例文:

She looks like she won the _miss con_.		She looks like she won a **_beauty contest_**.

彼女は、まるでミスコンで優勝したみたいに見える。

She looks like she won the _miss contest_.		She looks like she won a **_beauty contest_**.

彼女は、まるでミスコンテストで優勝したみたいに見える。

NAIVE

ナイーブ

Meaning in English:
英語の意味:

Having a lack of experience or judgment; simple, lacking critical thinking, unwilling or unable to believe negative or bad intentions, too trusting of others and their motives, often as a result of lacking experience

経験や判断力が未熟で、物事を疑わずに受け入れてしまう傾向がある。他人の裏の意図や悪意を疑わず、信じすぎてしまうことがある。これは、多くの場合、人生経験の浅さに起因している。

Say Instead:
適切な英語表現:

Overly sensitive

Example Sentences:
例文:

She always gets offended so easily. I feel like I can't say anything around her. She's so _naive_.		She always gets offended so easily. I feel like I can't say anything around her. She's so **_sensitive_**.

彼女はいつもすぐに気を悪くする。
何も言えない感じだ。本当にナイーブ（繊細）だ。

How English Speakers use "naive":
英語話者は（naive）をどのように使うか:

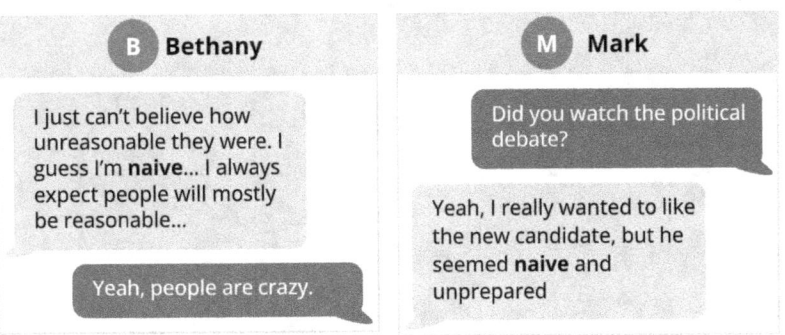

Neat / NEET

ニート

Meaning in English:
英語の意味:

1. Pleasant, cool
   心地よい、かっこいい
2. Organized
   きちんとしている

Say Instead:
適切な英語表現:

Willfully unemployed, Unemployed by choice,
Not actively seeking employment, education or training

Example Sentences:
例文:

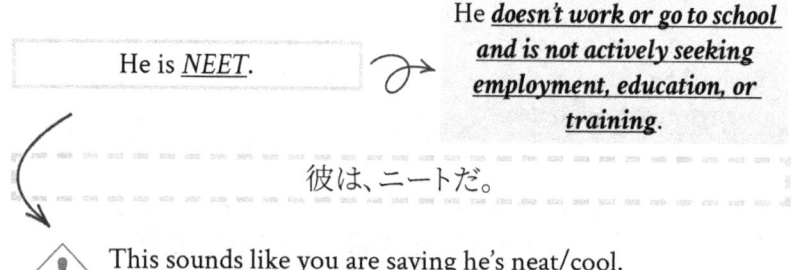

He is _NEET_.

He _doesn't work or go to school and is not actively seeking employment, education, or training_.

彼は、ニートだ。

 This sounds like you are saying he's neat/cool.
これは、彼がイケてる/カッコいい、と言っているように聞こえる。

How English Speakers use "neat":
英語話者は(neat)をどのように使うか:

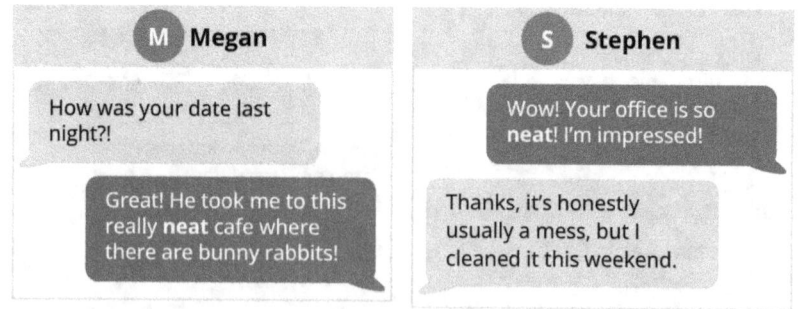

Megan

How was your date last night?!

Great! He took me to this really **neat** cafe where there are bunny rabbits!

Stephen

Wow! Your office is so **neat**! I'm impressed!

Thanks, it's honestly usually a mess, but I cleaned it this weekend.

NICE GUY

ナイスガイ

Meaning in English:
英語の意味:

A man who is nice/kind
優しくて感じのいい男性

Say Instead:
適切な英語表現:

Good-looking guy, Attractive guy

Example Sentences:
例文:

Thanks for showing me the
picture of your new
boyfriend!
He's such a *nice guy*!

Thanks for showing me the
picture of your new
boyfriend!
He's so ***good-looking***!

新しい彼氏の写真見せてくれてありがとう!
すごくナイスガイだね!

This sounds like your friend has already met or already
knows your new boyfriend and thinks he's really nice!
これは、あなたの友だちはもうこの人に会ったか知ってい
て、すごく感じのいい人だと思っているみたいに聞こえる。

How English speakers use "nice guy":
英語話者は(nice guy)をどのように使うか:

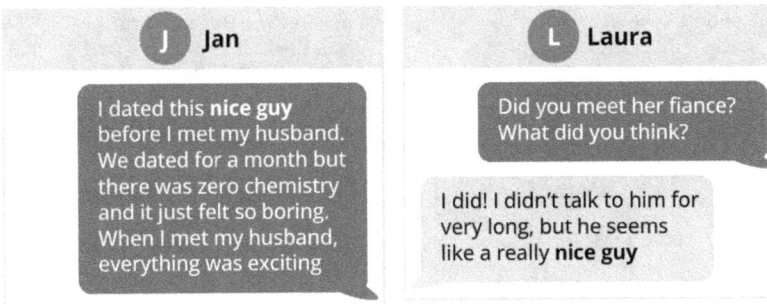

Jan

I dated this **nice guy**
before I met my husband.
We dated for a month but
there was zero chemistry
and it just felt so boring.
When I met my husband,
everything was exciting

Laura

Did you meet her fiance?
What did you think?

I did! I didn't talk to him for
very long, but he seems
like a really **nice guy**

ROMAN

Meaning in English:
英語の意味:

(Adjective) Related to Rome or the ancient Roman empire

(形容詞) 古代ローマ帝国に関する／古代ローマ帝国の

Say Instead:
適切な英語表現:

Far-fetched dream, Romanticized hypothetical adventure, Pipe dream

Example Sentences:
例文:

It seems like every man's _roman_ is to start his own company, become rich, and retire early.		It seems like every man's **_pipe dream_** is to start his own company, become rich, and retire early.

自分で会社を立ち上げてお金持ちになって早期リタイアするのが、男のロマンなのかもしれない。

How English Speakers use "Roman":
英語話者は(Roman)をどのように使うか:

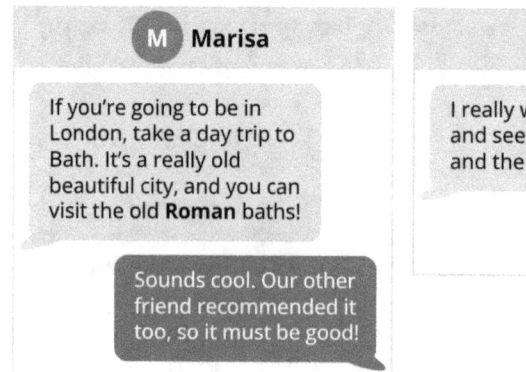

M Marisa

If you're going to be in London, take a day trip to Bath. It's a really old beautiful city, and you can visit the old **Roman** baths!

Sounds cool. Our other friend recommended it too, so it must be good!

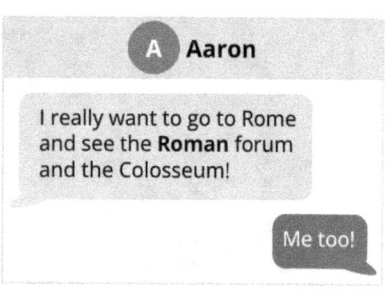

A Aaron

I really want to go to Rome and see the **Roman** forum and the Colosseum!

Me too!

ROMANCE GRAY

Meaning in English:
英語の意味:

Doesn't exist
英語には該当する単語がない

Say Instead:
適切な英語表現:

Silver fox, Salt and pepper hair

Example Sentences:
例文:

ロマンスグレー

I told my husband not to dye his hair because right now he's a *romance gray*!

→

I told my husband not to dye his hair because right now he's a ***silver fox***!

夫に「髪は染めないで」って言ったの。
今のロマンスグレーがいい感じだから。

ROUGH

ラフ

Meaning in English:
英語の意味:

1. Rough in texture, not smooth
手触りがざらざらしている、なめらかではない

2. If used to describe a person's appearance, *rough* means bad, untidy, not well-taken care of.

人の見た目について使われる場合"rough"は、見た目がだらしなかったり、身なりが整っていないように見えることを指す

3. An inexact form without details (E.g., a *rough* sketch of something would be a general sketch to show the main idea but without details)

細部を省いた大まかな形（例:ラフスケッチは、主なアイデアを示すためのもので、細かい部分までは描かれていない）

Say Instead:
適切な英語表現:

Casual, Plain, Informal
Laid back, Easy-going, Doesn't get caught up on minor details

Example Sentences:
例文:

| I wish I was more like him. He's so <u>rough</u>. | | I wish I was more like him. He's so ***laid back***. |

彼みたいにもっとラフに生きたいな。

 This sounds like he has a very unpolished personality.
彼が、すごくガサツな感じに聞こえる。

| She dresses really <u>rough</u> since she works from home. I'm so jealous. | | She dresses really ***casually*** since she works from home. I'm so jealous. |

彼女、在宅勤務だから服装もすごくラフでうらやましいよ。

 This sounds like she dresses very badly, maybe even unkempt.
彼女の服装がかなりひどくて、身だしなみもだらしないように聞こえる。

SMART

Meaning in English:
英語の意味:

Intelligent
カタカナでインテリ

Say Instead:
適切な英語表現:

Thin, Slim

Example Sentences:
例文:

スマート

| She became so _smart_! Did she diet? | | She became so **_thin_**. Did she lose weight? |

彼女は、とてもスマートになったね。ダイエットしたの?

This sounds like she is intelligent, but the question causes confusion because how is her intellect related to dieting?
彼女が知的であるように聞こえるが、質問内容が少し混乱を招く。彼女の知性がダイエットとどう関係しているのかが分かりにくい。

How English Speakers use "smart":
英語話者は(smart)をどのように使うか:

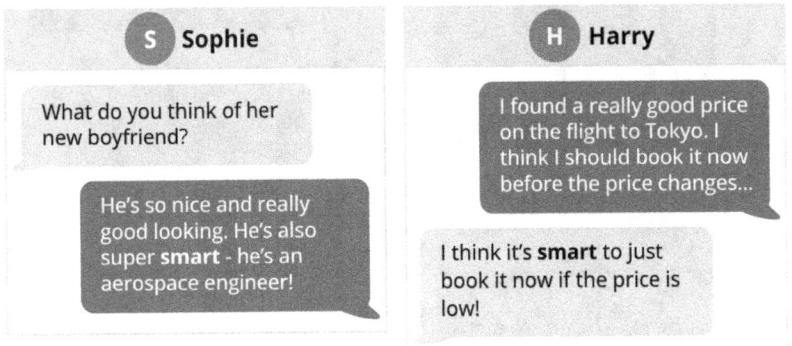

137

TALENT

タレント

Meaning in English:
英語の意味:

1. The skill or ability that someone has (most common use)
誰かが持っている技術や能力（最も一般的な用法）
2. A person who has great skill or talent in a specific area
特定の分野で優れた技術や才能を持っている人

Say Instead:
適切な英語表現:

Comedian who is also an actor/actress

Example Sentences:
例文:

> My favorite _talent_ is in the new drama! My favorite **_comedian_** is in the new TV show!

私の好きなタレントが新しいドラマに出てるのよ!

How English speakers use "talent":
英語話者は(talent)をどのように使うか:

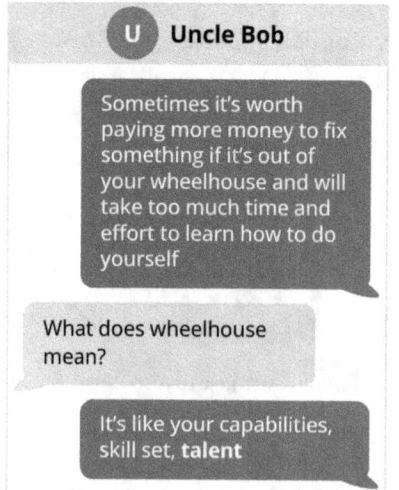

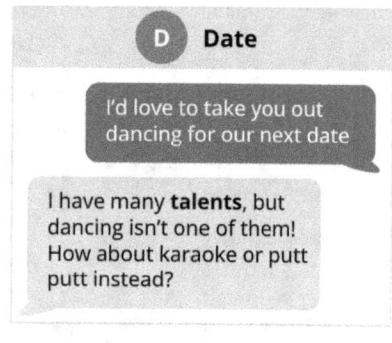

UNIQUE

ユ
ニ
ー
ク

Meaning in English:
英語の意味:

One of a kind, special
唯一無二の、特別な

Say Instead:
適切な英語表現:

Peculiar, Odd, Strange

Example Sentences:
例文:

My biology teacher is really _unique_.

My biology teacher is really _**peculiar**_ / _**odd**_ / _**strange**_.

私の生物の先生は、とてもユニークだ。

This sounds like your biology teacher is one of a kind, distinct, or special in a positive way.
これは、あなたの生物の先生が唯一無二で、際立っていて、いい意味で特別な存在であるように聞こえる。

How English Speakers use "unique":
英語話者は(**unique**)をどのように使うか:

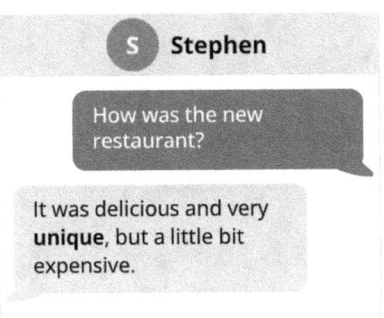

Megan: We're going to Japan next month, got any recommendations?!

Megan: Yes! You have to stay at a ryokan! It's a kind of traditional lodging that's **unique** to Japan!

Stephen: How was the new restaurant?

Stephen: It was delicious and very **unique**, but a little bit expensive.

VERY SHORT

ベリーショート

Meaning in English:
英語の意味:

Very short in height or length of time
身長が低い、または、時間の長さ
が非常に短い

Say Instead:
適切な英語表現:

Very short haircut, Pixie cut

Example Sentences:
例文:

She has very short. She has a *pixie cut* / *very short hair cut*.

彼女の髪はベリーショートだ。

 This sounds like you were trying to say, "She is very short."
この文では、「彼女がとても背が低い」と言おうとしてい
るように聞こえる。

How English Speakers use "very short":
英語話者は（**very short**）をどのように使うか:

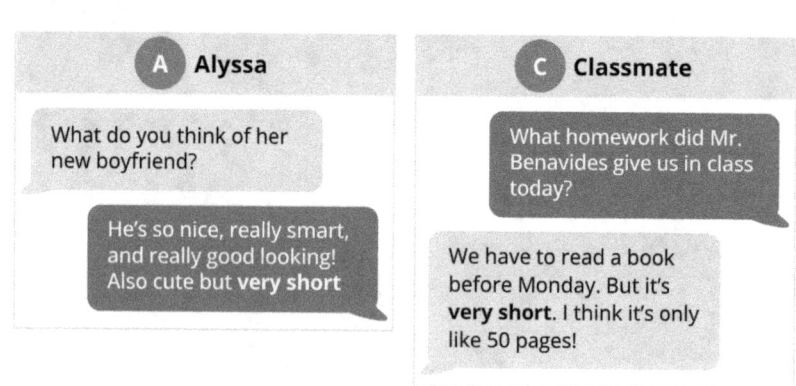

A Alyssa

What do you think of her new boyfriend?

He's so nice, really smart, and really good looking! Also cute but **very short**

C Classmate

What homework did Mr. Benavides give us in class today?

We have to read a book before Monday. But it's **very short**. I think it's only like 50 pages!

VIKING

バイキング

Meaning in English:

英語の意味:

The group of people from Scandinavia who often invaded, pirated, and settled in various parts of Northern Europe between the 8th and 10th centuries

8世紀から10世紀にかけて、
北ヨーロッパの各地に侵入・略奪・定住した
スカンジナビア出身の人々の集団

Say Instead:

適切な英語表現:

Buffet

Example Sentences:

例文:

We had a *viking* at our wedding.

We had a ***buffet*** at our wedding.

結婚式の食事はバイキング形式だった。

This sounds like you had a Viking at your wedding (or someone dressed up as a Viking!)

これは、結婚式にバイキング（あるいはバイキングの格好をした人）がいたように聞こえる。

YANKEE

ヤンキー

Meaning in English:
英語の意味:

1. (US) Anyone from the northern states, especially The Northeast. Historically, it meant anyone who was on the side of the Union (The North) during the American Civil War

（米）北部の州、特に北東部の出身者を指す言葉。歴史的には南北戦争において、北軍（Union）側に属していた人々のことを意味した。

2. (US) The Yankees are one of New York City's two MLB baseball teams

（米）「ヤンキース」は、ニューヨーク市にある2つのメジャーリーグ野球チームのうちの1つ。

3. (UK) This can be a negative term for anyone American

（英）アメリカ人全般に対して使われることがあり、時には否定的な意味合いを持つこともある。

Say Instead:
適切な英語表現:

Punk, Hooligan, Delinquent, Thug

Example Sentences:
例文:

He was a _yankee_ when he was a high school student.

He was a **_hooligan_** / **_punk_** when he was in high school.

彼は、高校生の時ヤンキーだった。

This sounds like you're slightly teasing that he lived in the Northeastern United States during high school.
彼が高校時代にアメリカ北東部に住んでいたことを、ちょっとからかっているように聞こえる。

EXPRESSING EMOTIONS & ENCOURAGEMENT

感情表現・励まし

Scan for Audio

ATTACK

アタック

Meaning in English:
英語の意味:

1. To try to criticize or hurt using words
言葉で批判したり傷つけようとすること

2. To try to hurt or damage using violence
暴力によって傷つけたり損害を与えようとすること

3. In sports, an offensive move to score points, advance
スポーツにおいて、得点を狙ったり前進する攻撃的な動き

4. To approach something in an aggressive way
何かに対して積極的または攻撃的に取り組むこと

Say Instead:
適切な英語表現:

Go for it! Go get it!

Example Sentences:
例文:

If you want to get that internship, then you should _attack_!	If you want to get that internship, then you should **_go for it_**!

そのインターンを獲得したいなら、攻めの姿勢で挑もう。

How English Speakers use "attack":
英語話者は(attack)をどのように使うか:

Coaching Exam Essay:
Analyze the pros and cons in sports coaching strategies that focus on <u>attack</u> vs. defense

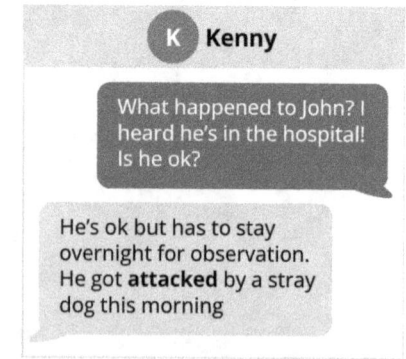

K Kenny

What happened to John? I heard he's in the hospital! Is he ok?

He's ok but has to stay overnight for observation. He got **attacked** by a stray dog this morning

CAPA

キャパ

Meaning in English:
英語の意味:

Doesn't exist
英語には該当する単語がない

Say Instead:
適切な英語表現:

Capacity, Limit

Example Sentences:
例文:

I have too much work today. I'm totally over my _capa_. → I have too much work today, and I'm totally **_overwhelmed_**!

今日は仕事が多すぎて、完全にキャパオーバーだ。

That person has a large _capa_ and is the type of person who doesn't worry about details. → That person **_can handle a lot_** and doesn't really worry about the details.

あの人はキャパが大きくて、細かいことは気にしないタイプだ。

This stadium has a _capa_ of 10,000 people. → This stadium has a **_capacity_** of 10,000 people.

このスタジアムのキャパは1万人だ。

DON MI

ドンマイ

Meaning in English:

英語の意味:

Doesn't exist

英語には該当する単語がない

Say Instead:

適切な英語表現:

It's okay! Good try! You'll get it next time! Don't worry about it!

Example Sentences:

例文:

Teammate in a volleyball game misses the ball and another teammate encourages her:
<u>Don mi</u>! <u>Don mi</u>! Next time!

Teammate in a volleyball game misses the ball and another teammate encourages her:
<u>It's okay</u>! **<u>Good try</u>**! You'll get it next time!

（バレーボールの試合でチームメイトがボールをミスする）
チームメイト：「ドンマイ！ドンマイ！次頑張ろう！」

Meaning in English:
英語の意味:

1. Physical violence or conflict (e.g., in boxing or in a physical fight or war)

身体的な暴力や戦い（例：ボクシングの試合、肉体的な喧嘩、戦争での戦闘）

2. Disagreement with words

☞ Example: A couple had a *fight* and now they are angry and hurt.

言葉での言い争いや口論
例：カップルが喧嘩をして、怒りや悲しみを抱えている。

3. Conflict between people

☞ Example: Two friends are *fighting,* so they aren't really talking to each other or hanging out right now.

人間関係における対立
例：友人同士が喧嘩をしてしまい、今はあまり話したり一緒に過ごしたりしていない。

Say Instead:
適切な英語表現:

Go! You got this! You can do it! Let's go team!
(general shout or cheer or encouragment)
Way to go! *(if you already did it)*

Example Sentences:
例文:

Fight! You can do it!

↝

Go team! You can do it!
(cheering for a team)
You got this! **You can do it**!
(encouraging a friend or person)

ファイト！君なら、できるよ！

ファイト

Goo

Meaning in English:
英語の意味:

Thick, sticky or slimy, usually gross substance
厚みのあるねばねば、またはぬるぬるしたもの。不快な物質であることが多い。

Say Instead:
適切な英語表現:

Good

Example Sentences:
例文:

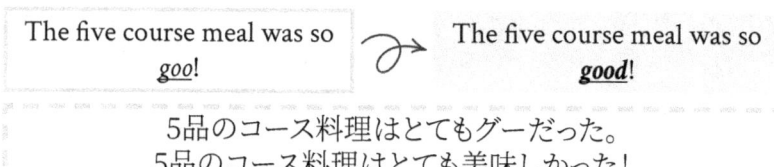

The five course meal was so _goo_! → The five course meal was so **_good_**!

5品のコース料理はとてもグーだった。
5品のコース料理はとても美味しかった！

How English Speakers use "goo":
英語話者は（goo）をどのように使うか:

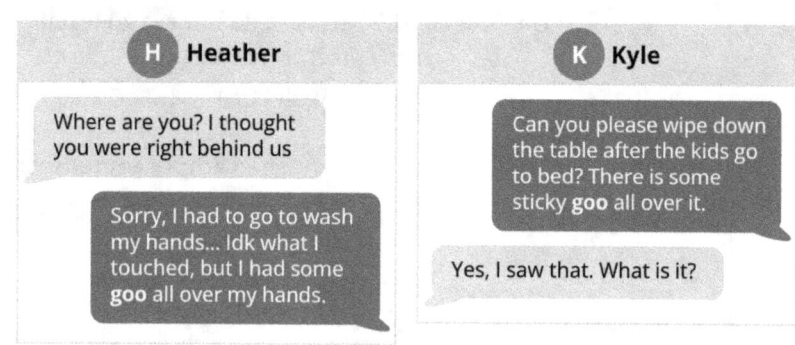

Heather

Where are you? I thought you were right behind us

Sorry, I had to go to wash my hands... Idk what I touched, but I had some **goo** all over my hands.

Kyle

Can you please wipe down the table after the kids go to bed? There is some sticky **goo** all over it.

Yes, I saw that. What is it?

GUTS POSE

ガッツポーズ

Meaning in English:
英語の意味:

Doesn't exist
英語には該当する単語がない

Say Instead:
適切な英語表現:

Fist pump, Pump your fist in the air

Example Sentences:
例文:

The team took a picture with _guts pose_ celebrating after their big win.

The team took a picture **_pumping their fists in the air_** celebrating after their big win.

チームは ガッツポーズ をして、大勝利を祝う写真を撮った。

HARD

ハード

Meaning in English:
英語の意味:

1. Opposite of soft
固い

2. Difficult
難しい

Say Instead:
適切な英語表現:

Busy, Hectic, Crazy (US)
Hardware

Example Sentences:
例文:

> I apologized to my professor, "I'm sorry, I didn't do my homework; this weekend was very _hard_."

> I apologized to my professor, "I'm sorry, I didn't do my homework; this weekend was very **_busy_**."

私は、教授に「宿題ができなくてすみませんでした。今週末は、とてもハードだったんです」と詫びた。

 This sounds like the weekend was very difficult and stressful, maybe emotionally and/or physically.
その週末は精神的にも肉体的にも、とても辛かったように聞こえる。

HIGH TENSION

Meaning in English:
英語の意味:

Doesn't exist
英語には該当する単語がない

Say Instead:
適切な英語表現:

Excited, Enthusiastic, Energetic

Example Sentences:
例文:

ハイテンション

Everyone was so *high tension* on the last day of school.

Everyone was so **excited** on the last day of school.

学校の最終日はみんなハイテンションだった。

This sentence sounds like everyone was feeling stressed and tense on the last day of school!
この文からすると、学年最後の日はみんなストレスを感じ、緊張していたようだ。

HIGH TOUCH

ハイタッチ

Meaning in English:
英語の意味:

Doesn't exist
英語には該当する単語がない

Say Instead:
適切な英語表現:

High five

Example Sentences:
例文:

We all did _high touch_ after our favorite team scored the winning goal.

We all **_high fived_** / did **_high fives_** after our favorite team scored the winning goal.

私たちは、好きなチームが決勝ゴールを決めた後、みんなでハイタッチした。

JINX

ジ
ン
ク
ス

Meaning in English:
英語の意味:

1. (Verb) To curse and cause bad luck
(動詞) 呪いをかけて不運をもたらす
2. (Noun) A curse or bad luck caused or brought on by a person
(名詞) 人によってもたらされた呪いや不運

Say Instead:
適切な英語表現:

Good luck, Bad luck, Good luck charm

Example Sentences:
例文:

I'll give you my *jinx* to win the game!

I'll give you my ***good luck charm*** to win the game!

この試合に勝つために、私のジンクスを教えてあげるよ!

This sounds confusing... if you want to help me win, why are you giving me a jinx? ⚠

これでは誤解されそうだ。私に勝ってほしいなら、なぜわざわざ縁起の悪いことを言うのか疑問に思われるだろう。

How English Speakers use "jinx":
英語話者は(jinx)をどのように使うか:

Tatiana

How did your interview go?

Really well, I think! But let's not talk about it becuase I don't want to **jinx** it!

Sam

How are you?! How is everything going?

Everything is going so well right now! I'm kind of afraid to **jinx** it because it's so good!

MOOD

ムード

Meaning in English:
英語の意味:

A person's general feeling at any specific time
ある特定の時点での人の一般的な気分

Say Instead:
適切な英語表現:

Ambiance, Atmosphere

Example Sentences:
例文:

> You'll love the _mood_ at the new restaurant!
> It's classy but chill.

> You'll love the **_ambiance/ atmosphere_** at the new restaurant! It's classy but chill.

新しいレストランのムード(雰囲気)はきっと気に入るよ！
上品だけど、気取ってなくてリラックスできる感じなんだ。

How English Speakers use "mood":
英語話者は(mood)をどのように使うか:

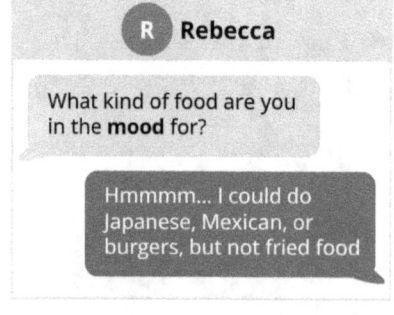

Rebecca

What kind of food are you in the **mood** for?

Hmmmm... I could do Japanese, Mexican, or burgers, but not fried food

Matt

We took the kids to the zoo yesterday, but it seemed like they were all in a bad **mood**! So much complaining!

Maybe it was the heat... yesterday was so hot!

NEUROSE

ノイローゼ

Meaning in English:
英語の意味:

Doesn't exist

英語には該当する単語がない

Say Instead:
適切な英語表現:

Postpartum depression, OCD, Anxiety, Neurosis

Example Sentences:
例文:

She got _neurose_ after having the baby, so she's started seeing a professional to get some help.

→ She had **_postpartum depression_** after having the baby, so she's started seeing a professional to get some help.

彼女は出産後にノイローゼになって、今は専門家に相談している。

NO TOUCH

ノータッチ

Meaning in English:
英語の意味:

An incorrect way of saying "don't touch"
"don't touch"を間違って言った言い方

Say Instead:
適切な英語表現:

Avoid the topic, Ignore, Don't bring up

Example Sentences:
例文:

They haven't told anyone else that they are moving abroad yet, so please _no touch_ about this topic at the party tonight.

→ They haven't told anyone else that they are moving abroad yet, so please **_don't bring up this topic_** at the party tonight.

彼らが海外に引っ越すことはまだ他の人には言ってないから、
今夜のパーティーではこの話題には、ノータッチで頼むよ。

OUTLOOK

アウトルック

Meaning in English:
英語の意味:

1. Attitude and view towards life and the future.
☞ Example: She has a positive *outlook* on things even though she has cancer and the situation is bad.

人生や将来に対する態度・考え方
例：彼女はがんで状況は悪いのに、物事に対して前向きな見方をしている。

2. A good viewpoint or place from which to see a good view

眺めのいい場所や眺めのポイント

Say Instead:
適切な英語表現:

Appearance, [He/she] looks...

Example Sentences:
例文:

His _outlook_ is bad today. Did he even take a shower? He _looks_ bad today. Did he even take a shower?

今日、彼のアウトルックは冴えないね。シャワーは浴びたのかな。

How English Speakers use "outlook":
英語話者は（outlook）をどのように使うか:

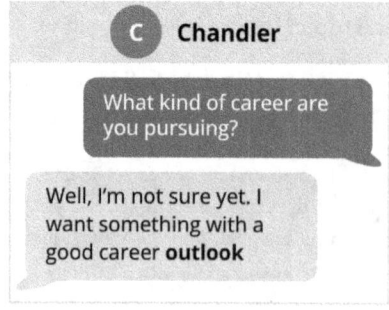

Chandler

What kind of career are you pursuing?

Well, I'm not sure yet. I want something with a good career **outlook**

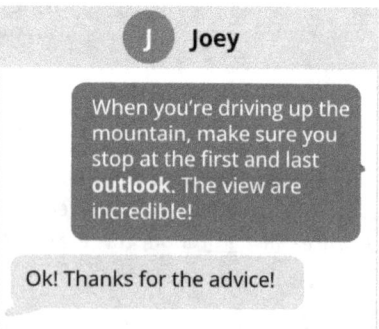

Joey

When you're driving up the mountain, make sure you stop at the first and last **outlook**. The view are incredible!

Ok! Thanks for the advice!

RETORTE

Meaning in English:
英語の意味:

Retort means to answer or respond to someone in a quick, sharp, impolite way showing anger and annoyance or sometimes humor

「レトルト」とは、相手に対して怒りや苛立ち、時にはユーモアを込めて、素早く鋭い、やや無礼な口調で返答すること

Say Instead:
適切な英語表現:

Pre-made, Microwaveable, Pouch of food, Instant, Ready-to-eat

Example Sentences:
例文:

You can find some delicious _retorte_ curry roux. → You can find some delicious **_instant_** Japanese curry **_pouches_**.

おいしいレトルトカレーが見つかるよ。

How English Speakers use "retort":
英語話者は(retort)をどのように使うか:

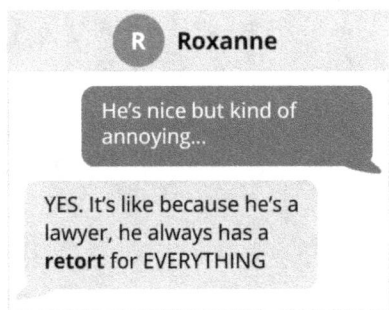

REVENGE

リベンジ

Meaning in English:
英語の意味:

Harm done to someone as punishment for some harm they did to another
誰かに危害を加えたことへの報いとして、自分が受ける危害
報復・復讐・仕返し

Say Instead:
適切な英語表現:

Rematch; Try again, A second chance

Example Sentences:
例文:

> It's okay that you didn't succeed this time. Just get back up and_revenge_.

> It's okay that you didn't succeed this time. Just get back up and ***try again***.

今回うまくいかなくても大丈夫。
また立ち上がって、リベンジすればいいんだ。

> ⚠ This sounds like you want to hurt or take action against someone who may have prevented you from having success the first time.
> 最初に自分の成功を妨げた誰かに対して、傷つけたり仕返しを
> しようとしているように聞こえる。

> We lost all of our baseball games, but at the last game, we _revenged_!

> We lost all of our baseball games, but at the last game, we ***finally beat one team that beat us before***!

野球の試合は、全部負けたけど、最後の試合でリベンジした。

> ⚠ This sounds like you really hated a specific team that beat you previously, and you finally "got your revenge" by beating them and showing you are better, likely in an unfriendly way.
> 以前、自分のチームを打ち負かした特定のチームのことを本当
> に嫌っていて、そのチームに勝つことで『仕返し』を果たし、自分
> たちのほうが上だと示したように聞こえる。――しかもあまり友好
> 的とは言えないやり方で。

SENSE

Meaning in English:
英語の意味:

1. Referring to the five senses: taste, touch, smell, sight, sound
   五感を指す：味覚、触覚、嗅覚、視覚、聴覚
2. Ability to have good judgment (e.g., common sense: basic understanding that everyone should have)
   判断力（例：常識＝誰もが持っているべき基本的な理解力）
3. A general feeling or understanding
   一般的な感覚や理解

Say Instead:
適切な英語表現:

Fashion sense, Sense of design, Style, Taste

Example Sentences:
例文:

| His _sense_ is so good; I love the colors! | | He has great **_taste_**; I love the color scheme! |

彼のセンスは最高！色の組み合わせが特に好き！

| Your _sense_ is so good! | | Your **_fashion sense_** is so good! |

あなたのセンス、すごく素敵！

This sounds like you have good senses, like maybe you could hear something that others couldn't hear well, or maybe you have a good sense of direction, or maybe you have good common sense, or a good general idea of what is happening around you, even if it's not clear to others.

これは、あなたが優れた感覚を持っているように聞こえる。例えば、他の人には聞き取りにくい音が聞こえるかもしれないし、方向感覚に優れているのかもしれない。または、常識があり、周囲で何が起きているのかを、他の人には分かりにくい状況でも把握できる力があるのかもしれない。

SUPER

スーパー

Meaning in English:
英語の意味:

1. Never a place. *Super* means excellent, great, wonderful, very, super...
場所ではない。「素晴らしい」「すごく良い」「最高」「非常に」
「超〜」など、賞賛や強調を表す言葉である。

2. *Super* can also be short for "superintendent" (manager of a building)
「superintendent（建物の管理人）」の略称として使われることも
ある。

Say Instead:
適切な英語表現:

Grocery store, Supermarket

Example Sentences:
例文:

| I went to the *super* this weekend. | ⟶ | I went to the ***supermarket*** this weekend. |

今週末、スーパーに行った。

How English Speakers use "super":
英語話者は(super)をどのように使うか:

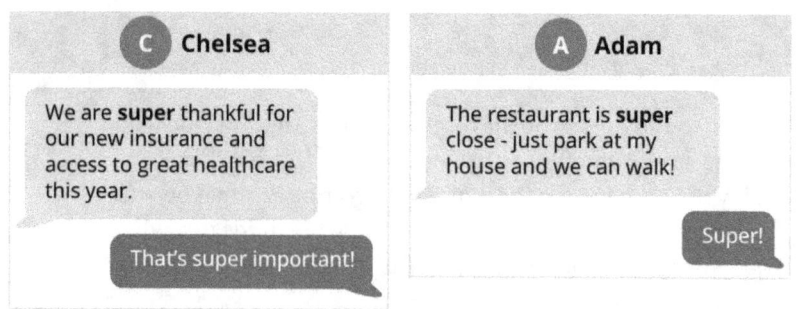

C Chelsea

We are **super** thankful for our new insurance and access to great healthcare this year.

That's super important!

A Adam

The restaurant is **super** close - just park at my house and we can walk!

Super!

Tension

Meaning in English:

英語の意味:

1. Stress

ストレス

2. Physical tightness and stiffness

身体の緊張やこわばり

3. Uneasiness or fragility in a situation

ある状況による不安感や脆弱さ

Say Instead:

適切な英語表現:

Energy level

Example Sentences:

例文:

My son is usually _high tension_, but my daughter is often _low tension_ due to her stress from the college application process.

My son is usually really **_enthusiastic and energetic_**, but my daughter is often **_down and tired_** due to her stress from the college application process.

息子はいつもテンションが高めなんだけど、
娘は大学の願書のストレスでよくテンションが低くなってるんだ。

How English Speakers use "tension":

英語話者は(tension)をどのように使うか:

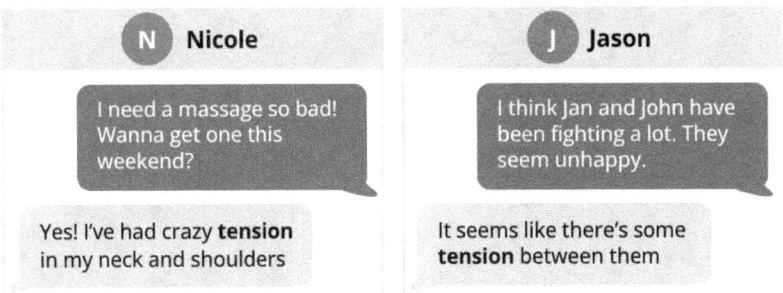

Nicole

I need a massage so bad! Wanna get one this weekend?

Yes! I've had crazy **tension** in my neck and shoulders

Jason

I think Jan and John have been fighting a lot. They seem unhappy.

It seems like there's some **tension** between them

TOUCH

タッチ

Meaning in English:

英語の意味:

1. To physically put part of your body onto something or someone else
☞ Example: Please don't *touch* me right now; it's so hot.

体の一部を何かまたは誰かに物理的に当てること
例:お願いだから、触らないで。暑いから。

2. When something comes into contact with another
☞ Example: My kids don't like their vegetables to *touch* their fruit.

何かが別のものに触れること
例:うちの子供は野菜が果物に触れるのを嫌がる。

3. To influence someone in an emotional way
☞ Example: I was so *touched* by her kindness.

誰かを感動させること
例:彼女の優しさにとても感動した。

Say Instead:

適切な英語表現:

Tap

Example Sentences:

例文:

She _touched_ me, so I turned around to see what she wanted.	She **_tapped_** me on the shoulder, so I turned around to see what she wanted.

彼女が私にタッチしたから、
何かあるのかなと思って振り向いた。

FOOD & DRINKS

食べ物・飲み物

Scan for Audio

AMERICAN COFFEE

アメリカンコーヒー

Meaning in English:
英語の意味:

Doesn't exist
英語には該当する単語がない

Say Instead:
適切な英語表現:

Drip coffee, Pour-over coffee, Weak drip coffee

Example Sentences:
例文:

Americans drink _American coffee_, not espresso. → Americans drink **_(weak) drip coffee_**, not espresso.

アメリカ人は、エスプレッソではなく、アメリカンコーヒーを飲む。

CHOCO

チョコ

Meaning in English:
英語の意味:

Doesn't exist
英語には該当する単語がない

Say Instead:
適切な英語表現:

Chocolate

Example Sentences:
例文:

Do you want some _choco_? → Do you want some **_chocolate_**?

チョコ食べたい？

164

CIDER

サイダー

Meaning in English:
英語の意味:

1. *Hard cider* is an alcoholic drink from apples

ハードサイダーは、リンゴから作られるアルコール飲料

2. *Hot cider* is a winter holiday drink - often homemade and made from apple juice and spices simmered together

ホットサイダーは冬のホリデーシーズンに飲まれる温かい飲み物で、リンゴジュースとスパイスを煮込んで作られることが多い

3. *Apple cider* is an unfiltered and less processed version of apple juice

アップルサイダーは、濾過されておらず、より自然な状態に近いリンゴジュースの一種

Cider could be any of these depending on the context.

「サイダー」という言葉は、文脈によってこれらのいずれかを指すことがある

Say Instead:
適切な英語表現:

Sprite, 7UP, Lemon-lime soda, Mitsuya, Lemonade (UK)

Example Sentences:
例文:

<u>Cider</u> is great because it doesn't have alcohol and can help your stomach feel better. It's also great for kids. Americans often drink <u>cider</u> when they have an upset stomach.	<u>*Sprite*</u> is great because it doesn't have alcohol and can help your stomach feel better. It's great for kids. Americans often drink <u>*7UP*</u> when they have an upset stomach.

サイダーはアルコールが入っていないので、
胃の調子を整えるのにいいし、子供にもぴったりだ。
アメリカでは、お腹の調子が悪いときにサイダーを飲む
ことがよくある。

165

COFFEE FRESH

コーヒーフレッシュ

Meaning in English:
英語の意味:

Doesn't exist
英語には該当する単語がない

Say Instead:
適切な英語表現:

Creamer, Non-dairy creamer

Example Sentences:
例文:

Would you like some *coffee fresh* in your coffee?

Would you like some ***creamer*** in your coffee?

コーヒーにコーヒーフレッシュいる？

! This sounds like maybe you want some fresher coffee or more freshly brewed coffee poured into your coffee cup.
これは、淹れたてのコーヒーをカップに注いでもらいたいように聞こえる。

COFFEE MILK

Meaning in English:
英語の意味:

Doesn't exist
英語には該当する単語がない

Say Instead:
適切な英語表現:

Creamer, Non-dairy creamer
Japanese coffee-flavored milk
Japanese milk coffee

Example Sentences:
例文:

コーヒーミルク

Many people enjoy drinking
coffee milk after a day at the
spa (onsen).

Many people enjoy drinking
Japanese coffee-flavored milk
after a day at the spa.

スパや温泉で沢山の人が、コーヒーミルクを楽しんでいる。

Would you like some
coffee milk in your coffee?

Would you like some **_creamer_**
in your coffee?

コーヒーにコーヒーミルクをいれる?

CONE

Meaning in English:
英語の意味:

1. Ice cream cone
アイスクリームのコーン

2. Cone shape
コーンの形

3. Sports cones
スポーツ用コーン
（または、トレーニングコーン）

4. Traffic cones
道路工事や交通整理などで使われるカラーコーン

Say Instead:
適切な英語表現:

Ice cream cone, Cone
Corn

Example Sentences:
例文:

| In Japan, sometimes there is <u>*cone*</u> on pizza. | | In Japan, sometimes there is <u>**corn**</u> on pizza. |

日本では、ピザにコーンが乗っていることがある。

CREAM PASTA

クリームパスタ

Meaning in English:
英語の意味:

Doesn't exist
英語には該当する単語がない

Say Instead:
適切な英語表現:

Alfredo pasta, Fettuccine Alfredo, Pasta with creamy sauce

Example Sentences:
例文:

That restaurant has good
cream pasta.

That restaurant has good
Alfredo pasta.

あのレストランのクリームパスタは、おいしい。

CREAM SODA

クリームソーダ

Meaning in English:
英語の意味:

A type of soda with a vanilla-based flavor
バニラ風味の炭酸飲料の一種

Say Instead:
適切な英語表現:

Melon soda ice-cream float

Example Sentences:
例文:

Cream soda is so good! I love
the green color and ice cream!

Melon soda ice-cream float is
so good! I love the green color
and the ice cream!

クリームソーダはおいしい。緑の色とアイスクリームが大好き。

Cup Ramen

カップラーメン

Meaning in English:
英語の意味:

Doesn't exist
英語には該当する単語がない

Say Instead:
適切な英語表現:

Instant ramen, Microwave ramen

Example Sentences:
例文:

| We always bring some _cup ramen_ when we travel. | ⟿ | We always bring some **_instant ramen_** when we travel. |

旅行するときはいつもカップラーメンを持っていく。

Curry Rice

カレーライス

Meaning in English:
英語の意味:

Doesn't exist, but sounds like rice flavored like curry
実際英語には対応する単語はないが、カレー風味のごはんのように聞こえる。

Say Instead:
適切な英語表現:

Japanese curry

Example Sentences:
例文:

| I ate _curry rice_ last night. | ⟿ | I ate **_Japanese curry_** last night. |

昨晩カレーライスを食べた。

CURRY ROUX

カレールー

Meaning in English:
英語の意味:

Doesn't really exist.. Some people may say "Japanese curry roux," but "Japanese curry mix" is much more common
英語にはこのような語は存在しない。「日本のカレールー」と言う人もいるが、「日本のカレーミックス」と言う方が一般的だ

Say Instead:
適切な英語表現:

Japanese curry mix

Example Sentences:
例文:

Do you use _curry roux_ or make your curry rice from scratch?

→

Do you use _(Japanese) curry mix_ or make your Japanese curry from scratch?

カレーを作るのにルーを使う?それとも、一から作るの?

DRY CURRY

ドライカレー

Meaning in English:
英語の意味:

Doesn't exist
英語には該当する単語がない

Say Instead:
適切な英語表現:

Japanese dry curry, Japanese pilaf, Japanese dry curry pilaf

Example Sentences:
例文:

| My husband cooks _dry curry_ for us every Tuesday night. | → | My husband cooks **_Japanese dry curry pilaf_** every Tuesday. |

夫は、毎週火曜日ドライカレーを作ってくれる。

FREE DRINK

フリードリンク

Meaning in English:
英語の意味:

A drink that is free
無料のドリンク

Say Instead:
適切な英語表現:

Drinks are free and included in the price, Drinks are included

Example Sentences:
例文:

| That karaoke is _free drink_ / has a _free drink_ system. | → | That karaoke **_includes free drinks in the price_**. |

あのカラオケは、フリードリンク制だ。

FRIED POTATO

フライドポテト

Meaning in English:
英語の意味:

Potatoes that are seasoned and fried, usually in cubes or chunks, (different from French fries)

味付けされて揚げられたジャガイモ。通常、小さいキューブ状や大きめのゴロゴロした角切り、または円形スライスの形で提供される（フレンチフライとは異なる）。

Say Instead:
適切な英語表現:

French fries (US), Chips (UK)

Example Sentences:
例文:

Do Americans always eat _fried potatoes_ with their burgers?

Do Americans always eat **_French fries_** with their burgers?

アメリカ人は、
いつもハンバーガーとフライドポテトを食べてるの？

FRUIT PUNCH

フルーツポンチ

Meaning in English:
英語の意味:

A party drink usually made by mixing a variety of fruit juices (both fresh and artificial), possibly soda or club soda, and possibly fruit pieces. This can be made with or without alcohol.

さまざまな種類のフルーツジュース（生搾りや人工のもの）を混ぜ合わせて作られるパーティードリンク。場合によっては炭酸飲料やクラブソーダが加えられ、フルーツの果肉が入ることもある。アルコールの有無に関わらず作ることができる。

Say Instead:
適切な英語表現:

Fruit salad, Fruit cocktail

Example Sentences:
例文:

I love eating *fruit punch* for dessert!   I love eating ***fruit salad*** for dessert!

デザートにフルーツポンチを食べるのが好きだ。

How English Speakers use "fruit punch":
英語話者は（fruit punch）をどのように使うか:

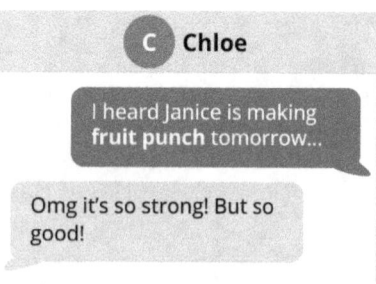

GREEN TEA

グリーンティー

Meaning in English:
英語の意味:

Any type of green tea including matcha, sencha, genmai, jasmine, etc.
抹茶、煎茶、玄米茶、ジャスミン茶などを含むあらゆる種類の緑茶

Say Instead:
適切な英語表現:

Matcha, Matcha green tea

Example Sentences:
例文:

I prefer to drink sencha, not _green tea_.

I prefer to drink sencha, not **_matcha green tea_**.

グリーンティーではなく、煎茶を飲む方が好きだ。

This sounds confusing... sencha is a type of green tea.
紛らわしいが、煎茶は緑茶の一種である。

How English Speakers use "green tea":
英語話者は(green tea)をどのように使うか:

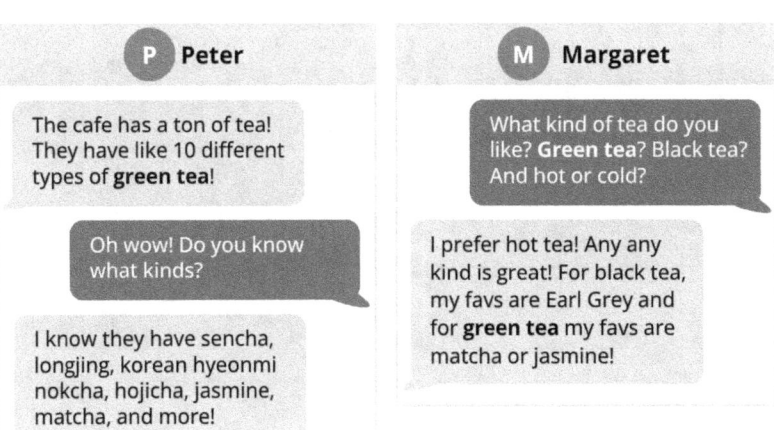

> **P** Peter
>
> The cafe has a ton of tea! They have like 10 different types of **green tea**!
>
> Oh wow! Do you know what kinds?
>
> I know they have sencha, longjing, korean hyeonmi nokcha, hojicha, jasmine, matcha, and more!

> **M** Margaret
>
> What kind of tea do you like? **Green tea**? Black tea? And hot or cold?
>
> I prefer hot tea! Any any kind is great! For black tea, my favs are Earl Grey and for **green tea** my favs are matcha or jasmine!

HAM EGG

ハムエッグ

Meaning in English:

英語の意味:

Doesn't exist
英語には該当する単語がない

Say Instead:

適切な英語表現:

Fried ham with a fried egg

Example Sentences:

例文:

> I thought Americans eat *ham egg* for breakfast, so I was really surprised when my friends told me they had never had it.

> I thought Americans eat ***fried ham with fried eggs*** for breakfast, so I was really surprised when my friends told me they had never had it.

アメリカ人は朝食にハムエッグを食べると思っていたので、友達に「食べたことがない」と言われて驚いた。

HASH(ED) POTATOES

Meaning in English:
英語の意味:

Doesn't exist, but "Potato hash" or "Hash" is a dish where diced potatoes are fried together with vegetables like onions and bell peppers

英語には、該当する単語がないが、「ポテト・ハッシュ」または、「ハッシュ」は、さいの目に切ったポテトを玉ねぎやパプリカなどの野菜と一緒に炒めた料理である。

Say Instead:
適切な英語表現:

Hash browns

Example Sentences:
例文:

I like eating _hash potatoes_ for breakfast at fast food restaurants.

I like eating **_hash browns_** for breakfast at fast food restaurants.

ファストフード店で朝食にハッシュドポテトを食べるのが好きだ。

ハッシュドポテト

HOT TEA

ホットティー

Meaning in English:
英語の意味:

Any tea that is hot
あたたかいお茶なら何でもホットティーという。

Say Instead:
適切な英語表現:

Hot black tea

Example Sentences:
例文:

| I prefer to drink *hot tea*, not green tea. | | I prefer to drink ***hot black tea***, not matcha. |

私は緑茶ではなく、ホットティーを飲むのが好きだ。

 This sounds confusing... green tea can be hot or cold.
紛らわしいが...緑茶は温かい場合もあれば冷たい場合もある。

How English Speakers use "hot tea":
英語話者は(**hot tea**)をどのように使うか:

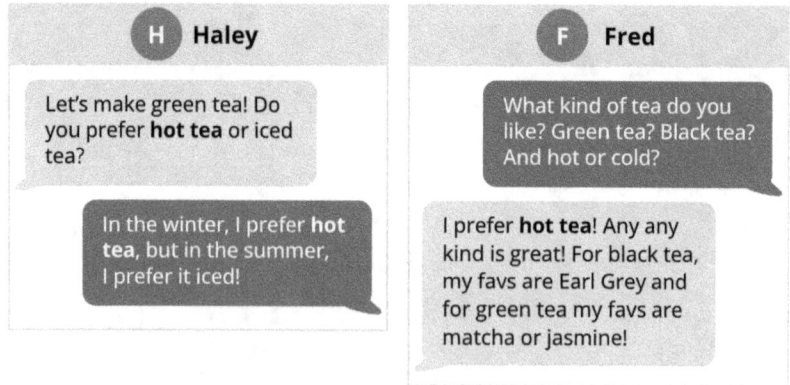

H Haley

Let's make green tea! Do you prefer **hot tea** or iced tea?

In the winter, I prefer **hot tea**, but in the summer, I prefer it iced!

F Fred

What kind of tea do you like? Green tea? Black tea? And hot or cold?

I prefer **hot tea**! Any any kind is great! For black tea, my favs are Earl Grey and for green tea my favs are matcha or jasmine!

HOTCAKE

Meaning in English:
英語の意味:

Hotcake can be found in the USA as a regional word for pancake; however, in most regions, it is more common to say "pancake." In some regions, people may call them "flapjacks." There is a common phrase *"selling/going like hotcakes"* that means something is selling out quickly.

この単語（ホットケーキ）はアメリカ英語では、一部の地域でパンケーキを指す言葉として使われる。しかし、ほとんどの地域では「パンケーキ」と呼ばれるのが一般的。また、地域によってはパンケーキを「フラップジャック」と呼ぶこともある。さらに、「売れ行きが非常に良い」ことを意味する慣用句として、"hot cake"のように売れる"selling/going like hot cakes"という表現があり、これは、何かが非常に人気があって、急速に売り切れることを表すフレーズである。

Say Instead:
適切な英語表現:

Pancake (US), American pancake (UK)

Example Sentences:
例文:

Hotcakes in Japan are usually fluffier than *hotcakes* in the USA.

Pancakes in Japan are usually fluffier than *pancakes* in the USA.

日本のホットケーキは、
アメリカのホットケーキよりもふわふわしていることが多い。

ICE

アイス

Meaning in English:
英語の意味:

Frozen water
氷

Say Instead:
適切な英語表現:

Ice cream bar

Example Sentences:
例文:

Do you prefer _ice_ or ice candy? → Do you prefer an _**ice cream bar**_ or a popsicle?

アイスとアイスキャンディー、どちらが好き?

ICE CANDY

アイスキャンディー

Meaning in English:
英語の意味:

Doesn't exist
英語には該当する単語がない

Say Instead:
適切な英語表現:

Popsicle

Example Sentences:
例文:

Do you prefer ice or _ice candy_? → Do you prefer an ice cream bar or a _**popsicle**_?

アイスとアイスキャンディー、どちらが好き?

JELLY / JELLO

Meaning in English:
英語の意味:

(US) Similar to jam
(米) ジャム

(UK) Same meaning as in Japanese
(英) ゼリー
ジェロ（日本語と同じ意味）

Say Instead:
適切な英語表現:

Jello (US), Gummies (US), Jelly (UK), Jelly sweets (UK)

Example Sentences:
例文:

ゼリー・ジェロ

My kids love *jelly*. ⟶ My kids love ***gummies*/*jello***.

子供たちはゼリーが大好きだ。

I love taking *jelly* vitamins. ⟶ I love taking ***gummy*** vitamins.

私はゼリータイプのサプリを飲むのが好きだ。

How English speakers use "jelly":
英語話者は（jelly）をどのように使うか:

Jenny

I made peanut butter and **jelly** sandwiches to take with us for lunch on our hike today

Awesome! I can bring some fruit and nuts to snack on

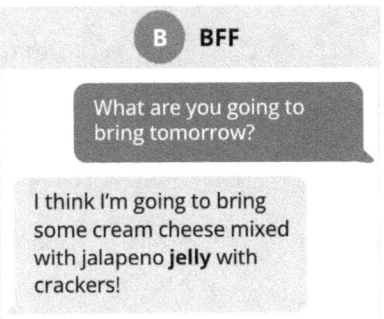

BFF

What are you going to bring tomorrow?

I think I'm going to bring some cream cheese mixed with jalapeno **jelly** with crackers!

LAURIER

ローリエ

Meaning in English:
英語の意味:

Doesn't exist
英語には該当する単語がない

Say Instead:
適切な英語表現:

Bay leaf

Example Sentences:
例文:

Put two or three _laurier_ to help season the soup. Put two or three **_bay leaves_** to help season the soup.

スープに風味をつけるために、
ローリエを2〜3枚入れてください。

Bay leaf

レフトオーバー

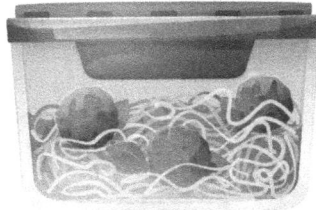

Meaning in English:
英語の意味:

An amount remaining, usually food
☞ Example: We have *left over* chicken; let's eat it for dinner tomorrow night.

残り物（通常、食べ物）
例: 残ったチキンがあるから、明日の晩ご飯に食べよう。

Say Instead:
適切な英語表現:

Hit to left field (that goes over the fielder's head)

Example Sentences:
例文:

| He did a huge *left over* at the end of the game. | ➔ | He had a huge ***hit to left field*** at the end of the game. |

彼は試合の終盤で大きなレフトオーバーの打球を決めた。

How English Speakers use "left over":
英語話者は（left over）をどのように使うか:

W **Wife**

What's the plan for dinner tonight?

I told the kids there's **leftover** chicken in the fridge or they can make macaroni

R **Roommate**

We had a lot of pizza **left over** from the party, so I put it in the fridge... I think we can eat that for lunch tomorrow

Great plan!

LEMON TEA

レモンティー

Meaning in English:
英語の意味:

Any tea where lemon is the main focus, often herbal tea with lemon and simple additional ingredients such as honey and ginger

レモンをメインにしたお茶。レモンが入ったハーブティーに、しばしばはちみつや生姜なども入れられる。

Say Instead:
適切な英語表現:

Black tea with lemon

Example Sentences:
例文:

Lemon tea is great, and it can also give you a good caffeine boost.	**_Black tea with lemon_** is great, and it can also give you a good caffeine boost.

レモンティーはおいしいし、カフェイン効果も期待できる。

 This sounds confusing... Lemon tea is usually a caffeine-free herbal tea.

これは、紛らわしい。なぜなら、レモンティーはノンカフェインのハーブティーであることが多いからだ。

How English Speakers use "lemon tea":
英語話者は（**lemon tea**）をどのように使うか:

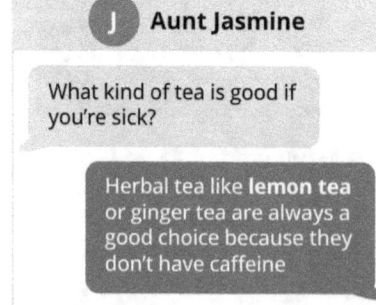

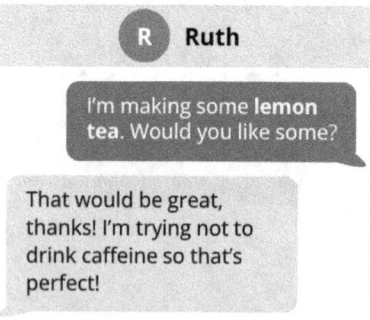

184

Mac / MacDo

Meaning in English:
英語の意味:

Doesn't exist
英語には該当する単語がない

Say Instead:
適切な英語表現:

McDonald's

Example Sentences:
例文:

マック・マクド

Mac in Japan has a teriyaki burger. _McDonald's_ in Japan has a teriyaki burger.

日本のマックには、てりやきバーガーがある。

MacDo in Japan has a teriyaki burger. _McDonald's_ in Japan has a teriyaki burger.

日本のマクドには、てりやきバーガーがある。

MACARONI

マカロニ

Meaning in English:
英語の意味:

1. Usually macaroni and cheese
マカロニとチーズ

2. A specific type of elbow-shaped pasta
特定の形状をしたエルボー
マカロニ(肘型パスタ)

Say Instead:
適切な英語表現:

Pasta

Example Sentences:
例文:

| We're having _macaroni_ and meatballs for dinner. | | We're having **_spaghetti_** and meatballs for dinner. |

晩御飯は、マカロニとミートボールだ。

 This sounds like you're having macaroni and cheese together with meatballs for dinner.
夕食にマカロニ&チーズとミートボールを
一緒に食べているように聞こえる。

How English Speakers use "macaroni":
英語話者は(macaroni)をどのように使うか:

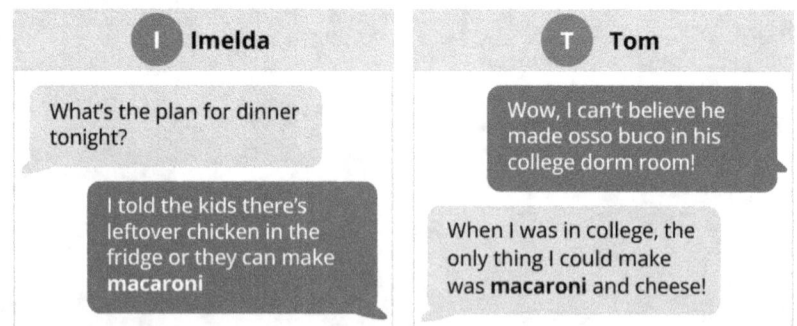

MILK TEA

ミルクティー

Meaning in English:
英語の意味:

Any kind of tea mixed with milk
ミルクを混ぜた紅茶

Say Instead:
適切な英語表現:

Black tea with milk

Example Sentences:
例文:

She wants green tea with milk, not _milk tea._

She wants green tea with milk, not **_black tea with milk_**.

彼女はミルクティーではなく、ミルク入りのグリーンティーを欲しがっている。

MINCHI

ミンチ

Meaning in English:
英語の意味:

Doesn't exist
英語には該当する単語がない

Say Instead:
適切な英語表現:

Ground meat (US), Minced meat (UK)

Example Sentences:
例文:

The recipe calls for two pounds of _minchi._

The recipe calls for two pounds of **_ground beef_**.

そのレシピでは、ミンチを2ポンド使う。

MUSHROOM

マ
ッ
シ
ュ
ル
ー
ム

Meaning in English:
英語の意味:

Any type of mushroom
全てのキノコの種類

Say Instead:
適切な英語表現:

Button mushroom, White button mushroom, White mushroom, Cremini mushroom, Baby Bella mushroom, Portobello mushroom

Example Sentences:
例文:

What's your favorite type of _mushroom キノコ_? I especially like _mushrooms マッシュルーム_, _shiitake mushrooms シイタケ_, _king oyster mushrooms エリンギ_, and _enoki mushrooms エノキ_.

What's your favorite type of **_mushroom_**? I especially like **_white mushrooms_**, **_shiitake mushrooms_**, **_king oyster mushrooms_**, and **_enoki mushrooms_**.

「好きなキノコの種類は何?」「私はホワイトマッシュルーム、シイタケ、エリンギ、それとエノキが特に好き。」

How English Speakers use "mushroom":
英語話者は(mushroom)をどのように使うか:

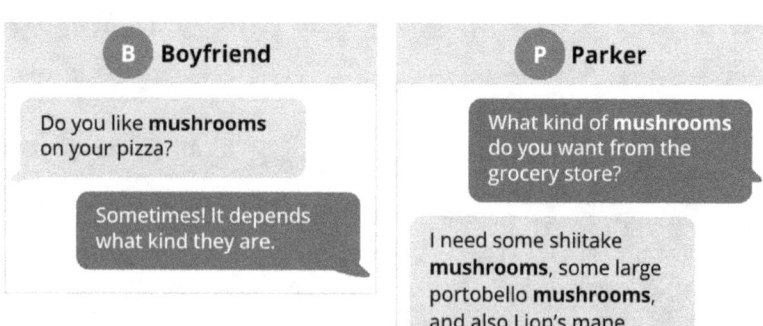

B **Boyfriend**

Do you like **mushrooms** on your pizza?

Sometimes! It depends what kind they are.

P **Parker**

What kind of **mushrooms** do you want from the grocery store?

I need some shiitake **mushrooms**, some large portobello **mushrooms**, and also Lion's mane

POOCHI TOMATO

プチトマト

Meaning in English:
英語の意味:

Doesn't exist
英語には該当する単語がない

Say Instead:
適切な英語表現:

Cherry tomato

Example Sentences:
例文:

I'm going to add _poochi tomatoes_ to the salad. ➔ I'm going to add **_cherry tomatoes_** to the salad.

サラダにプチトマトをいれるつもり。

POTATO FRIES

ポテトフライ

Meaning in English:
英語の意味:

Doesn't exist
英語には該当する単語がない

Say Instead:
適切な英語表現:

French fries (US), Chips (UK)

Example Sentences:
例文:

Do Americans always eat _potato fries_ with their burgers? Do Americans always eat **_French fries_** with their burgers?

アメリカ人は、いつもハンバーガーとポテトフライを食べてるの？

RANGE FOOD

レンジフード

Meaning in English:
英語の意味:

Doesn't exist
英語には該当する単語がない。

Say Instead:
適切な英語表現:

Microwave meal, Frozen meal, TV dinner

Example Sentences:
例文:

I taught my sons how to cook because I don't want them relying on fast food or _range food_ or expecting their wives to do all the cooking.

I taught my sons how to cook because I don't want them relying on fast food or **_microwave meals_** or expecting their wives to do all the cooking.

息子たちには料理の仕方を教えた。
ファストフードやレンジフード(電子レンジ用食品)ばかりに頼ったり、
将来奥さんに全部まかせたりしてほしくないからだ。

ROYAL MILK TEA

Meaning in English:
英語の意味:

Doesn't exist
英語には該当する単語がない

Say Instead:
適切な英語表現:

Japanese (royal) milk tea

Example Sentences:
例文:

ロイヤルミルクティー

I want to learn how to make _royal milk tea_ since it's really difficult to find in the U.S.

I want to learn how to make _**Japanese royal milk tea**_ since it's really difficult to find in the U.S.

アメリカではなかなか見つからないから、
ロイヤルミルクティーの作り方を学びたい。

SNACK

スナック

Meaning in English:
英語の意味:

A small amount of food eaten between meals
間食

Say Instead:
適切な英語表現:

Local bar (US), local pub (UK)

Example Sentences:
例文:

> There are no food places around here, only a _snack_ on the corner.

> There are no food places around here, only a **_local bar_** on the corner **_that has some salty appetizers_**.

このあたりに食べるところはないけれど、
角にスナックがひとつだけあるよ。

 This sounds you can buy a snack at a shop on the corner.
角の店で、スナックが買える、と言っているように聞こえる。

How English Speakers use "snack":
英語話者は（snack）をどのように使うか:

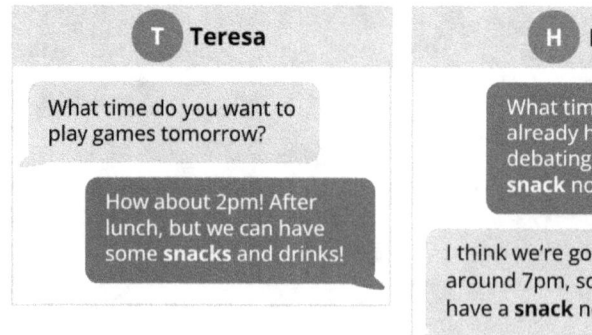

T Teresa

What time do you want to play games tomorrow?

How about 2pm! After lunch, but we can have some **snacks** and drinks!

H Harvey

What time is dinner? I'm already hungry, so debating if I should have a **snack** now or just wait...

I think we're gonna eat around 7pm, so maybe have a **snack** now

SOFT CREAM

Meaning in English:
英語の意味:

Doesn't exist
英語には該当する単語がない

Say Instead:
適切な英語表現:

Soft-serve ice cream

Example Sentences:
例文:

Do you prefer *soft cream* or ice? Do you prefer ***soft-serve ice cream*** or ice cream bars?

ソフトクリームとアイス、どっちが好き?

SOUP PASTA

Meaning in English:
英語の意味:

Doesn't exist
英語には該当する単語がない

Say Instead:
適切な英語表現:

Pasta with a soupy base, Pasta soup

Example Sentences:
例文:

I love *soup pasta*, but my kids prefer macaroni. I love ***pasta with a soupy base***, but my kids prefer spaghetti.

私はスープパスタが大好きだけど、
子どもたちはマカロニのほうが好きみたい。

SWEET POTATO

スイートポテト

Meaning in English:
英語の意味:

Sweet potato vegetable
サツマイモ

Say Instead:
適切な英語表現:

Japanese sweet potato dessert

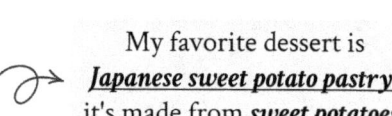

Example Sentences:
例文:

My favorite dessert is
sweet potato スイートポテト;
it's made from
sweet potatoes さつまいも.

My favorite dessert is
Japanese sweet potato pastry;
it's made from **_sweet potatoes_**.

私の好きなデザートはスイートポテトだ。
さつまいもから作られている。

How English Speakers use "sweet potato":
英語話者は(**sweet potato**)をどのように使うか:

F Family Chat

For Christmas dinner, let's all message what we're going to bring, so we don't have multiples!

I'm planning to bring **sweet potato** casserole

K Kara

My favorite mochi flavor is ube! It's a kind of purple **sweet potato**!

Oh yes, I love that kind!

TEA

ティー

Meaning in English:
英語の意味:

Any type of tea including black tea, green tea, herbal tea, etc.
紅茶、緑茶、ハーブティーなどを含むあらゆる種類のお茶

Say Instead:
適切な英語表現:

English black tea

Example Sentences:
例文:

I prefer to drink _tea_,
not green tea.

I prefer to drink **_black tea_**,
not matcha.

グリーンティーではなく、ティーを飲むのが好きだ。

This sounds confusing... green tea is a type of tea.
紛らわしいが...グリーンティーはお茶の一種だ。

How English Speakers use "tea":
英語話者は(tea)をどのように使うか:

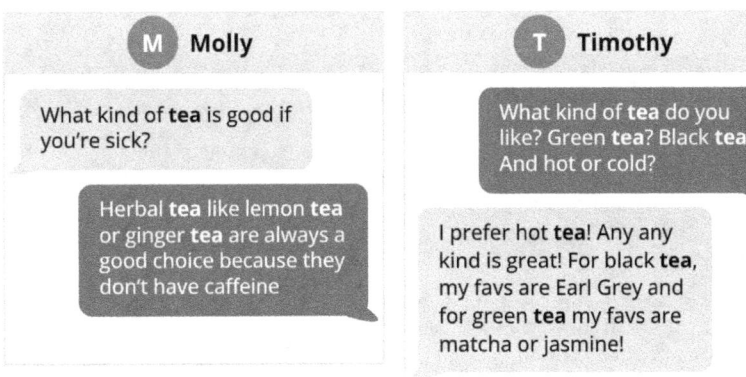

M Molly

What kind of **tea** is good if you're sick?

Herbal **tea** like lemon **tea** or ginger **tea** are always a good choice because they don't have caffeine

T Timothy

What kind of **tea** do you like? Green **tea**? Black **tea**? And hot or cold?

I prefer hot **tea**! Any any kind is great! For black **tea**, my favs are Earl Grey and for green **tea** my favs are matcha or jasmine!

WRAP

ラップ

Meaning in English:

英語の意味:

1. (Verb) To fully cover something in paper or plastic, like to wrap a gift or wrap up some bread so it doesn't get stale

(動詞)紙やビニールで物を完全に包むこと
(例えばプレゼントを包んだり、パンが乾かないように包むなど)

2. (Noun) A loose skirt or dress that's made by wrapping a large piece of fabric around the body (like a sarong)

(名詞)大きな布を体に巻きつけて着る、ゆったりしたスカートやドレス(サロンのような衣類)

3. (Noun) Similar to a sandwich, but the ingredients are wrapped with a flatbread like a tortilla instead of put between two slices of bread

(名詞)サンドイッチに似ているが、主な具材を平たいパン(トルティーヤなど)で包んだもの

Say Instead:

適切な英語表現:

Plastic wrap, Saran wrap, Cling wrap

Example Sentences:

例文:

Wrap is made of plastic. → **_Saran wrap_** is made of plastic.

ラップはプラスチック製です。

How English speakers use "wrap":

英語話者は(wrap)をどのように使うか:

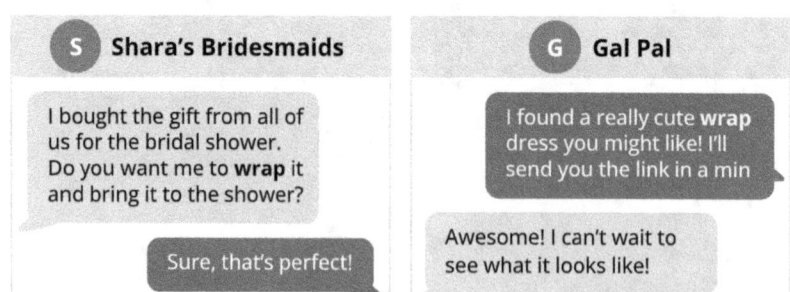

S **Shara's Bridesmaids**

I bought the gift from all of us for the bridal shower. Do you want me to **wrap** it and bring it to the shower?

Sure, that's perfect!

G **Gal Pal**

I found a really cute **wrap** dress you might like! I'll send you the link in a min

Awesome! I can't wait to see what it looks like!

GAMES, TOYS, HOBBIES

ゲーム
おもちゃ・趣味

9

Scan for Audio

AMA

Meaning in English:
英語の意味:

Doesn't exist
英語には該当する単語がない

Say Instead:
適切な英語表現:

Amateur, Non-professional, A hobby

Example Sentences:
例文:

My son is in a band, but it's just _ama_.	My son is in a band, but it's just a _**hobby**_.

私の息子は、バンドをしてるけど、アマなんだ。

ARCADE

アーケイド

Meaning in English:
英語の意味:

1. Video game arcade
ゲームセンター・ゲーセン

2. In architecture, a continuous set of arches supported by columns or piers, sometimes with a roof to create a covered walkway
建築に用いられる柱に支えられた連続アーチで、屋根付きの通路として設けられることもある

Say Instead:
適切な英語表現:

Covered outdoor shopping center, Shopping arcade

Example Sentences:
例文:

We went to an _arcade_ Friday afternoon.

→ We went to a **_covered outdoor shopping center_** Friday afternoon.

私たちは、金曜日の午後アーケード商店街に行った。

This sounds like you went to a place to play games! これは、ゲームをする場所（ゲームセンター）に行ったように聞こえる！

199

Cosplay

コスプレ

Meaning in English:
英語の意味:

Cosplay is more specific in English than "dressing up" or "wearing a costume." For Halloween, children often "dress up," and adults sometimes go to a "costume" party. *Cosplay* usually involves dressing up in costumes that represent a specific character, usually from cartoons, anime, comics, movies, books, or video games, often including science fiction and fantasy genres. People may also role-play to act like the character they are dressed as. *Cosplay* can be considered a specific sub-culture in the West, and participants often attend events and conventions based on their preferred theme.

コスプレは、単に「仮装」や「衣装を着る」といった言葉よりも、より具体的な意味を持つ。例えば、ハロウィンでは子供が「仮装」を楽しみ、大人は「コスチュームパーティー」に参加することがあるが、コスプレの場合は、特定のキャラクターを再現する衣装を着ることが一般的。コスプレでは、アニメ、漫画、映画、本、ビデオゲームなどに登場するキャラクターになりきることが多く、特にSFやファンタジーのジャンルが人気である。さらに、衣装を着るだけでなく、そのキャラクターの動きや話し方を真似して「ロールプレイ」を行うこともある。欧米ではコスプレは一つのサブカルチャーとして認識されており、コスプレを楽しむ人々は、自分の好きなテーマに沿ったイベントやコンベンションに参加することが多い。

Say Instead:
適切な英語表現:

Dress up, Wear a costume

Example Sentences:
例文:

We're going to do *cosplay* for Halloween. We're going to ***dress up*** for Halloween.

ハロウィンにコスプレをする。

 This sounds like you will be attending a special ComiCon-type of event dressed in costume and character for Halloween.

ハロウィーンの仮装をして、キャラクターになりきりながら、コミコンのような特別なイベントに参加するように聞こえる。

200

FAMI COM

Meaning in English:
英語の意味:

Doesn't exist
英語には該当する単語がない

Say Instead:
適切な英語表現:

(Retro) video game console

Example Sentences:
例文:

We don't have a _fami com_, but we love playing old games at my cousins' house on their N64.

→

We don't have a **_video game console_**, but we love playing old games at my cousins' house on their N64.

ファミコンは持っていないけど、いとこの家でN64の古いゲームで遊ぶのが大好きなんだ。

GAME SOFT

Meaning in English:
英語の意味:

Doesn't exist
英語には該当する単語がない

Say Instead:
適切な英語表現:

Video game

Example Sentences:
例文:

What's your favorite _game soft_? → What's your favorite **_video game_**?

好きなゲームソフトは何?

GA CEN / GAME CENTER

ゲーセン・ゲームセンター

Meaning in English:
英語の意味:

Ga cen doesn't exist

英語には該当する単語がない

Game center doesn't exist; however, there is a specific social gaming network service with this name from a popular company

英語には該当する単語はないが、有名な企業による特定のソーシャルゲームネットワークサービスとしてこの名称が使われている

Say Instead:
適切な英語表現:

Arcade, Gaming arcade, Video arcade

Example Sentences:
例文:

When I was a teenager, I went to the *ga cen* almost every day after school with my friends. 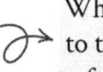 When I was a teenager, I went to the *arcade* almost every day after school with my friends.

10代の頃、友達と放課後ほぼ毎日ゲーセンに行っていた。

When I was a teenager, I went to the *game center* almost every day after school with my friends. When I was a teenager, I went to the *arcade* almost every day after school with my friends.

10代の頃、友達と放課後ほぼ毎日ゲームセンターに行っていた。

MAGIC

Meaning in English:
英語の意味:

Magic, like a magician does
マジシャンがする手品

Say Instead:
適切な英語表現:

Magic Marker, Permanent marker,
Sharpie

Example Sentences:
例文:

I'd like to write this with a *magic*.

I'd like to write this with a ***permanent marker***.

マジックでこれを書きたい。

This sounds like you are going to write it using magic.
魔法を使って書こうとしているみたいだ。

How English speakers use "magic":
英語話者は(magic)をどのように使うか:

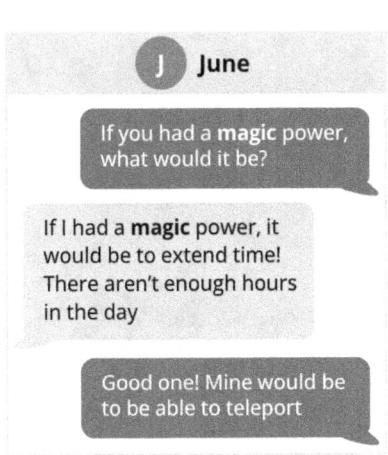

June

If you had a **magic** power, what would it be?

If I had a **magic** power, it would be to extend time! There aren't enough hours in the day

Good one! Mine would be to be able to teleport

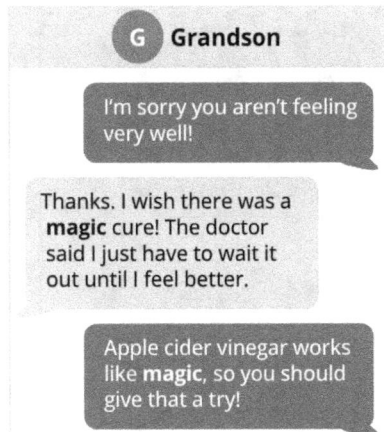

Grandson

I'm sorry you aren't feeling very well!

Thanks. I wish there was a **magic** cure! The doctor said I just have to wait it out until I feel better.

Apple cider vinegar works like **magic**, so you should give that a try!

203

NUM PLAY

ナンプレ

Meaning in English:
英語の意味:

Doesn't exist
英語には該当する単語がない

Say Instead:
適切な英語表現:

Sudoku

Example Sentences:
例文:

> I do the _num play_ every morning in the newspaper appli.

> I do the **_sudoku_** every morning in the newspaper app.

新聞のアプリで、毎朝ナンプレやってるんだ。

PLA MO

プラモ

Meaning in English:
英語の意味:

Doesn't exist
英語には該当する単語がない

Say Instead:
適切な英語表現:

Action figures, Model kit

Example Sentences:
例文:

> He collects _pla mo_ of airplanes and action figures and has a room with over 50 of them!

> He collects **_airplane models and action figures_** and has a room with over 50 of them!

彼は飛行機のプラモやアクションフィギュアを集めていて、
それらが50個以上並ぶ専用の部屋もあるんだ！

Pla Rail

プラレール

Meaning in English:
英語の意味:

Doesn't exist
英語には該当する単語がない

Say Instead:
適切な英語表現:

Toy railroad, Plastic railroad, Toy train

Example Sentences:
例文:

My uncle collects *pla rail*, and my cousin and I loved playing with them as kids.

My uncle collects ***toy trains***, and my cousin and I loved playing with them as kids.

私の叔父はプラレールを集めていて、子どもの頃いとこと一緒によく遊んだ。

Prin Clu

プリクラ

Meaning in English:
英語の意味:

Doesn't exist
英語には該当する単語がない

Say Instead:
適切な英語表現:

Photo booth, Sticker photo booth

Example Sentences:
例文:

In Tokyo, some of the train stations have *prin clu*! So fun!

In Tokyo, some of the train stations have ***photo booths that print stickers***! So fun!

東京の駅周辺には、プリクラがとれるところがあって、すごく楽しい。

PRIVATE TIME

プライベートタイム

Meaning in English:
英語の意味:

Time only for your self, but this phrase is not so common and sounds more secretive and individual than "free time."

自分だけの時間ではあるが、この表現はあまり一般的ではなく、『free time（自由時間）』よりも、より個人的で少し秘密めいた響きをもつ。

Say Instead:
適切な英語表現:

Free time, Leisure time

Example Sentences:
例文:

In my _private time_, I love to play basketball. In my **_free time_**, I love to play basketball.

プライベートタイムに、バスケットボールをするのが大好きだ。

How English Speakers use "private time":
英語話者は（private time）をどのように使うか:

X XYZ Company

Next week, we will install new website-blocking programs on all company computers. We strongly believe that many websites may be great during your **private time** but are inappropriate during work hours.

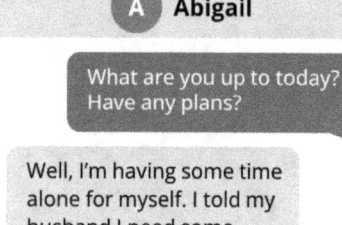

A Abigail

What are you up to today? Have any plans?

Well, I'm having some time alone for myself. I told my husband I need some **private time**, so he is taking the kids to the park

Puzzle

Meaning in English:
英語の意味:

Any situation, toy, or game that is difficult to solve or put together

解くのが難しかったり、組み立てるのが難しい状況、おもちゃ、
ゲームのこと

Say Instead:
適切な英語表現:

Puzzle, Jigsaw puzzle

Example Sentences:
例文:

I like *jigsaw puzzles*
ジグソーパズル but not other
types of *puzzles* パズル.

> I like *jigsaw puzzles* but not other types of *puzzles*.

ジグソーパズルは好きなんだけど、
それ以外のパズルは苦手なんだよね。

How English Speakers use "puzzle":
英語話者は(puzzle)をどのように使うか:

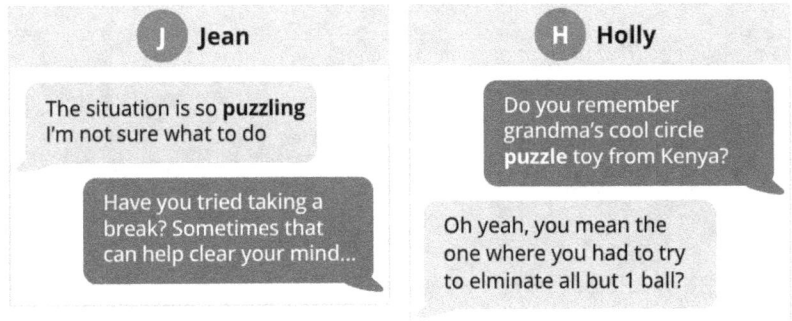

Jean

The situation is so **puzzling** I'm not sure what to do

Have you tried taking a break? Sometimes that can help clear your mind...

Holly

Do you remember grandma's cool circle **puzzle** toy from Kenya?

Oh yeah, you mean the one where you had to try to elminate all but 1 ball?

WAPPEN

Meaning in English:

英語の意味:

Doesn't exist

英語には該当する単語がない

Say Instead:

適切な英語表現:

Iron-on-patch

Example Sentences:

例文:

I love collecting _wappens_ from the places I travel to.

I love collecting **_iron-on patches_** from the places I travel to.

旅行に行った所のワッペンを集めるのが好きだ。

HEALTH & BODY

健康・身体

10

Scan for Audio

BODYLINE

ボ
デ
ィ
ー
ラ
イ
ン

Meaning in English:
英語の意味:

Doesn't exist
英語には該当する単語がない

Say Instead:
適切な英語表現:

Figure, shape

Example Sentences:
例文:

She has a good _bodyline_. She has a good **_figure_**.

彼女はきれいなボディーラインをしている。

I need to exercise to improve my _bodyline_. I need to exercise to improve my **_figure_**.

ボディラインを引き締めるために運動が必要だ。

DIET

ダイエット

Meaning in English:
英語の意味:

1. *(Go/be) on a diet* means changing or restricting the foods you usually eat for medical reasons, healthier habits, or weight loss.

☞ Example: She has diabetes, so she needs to go on a low-sugar *diet*.

☞ Example: Someone with high cholesterol might need to go on a low-sodium *diet*.

「ダイエットをする」「ダイエット中である」とは、健康のため、医療的な理由、または減量のために、普段の食事内容を変更したり制限したりすることを指す

例：彼女は糖尿病のため、低糖質の食事をとる必要がある。

例：コレステロール値が高い人は、低ナトリウムの食事を取る必要がある場合がある。

2. *Diet* can also mean food one usually eats

☞ Example: A typical Japanese *diet* includes rice, vegetables, and fish.

「ダイエット」は、普段食べている食事全般を指すこともある

例：典型的な日本の食事は、ご飯、野菜、魚を含む。

Say Instead:
適切な英語表現:

Trying to lose weight

Example Sentences:
例文:

I'm going to the gym because I'm on a _diet_.	I'm going to the gym because I'm ***trying to lose weight***. I'm trying to get in shape.

ダイエット中なので、ジムに行くよ。

DOCTOR STOP

Meaning in English:
英語の意味:

Doesn't exist
英語には該当する単語がない

Say Instead:
適切な英語表現:

My doctor told me (not) to...

Example Sentences:
例文:

I have a *doctor stop* about sugar.

My doctor told me I need to cut sugar out of my diet.

私は糖分についてドクターストップがかかっている。

Sports/exercise is a *doctor stop* for me right now.

My doctor told me I shouldn't do any strenuous activity right now.

今、ちょうどスポーツ/運動は、ドクターストップがかかっている。

ド
ク
タ
ー
ス
ト
ッ
プ

FITNESS

Meaning in English:
英語の意味:

The practice of being physically fit and healthy; never a place
身体を健康に保ち、体力を維持することを目的とした習慣や
取り組み（場所を指す言葉ではない）

Say Instead:
適切な英語表現:

Gym, Fitness center

Example Sentences:
例文:

I go to the _fitness_ every day. I go to the **gym** every day.

私は、毎日フィットネスに行っている。

How English Speakers use "fitness":
英語話者は（**fitness**）をどのように使うか:

L LL Apartments

You have received a package. Your package is located in locker 15 in the hallway across from the **fitness** room.

This is an automated message. Please contact your leasing office with any additional questions.

V Volleyball Coach

What do you have in mind for volleyball practice today?

I want to start practice with at least 30 minutes of **fitness**. Maybe have the team warm up and do some **fitness** stuff first

HEALING

ヒーリング

Meaning in English:
英語の意味:

The process of becoming well or whole again after illness or injury (physical or emotional)
病気や怪我(身体的または精神的)の後、健康な状態に戻る、または完全に治る過程のこと

Say Instead:
適切な英語表現:

Relaxing, Stress-relieving, Calming

Example Sentences:
例文:

This music has _healing_ effect. ⟶ This music is **_relaxing_**.

この音楽にはヒーリング効果がある。

⚠ This sounds like the music can heal you.
音楽があなたを癒してくれるように聞こえる。

How English Speakers use "healing":
英語話者は(**healing**)をどのように使うか:

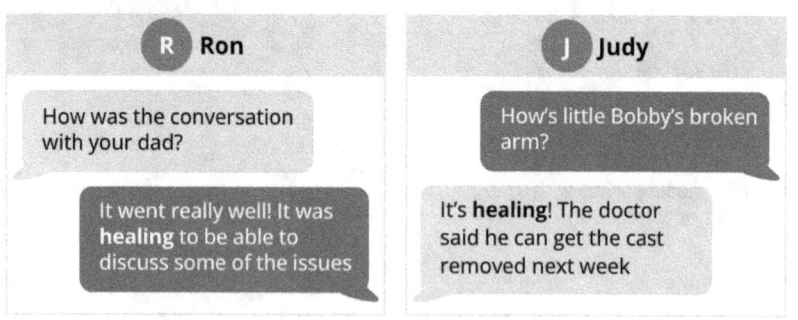

R Ron

How was the conversation with your dad?

It went really well! It was **healing** to be able to discuss some of the issues

J Judy

How's little Bobby's broken arm?

It's **healing**! The doctor said he can get the cast removed next week

214

HIP

Meaning in English:
英語の意味:

You have two hips on the sides. It includes the bones and joints where your femur connects to your pelvis. The back part is not usually called your hip.

両側に二つの臀部（ヒップ）がある。それは、大腿骨が骨盤に接続する骨や関節を含む。通常、背面部分はヒップとは呼ばれない。

Say Instead:
適切な英語表現:

Buttocks, Butt, Bottom, Behind, Backside, Derriere

Example Sentences:
例文:

She has a big _hip_. She has a big **_butt_**/**_behind_**.

彼女のヒップは大きい。

This sounds like she has wide hips.
これは、彼女のヒップが広いように聞こえる。

How English speakers use "hip":
英語話者は（hip）をどのように使うか:

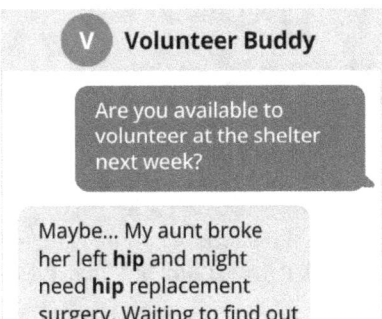

Volunteer Buddy

Are you available to volunteer at the shelter next week?

Maybe... My aunt broke her left **hip** and might need **hip** replacement surgery. Waiting to find out the surgery date...

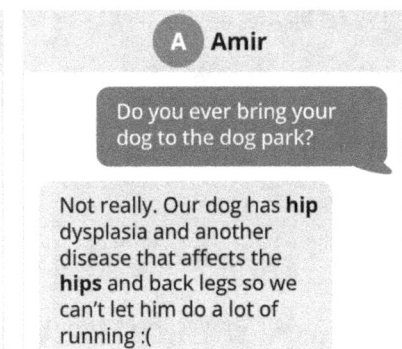

Amir

Do you ever bring your dog to the dog park?

Not really. Our dog has **hip** dysplasia and another disease that affects the **hips** and back legs so we can't let him do a lot of running :(

HEALTH METER

Meaning in English:
英語の意味:

Doesn't exist
英語には該当する単語がない

Say Instead:
適切な英語表現:

(Bathroom) scale

Example Sentences:
例文:

| We have a _health meter_ in our bathroom. | | We have a **_(bathroom) scale_** in our bathroom. |

私たちのバスルームにはヘルスメーターがある。

HOME DOCTOR

Meaning in English:
英語の意味:

Doesn't exist
英語には該当する単語がない

Say Instead:
適切な英語表現:

Primary care physician (PCP), Family medicine doctor

Example Sentences:
例文:

| You should take your kids to the _home doctor_ if you think they're sick. | | You should take your kids to your **_PCP_** if you think they're sick. |

子どもが体調を壊していると思うなら、
ホームドクター（かかりつけの医者）に診てもらったほうがいい。

HUMAN DOCK

人間ドック

Meaning in English:
英語の意味:

Doesn't exist
英語には該当する単語がない

Say Instead:
適切な英語表現:

Annual checkup

Example Sentences:
例文:

I always get my *human dock* when I go back to Japan in the summer. ➜ I always get my **_annual checkup_** when I go back to Japan in the summer.

私は毎年夏に日本へ帰ったときに人間ドックを受ける。

KARTE

カルテ

Meaning in English:
英語の意味:

Doesn't exist
英語には該当する単語がない

Say Instead:
適切な英語表現:

Medical records

Example Sentences:
例文:

Can I get a copy of my _karte_ to bring to my new doctor? Can I get a copy of my **_medical records_** to bring to my new doctor?

新しい先生のところに持っていくために、
カルテのコピーをもらえますか?

LIVER / LEVER

レバー

Meaning in English:
英語の意味:

1. Liver - body part
肝臓

2. Liver - food
レバー

3. Lever
梃子

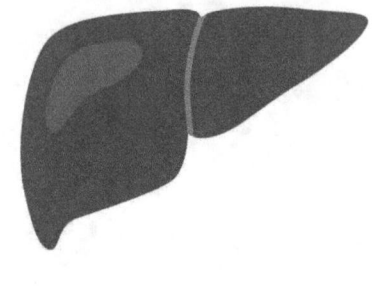

Say Instead:
適切な英語表現:

Liver

Example Sentences:
例文:

My uncle has fatty _liver_ 肝 disease, so his doctor told him he can't eat chicken _liver_ レバー or beef _liver_ レバー anymore.

→

My uncle has fatty **_liver_** disease, so his doctor told him he can't eat chicken **_liver_** or beef **_liver_** anymore.

　　私の叔父は脂肪肝の病気を持っているので、
医者に鶏レバーや牛レバーを食べてはいけないと言われた。

How English Speakers use "liver":
英語話者は(liver)をどのように使うか:

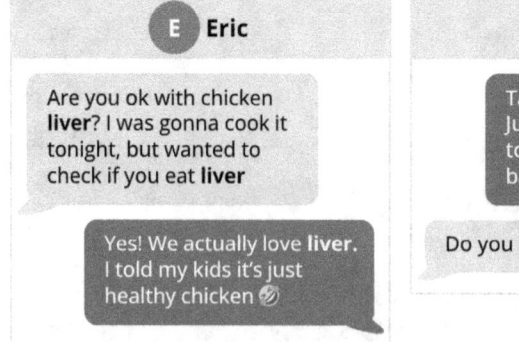

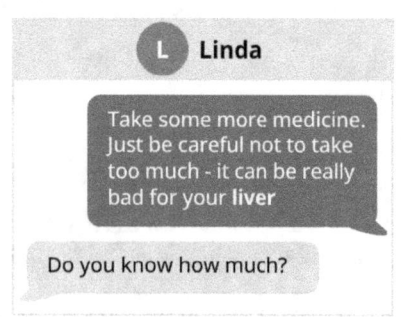

MANIA

マニア

Meaning in English:
英語の意味:

1. Excessive or unusual excitement, enthusiasm, or obsession. This is usually negative in meaning and never refers to a person.
何かに対する過剰または異常な興奮、熱狂、執着（通常、否定的な意味を持ち、人には使われない）

2. Mania in a psychiatric disorder like bipolar disorder
マニアとは、双極性障害などの精神疾患における躁状態

Say Instead:
適切な英語表現:

Connoisseur, Enthusiast *(positive, also means you know a lot about the topic, usually used for the arts and food related topics (e.g., a wine connoisseur))*
A (big) fan of *(positive)*
To be really into *(neutral)*
Fanatic, Obsessed with *(can be positive or negative)*
Obsession [for the thing] *(somewhat negative)*
Maniac [for the person] *(negative)*

Example Sentences:
例文:

| She is a coffee _mania_. She goes to specialty coffee tastings in her free time and experiments with different ways of roasting coffee beans on the weekends. | | She is a coffee **_enthusiast_**. She goes to specialty coffee tastings in her free time and experiments with different ways of roasting coffee beans on the weekends. |

彼女はコーヒーマニアだ。
暇なときにはスペシャルティコーヒーのテイスティングに出かけ、
週末にはコーヒー豆のさまざまな焙煎方法を試している。

NECK

ネック

Meaning in English:
英語の意味:

The part of your body between your head and back
首

Say Instead:
適切な英語表現:

Obstacle, Setback, Holdup

Example Sentences:
例文:

> The _neck_ of this project is money; our budget is too small.

> The **_biggest obstacle_** to this project is money; our budget is too small.

このプロジェクトのネックは資金。予算が少なすぎる。

How English Speakers use "neck":
英語話者は(neck)をどのように使うか:

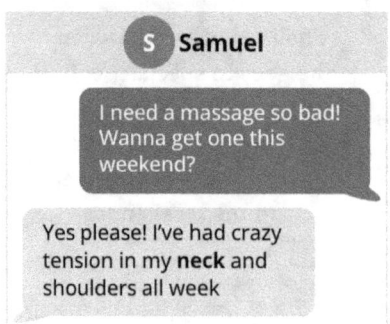

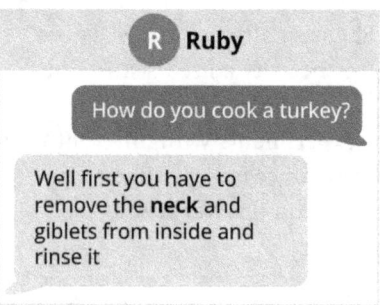

OB

オービー

Meaning in English:
英語の意味:

Obstetrics, Obstetrician
産科または産婦人科医

Say Instead:
適切な英語表現:

He went to my university,
A male alumnus from my university who graduated before me

Example Sentences:
例文:

He's an *OB* from my university. He was part of our business club and graduated two years before me.

He's an ***alumnus*** from my university. He was part of the business club and graduated two years before me.

彼は私の大学のOBだ。
ビジネスクラブのメンバーで、私より2年早く卒業した。

This sounds like he now works as an obstetrician.
今、彼は、産婦人科医として働いているように聞こえる。

How English Speakers use "OB":
英語話者は（OB）をどのように使うか:

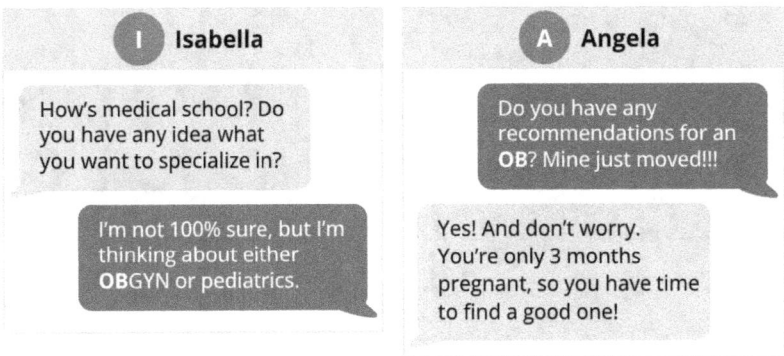

Pill

Meaning in English:
英語の意味:

Any type of medicine that is
swallowed whole without chewing
噛まずにそのまま飲み込むタイプの薬
全般

ピ
ル

Say Instead:
適切な英語表現:

Birth control (pill), Contraception

Example Sentences:
例文:

> My grandma has to take 10
> _pills_ 錠も薬 a day! Basically the
> only _pill_ 薬 she doesn't take is
> _birth control_ ピル since she's
> post-menopausal.

> My grandma has to take 10
> **_pills_** a day! Basically, the only
> **_pill_** she doesn't take is **_birth
> control_** since she's
> post-menopausal.

うちのおばあちゃん、
1日に10錠も薬を飲まなきゃいけないの!更年期を過ぎてるから、
唯一飲んでいない薬は避妊薬くらいかな。

How English Speakers use "pill":
英語話者は(pill)をどのように使うか:

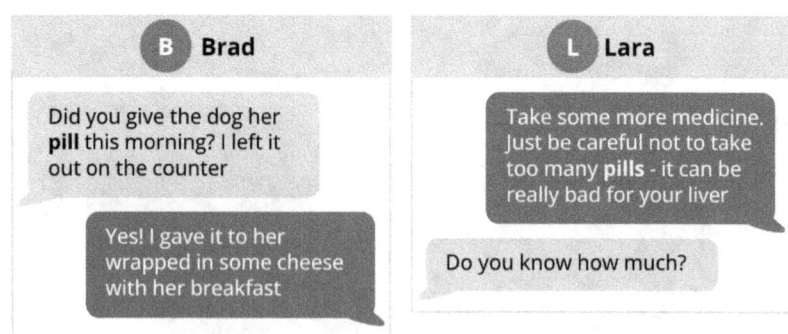

B Brad

Did you give the dog her
pill this morning? I left it
out on the counter

Yes! I gave it to her
wrapped in some cheese
with her breakfast

L Lara

Take some more medicine.
Just be careful not to take
too many **pills** - it can be
really bad for your liver

Do you know how much?

PROPORTION

$$\frac{a}{b} = \frac{c}{d}$$

Meaning in English:
英語の意味:

1. A ratio or comparative relationship of size or amount between two things
2つのものの大きさや量の割合、または比較的な関係

2. Symmetry or balance (often used in art and design)
対称性やバランス(アートやデザインでよく使われる)

Say Instead:
適切な英語表現:

Body shape

Example Sentences:
例文:

In Japan, you can find many services that offer to help you find your ideal *proportions*. → In Japan, you can find many services that offer to help you find your ideal ***body shape***.

日本では、自分にとって理想のプロポーション探しをサポートしてくれるサービスが数多く存在する。

How English Speakers use "proportion":
英語話者は(proportion)をどのように使うか:

A Alice

They fired him because he arrived 5 minutes late? That seems out of **proportion**. There must be more details to what happened...

M Matthew

What **proportion** of coffee to water do you usually use for French press coffee?

Let me ask TJ and get back to you. He usually makes the coffee at our house!

223

REHABILI

リハビリ

Meaning in English:
英語の意味:

Doesn't exist
英語には該当する単語がない

Say Instead:
適切な英語表現:

Rehab, Physical therapy, PT, Occupational therapy

Example Sentences:
例文:

He had to do a lot of _rehabili_ after the injury.

He had to do a lot of **_rehab/ physical therapy_** after the injury.

彼はケガのあと、長期間にわたってリハビリに取り組まなければ ならなかった。

SELF

セ
ル
フ

Meaning in English:
英語の意味:

Doesn't usually exist alone except for meaning "the self" in a psychological sense. Typically it's only used as myself, yourself, himself, herself, itself, oneself, themselves, ourselves, or when combined with other words to form an adjective (e.g., self-checkout, self-explanatory)

心理学的な意味で「自己」を指す場合を除き、「self」は通常、単独で使われることはない。一般的には、myself, yourself, himself, herself, itself, oneself, themselves, ourselvesのような形で用いられるか、self-checkoutやself-explanatoryのように他の語と組み合わせて形容詞をつくる場合に使われる。

Say Instead:
適切な英語表現:

Self-serve, Self-service

Example Sentences:
例文:

The water is _self_.   The water is **_self-serve_**.

水は、セルフとなっております。

How English Speakers use "self":
英語話者は (self) をどのように使うか:

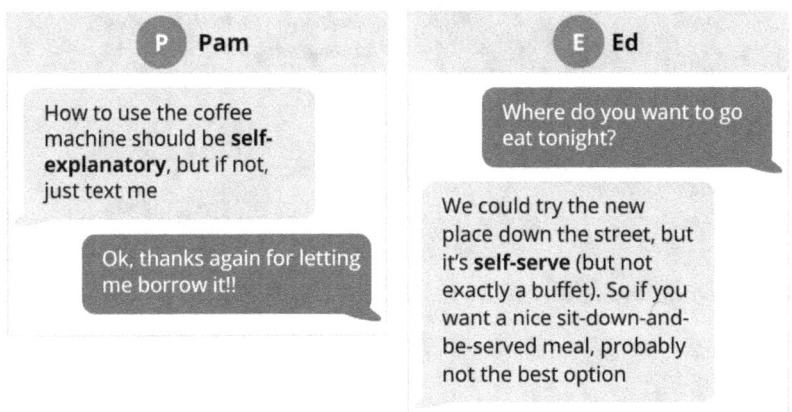

SWEAT

スウェット

Meaning in English:
英語の意味:

Perspiration from one's body
身体からの汗

Say Instead:
適切な英語表現:

Sweatsuit (US), Jogger (UK)

Example Sentences:
例文:

> He always wears _sweat_, even in the summer.

> He always wears **_sweatshirts_**, even in the summer.

彼は夏でもいつもスウェットを着ている。

How English Speakers use "sweat":
英語話者は(sweat)をどのように使うか:

E Erica

Why don't more people walk to work in your city?

Well, one reason is that it's just really hot - people don't want to show up to work covered in **sweat**

R Richard

Sweat is really good for your body - it helps remove toxins

Yes, I believe that! I always feel great after a workout with a good **sweat**

Houses, Homes, & Living

11

家・住まい・生活

Scan for Audio

AIR CON

エアコン

Meaning in English:
英語の意味:

Doesn't exist
英語には該当する単語がない

Say Instead:
適切な英語表現:

Air conditioner, A/C
Heater

Example Sentences:
例文:

> It's so cold in here; can we turn on the *air con*?

> It's so cold in here; can we turn on the **_heater_**?

とても寒いから、エアコンつけてもいいかな。

This sounds like you are cold but asking to make it colder!
これは、寒いのにさらに寒くしてほしいと言っているように聞こえる！

228

APART

アパート

Meaning in English:
英語の意味:

Separated, not together
別々/離れている/一緒ではない

Say Instead:
適切な英語表現:

Apartment, Affordable/older apartment, 2-story apartment building

Example Sentences:
例文:

My *apart* is really old. ⟶ My ***apartment*** is really old and affordable but not very fancy.

私のアパートは、とても古い。

How English speakers use "apart":
英語話者は(apart)をどのように使うか:

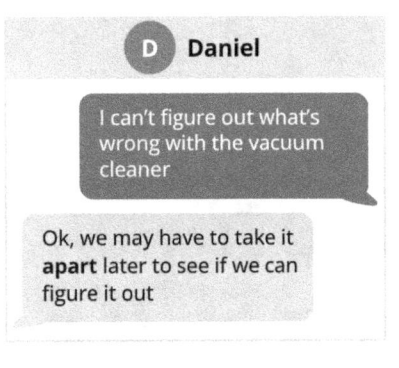

Daniel

I can't figure out what's wrong with the vacuum cleaner

Ok, we may have to take it **apart** later to see if we can figure it out

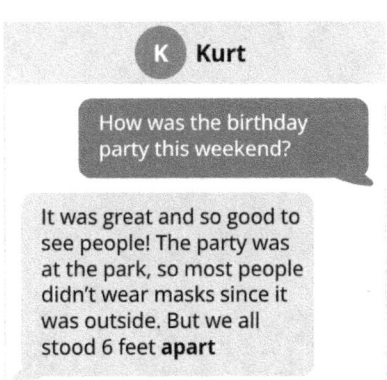

Kurt

How was the birthday party this weekend?

It was great and so good to see people! The party was at the park, so most people didn't wear masks since it was outside. But we all stood 6 feet **apart**

AT HOME

Meaning in English:
英語の意味:

At one's own house or place of residence
自宅でまたは居住地で

Say Instead:
適切な英語表現:

Cozy, Relaxed, Comfortable (atmosphere)

Example Sentences:
例文:

I love that coffee shop; it's _at home_.

I love that coffee shop; it **_has such a cozy, relaxed comfortable atmosphere_**.

私は、あのカフェが大好き。アットホームな雰囲気だから。

 This sounds like the coffee shop is at your house!
あなたの家にコーヒーショップがあるみたいに聞こえる。

How English Speakers use "at home":
英語話者は(**at home**)をどのように使うか:

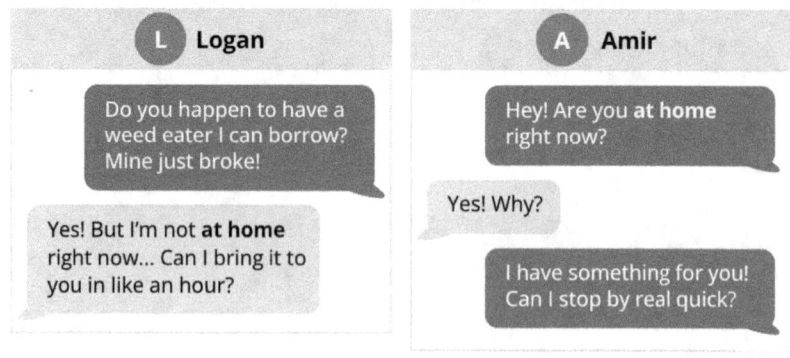

Logan

Do you happen to have a weed eater I can borrow? Mine just broke!

Yes! But I'm not **at home** right now... Can I bring it to you in like an hour?

Amir

Hey! Are you **at home** right now?

Yes! Why?

I have something for you! Can I stop by real quick?

BED COVER

Meaning in English:

英語の意味:

Bed cover sounds extremely vague and unclear. It could mean any of the items you put on top of your bed, including sheets, and would likely be unclear to most people as it could include a comforter, duvet cover, blanket, or anything on top of your bed for warmth or decoration.

『ベッドカバー』という言葉は非常にあいまいで、多くの人にとって意味が分かりにくい。これは、シーツを含めてベッドの上に置かれるさまざまなアイテム——例えば、掛け布団、布団カバー、毛布、あるいは防寒・装飾用のものまで——が含まれる可能性があるからだ。

Say Instead:

適切な英語表現:

Bedspread, Comforter

Example Sentences:

例文:

That store sells really nice _bed covers_. That store sells really nice **_comforters_**.

あの店は、本当に素敵なベッドカバーを売っている。

BED TOWN

ベッドタウン

Meaning in English:
英語の意味:

Doesn't exist
英語には該当する単語がない

Say Instead:
適切な英語表現:

Commuter town (US), Bedroom community (US)
Dormitory town (UK)

Example Sentences:
例文:

| Are there many _bed towns_ near Tokyo? | ➔ | Are there many **_commuter towns_** near Tokyo? |

東京の近くにたくさんベッドタウンがあるの?

クリーニング

Meaning in English:

英語の意味:

1. (Noun) Usually a professional service that cleans. Used alone, *cleaning* sounds like house-cleaning but could be used in other contexts with an adjective (e.g., teeth cleaning)

（名詞）通常、専門的な清掃サービスを指す。「クリーニング」だけではハウスクリーニングを連想させるが、形容詞をつけることで他の文脈でも使われる。（例：「歯のクリーニング（teeth-cleaning）」）

2. (Verb) Progressive participle of "to clean"

（動詞）「to clean」の進行形で、掃除や清潔にする動作を指す。

Say Instead:

適切な英語表現:

Dry cleaning

Example Sentences:

例文:

I need to take my clothes for <u>cleaning</u>.	I need to take my clothes for <u>**dry cleaning**</u>.

服をクリーニングに出さないといけない。

DRIVEWAY

Meaning in English:
英語の意味:

In a typical American house, a *driveway* is the short private road that leads from the street to your house (or your garage if you have one). This is usually where people park their cars.

一般的なアメリカの家では、道路から家（またはガレージ）へと続く短い私道のことを指す。通常、ここに車を駐車する。

Say Instead:
適切な英語表現:

Highway (US), Motorway (UK), Road

Example Sentences:
例文:

> There is a good new <u>*driveway*</u> to get to that city. It's faster than using the old roads.

> There is a good new **_highway_** to get to that city. It's faster than using the old roads.

その町へ行くには新しくできた良いドライブウェイがある。
昔の道を使うより速いよ。

How English Speakers use "driveway":
英語話者は(driveway)をどのように使うか:

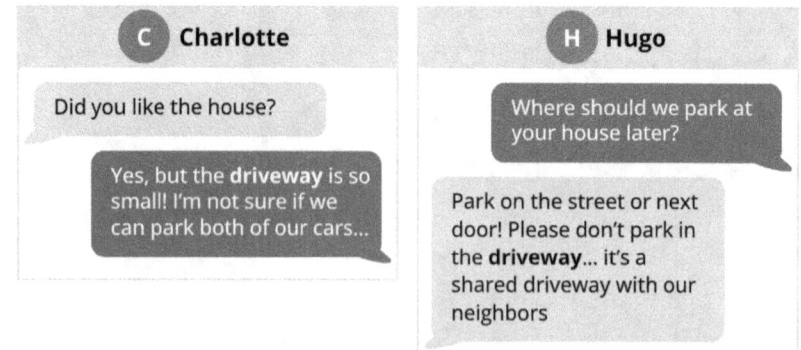

C Charlotte

Did you like the house?

Yes, but the **driveway** is so small! I'm not sure if we can park both of our cars...

H Hugo

Where should we park at your house later?

Park on the street or next door! Please don't park in the **driveway**... it's a shared driveway with our neighbors

DRYER

ドライヤー

Meaning in English:
英語の意味:

A machine that dries things,
usually a dryer for clothes
物を乾燥させる機械
通常は衣類用の乾燥機

Say Instead:
適切な英語表現:

Hair dryer, Blow dryer

Example Sentences:
例文:

I need to use the *dryer* to make my hair look pretty. → I need to use the **hair dryer** to make my hair look good.

髪をきれいに整えるためにドライヤーを使わないといけない。

How English Speakers use "dryer":
英語話者は(dryer)をどのように使うか:

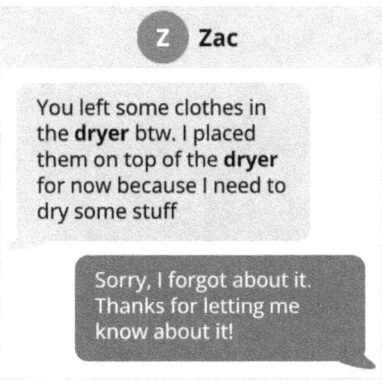

Zac

You left some clothes in the **dryer** btw. I placed them on top of the **dryer** for now because I need to dry some stuff

Sorry, I forgot about it. Thanks for letting me know about it!

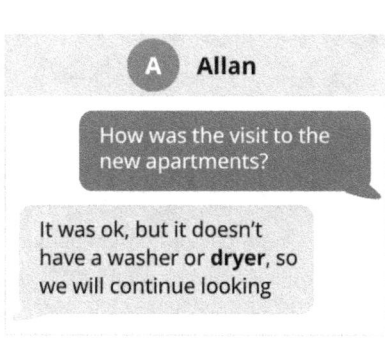

Allan

How was the visit to the new apartments?

It was ok, but it doesn't have a washer or **dryer**, so we will continue looking

FLOORING

Meaning in English:
英語の意味:

Any type of material on your floor
(e.g., wood flooring, vinyl flooring,
tile flooring, carpet flooring)

床に使用されるあらゆる種類の
素材(例：木製フローリング、ビ
ニールフローリング、タイルフロ
ーリング、カーペットなど)

BASIC TYPES OF FLOORING

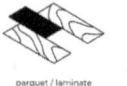
parquet / laminate

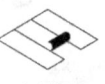
quartz-vinyl laminate

quartz-vinyl tile

carpet

linoleum

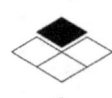
tile

Say Instead:
適切な英語表現:

Wood floors, Wood flooring, Hardwood floors, Hardwood flooring

Example Sentences:
例文:

I don't have any _flooring_ in my house.

I don't have any **_wood flooring_** in my house.

私の家には、フローリングがない。

⚠ This sounds like your house doesn't have any finished flooring!
家の床はまだ仕上がっていないように聞こえる。

How English Speakers use "flooring":
英語話者は(**flooring**)をどのように使うか:

to: Me <homeowner@propertytax.com>
subject: Re: Property Tax Info 2017

Here is the information requested:

Interior, Utilities, and Additional Information:
Microwave: Yes
Dishwasher: Yes
Connect: Electric Dryer Connections, Gas Dryer Connections
Oven: Electric Oven, Freestanding Oven
Range: Freestanding Range, Gas Range
Flooring: Carpet, Tile

IH

Meaning in English:
英語の意味:

Doesn't exist
英語には該当する単語がない

Say Instead:
適切な英語表現:

Stove, Induction cooktop

Example Sentences:
例文:

Please turn off the _IH_ before you go out.

Please turn off the **_stove_** before you leave the house.

家を出る前にIHコンロの電源を消してください。

INTERPHONE

Meaning in English:
英語の意味:

Doesn't exist
英語には該当する単語がない

Say Instead:
適切な英語表現:

Intercom

Example Sentences:
例文:

Call me on the _interphone_ when you arrive.

Call me on the **_intercom_** when you arrive, and I'll buzz you up.

到着したらインターホンで呼んでね。

MANSION

Meaning in English:
英語の意味:

A very big and luxurious house
豪邸、大邸宅

Say Instead:
適切な英語表現:

Apartment, Nice apartment,
High-rise apartment

Example Sentences:
例文:

After living in a small DK for five years, we finally moved to a _mansion_.

After living in a small studio apartment for five years, we finally moved to a **_nice apartment_**.

5年間小さなDKに住んだ後、ついにマンションに引っ越しした。

 This sounds like you moved to an extremely large, luxurious house!
とても大きくて豪華な家（豪邸）に引っ越したみたいだ。

How English Speakers use "mansion":
英語話者は（**mansion**）をどのように使うか:

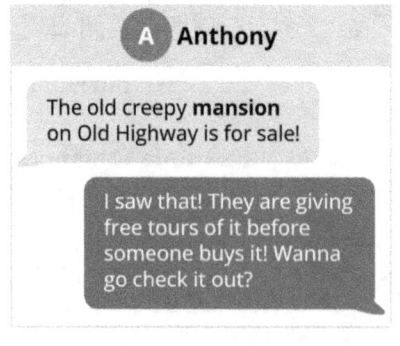

MY HOME

Meaning in English:
英語の意味:

The place where I live
私の家

Say Instead:
適切な英語表現:

[I] own/bought this house

Example Sentences:
例文:

- Wow, your house is
beautiful!
- Thanks! It's _my home_!

- Wow, your house is
beautiful!
- Thanks! **_We bought it_**
last year.

お家、綺麗ですね！ありがとう。マイホームなんだ。

How English Speakers use "my home":
英語話者は（my home）をどのように使うか:

Patrick

Did your phone die?

Kind of... I'm sorry, I lost connection. The phone service in **my home** is terrible. I'll go outside and call you back

Mary

Bobby is sick, so we can't host the world cup party at our house. Is anyone else available to host?

My home is available! I'd love to host!

ONE ROOM MANSION

ワンルームマンション

Meaning in English:
英語の意味:

Doesn't exist
英語には該当する単語がない

Say Instead:
適切な英語表現:

Studio apartment

Example Sentences:
例文:

Last week, we moved into a _one room mansion_. It's still small, but it's much better than our apart.

Last week, we moved into a **_studio apartment in a nicer building_**. It's still small, but it's much better than our old apartment.

先週、ワンルームマンションに引っ越したんだ。まだ狭いけど、前のアパートよりずっといいよ。

 This sounds like you live in a giant, luxurious house with only one giant room!
広々とした部屋が一つだけの超豪華な家に住んでるみたいに聞こえる。

OVEN RANGE

Meaning in English:
英語の意味:

This is not a common phrase, but an "oven range" or a "range oven" could mean a combination stovetop and oven. However, this combination appliance is most commonly called simply a "range" or "stove" depending on one's style of English.

これは一般的な表現ではないが、「オーブンレンジ」や「レンジオーブン」は、コンロとオーブンを組み合わせたものを意味することもある。ただし、このような一体型の調理家電は、地域や言語の使い方によって、通常は「レンジ」または「ストーブ」と呼ばれている。

Say Instead:
適切な英語表現:

Convection microwave, Microwave oven combo

Example Sentences:
例文:

Most kitchens only have an _oven range_, not an oven. Most kitchens only have a **_microwave oven combo_**, not a conventional oven.

大抵のキッチンにはオーブンレンジしかなくて、
ちゃんとしたオーブンはないんだよね。

Post

ポスト

Meaning in English:
英語の意味:

1. (UK) Letters, mail, and the postal system
(英)手紙と郵便制度

2. Social media or blog post
ソーシャルメディアやブログへの投稿

3. A vertical, supporting pole, often made of metal or wood
(e.g., fence post, lamppost)
金属や木でできた垂直の支柱（フェンスの柱、街灯など）

Say Instead:
適切な英語表現:

Mail box (US), Post box (UK)

Example Sentences:
例文:

I need to check my _post_; my friend said he sent me something important.

I need to check my **_mailbox_**; my friend said he sent me something important.

ポストを確認しなくては。
友達が大事なものを送ったと言ったので。

 This sounds like you might be checking a social media post.
貴方が、SNSの投稿をチェックしてる感じに聞こえる。

(DENSHI) RANGE

Meaning in English:

英語の意味：

1. (Noun) Span, scope, spread

（名詞）スパン、範囲、広がり

2. (Verb) To vary within a specific upper and lower limit

（動詞）「（一定の）範囲で変動する」「〜の幅がある」

3. (Noun) In some varieties of English, *range* means an appliance that combines a stovetop and an oven into one.

（名詞）一部の英語話者による表現：コンロとオーブンが一体化された調理器具 →「レンジ」「調理用レンジ」「加熱器具」など

Say Instead:

適切な英語表現：

Microwave, Microwave oven

Example Sentences:

例文：

My stove and oven are both broken, so we have been using the *range*.	My stove and oven are both broken, so we have been using the ***microwave***.

コンロとオーブンの両方が壊れてしまったので、
最近は電子レンジを使っている。

SEMI DOUBLE

セ
ミ
ダ
ブ
ル

Meaning in English:
英語の意味:

Doesn't exist
英語には該当する単語がない

Say Instead:
適切な英語表現:

Bed that's bigger than a twin but smaller than a double

Example Sentences:
例文:

I prefer a *semi double* to a twin since it's a little more spacious.

I prefer a Japanese *semi double, a bed that's bigger than a twin but smaller than a double*, since it's a little more spacious than a twin.

ツインよりもセミダブルの方が少し広くて好きだ。

ストーブ

Meaning in English:
英語の意味:

Any kind of cooktop
あらゆる種類の調理器具／コンロ
（ガスコンロ、IHクッキングヒーターなど）

Say Instead:
適切な英語表現:

Space heater, Portable heater,
Electric heater

Example Sentences:
例文:

Sometimes my buil is so cold because of the cooler, so I bought a _stove_ to warm me up.

Sometimes my office building is so cold because of the air conditioner, so I bought a **_space heater_** to warm me up.

オフィスの建物がクーラーで寒すぎるときがあるから、
暖かくするためにストーブを買ったんだ。

How English Speakers use "stove":
英語話者は（stove）をどのように使うか:

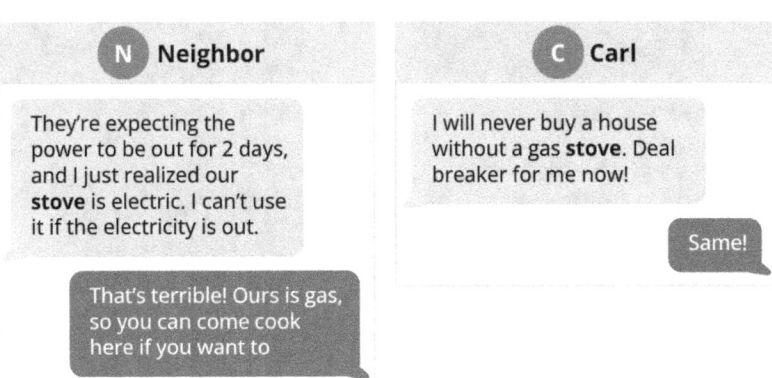

N Neighbor

They're expecting the power to be out for 2 days, and I just realized our **stove** is electric. I can't use it if the electricity is out.

That's terrible! Ours is gas, so you can come cook here if you want to

C Carl

I will never buy a house without a gas **stove**. Deal breaker for me now!

Same!

TENANT

テナント

Meaning in English:
英語の意味:

A person who rents and/or lives on land, space, or property from an owner or landlord

所有者または貸主から土地や建物などを借りている、またはそこに居住している人

Say Instead:
適切な英語表現:

Available for rent, Vacancy

Example Sentences:
例文:

We need to find a place that's _tenant_ in the mall. We need to find a place that's **_available for rent_** in the mall.

ショッピングモールでテナントを探す必要があるね。

How English Speakers use "tenant":
英語話者は(tenant)をどのように使うか:

TOWELKET

タオルケット

Meaning in English:
英語の意味:

Doesn't exist
英語には該当する単語がない

Say Instead:
適切な英語表現:

Blanket made out of towel material

Example Sentences:
例文:

I always bring my towelket when I travel because it's so versatile.	I always bring my _**Japanese towel blanket**_ when I travel because it's so versatile.

旅行のときはいつもタオルケットを持って行くよ。
いろんな用途に使えて便利なんだ。

Unit Bath

ユニットバス

Meaning in English:
英語の意味:

Doesn't exist
英語には該当する単語がない

Say Instead:
適切な英語表現:

The toilet and bathtub are together in one room

Example Sentences:
例文:

The hotel room has a _unit bath_.

The hotel room has _**a bathroom with the toilet and bathtub combined in the same room**_.

ホテルの部屋には、ユニットバスがついている。

VERANDA

Meaning in English:
英語の意味:

ベ
ラ
ン
ダ

A covered patio on the ground floor, but this word is uncommon in some varieties of English.

1階にある屋根付きのパティオだが、一部の英語圏ではこの語はあまり使われない

Say Instead:
適切な英語表現:

Balcony

Example Sentences:
例文:

I have a lot of plants on my *veranda*.

→

I have a lot of plants on my ***balcony***.

ベランダで、たくさんの植物を育てている。

How English speakers use "veranda":
英語話者は（veranda）をどのように使うか:

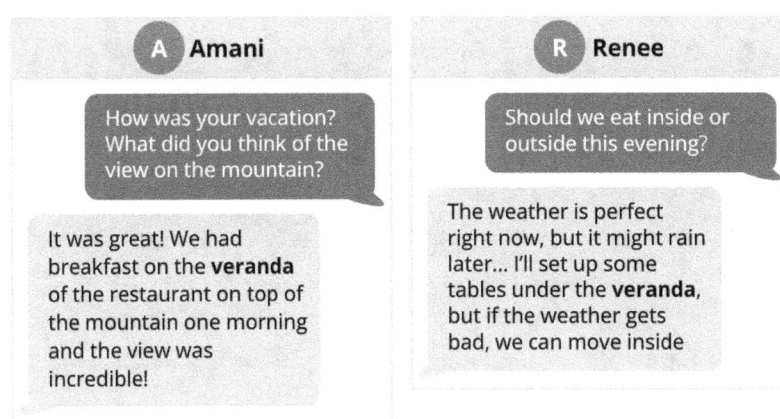

A Amani

How was your vacation? What did you think of the view on the mountain?

It was great! We had breakfast on the **veranda** of the restaurant on top of the mountain one morning and the view was incredible!

R Renee

Should we eat inside or outside this evening?

The weather is perfect right now, but it might rain later... I'll set up some tables under the **veranda**, but if the weather gets bad, we can move inside

Washlet

ウォシュレット

Meaning in English:
英語の意味:

Doesn't exist
英語には該当する単語がない

Say Instead:
適切な英語表現:

Bidet, Bidet toilet

Example Sentences:
例文:

Many nice hotels in Asia have _washlets_ in each room. Many nice hotels in Asia have **_bidet toilets_** in each room.

アジアの良いホテルには、部屋ごとにウォシュレットが付いてる。

 One might imagine a washlet is a small washing area separate from the bathroom, like a small sink outside of the bathroom.

ウォシュレットという言葉からは、浴室とは別に設けられた小さな洗い場、たとえば小さな洗面台のようなものを想像するかもしれない。

250

Hygeine, Makeup, Skincare, Haircare

12

衛生・メイクアップ・スキンケア・ヘアケア

Scan for Audio

BARIKAN (BARRIQUAND)

バリカン

Meaning in English:
英語の意味:

Doesn't exist
英語には該当する単語がない

Say Instead:
適切な英語表現:

Electric hair trimmer/clippers

Example Sentences:
例文:

| He asked for a _barikan_ for a Christmas gift. | | He asked for an _**electric hair trimmer**_ for a Christmas gift. |

彼は、クリスマスプレゼントにバリカンをたのんだ。

BODY SHAMPOO

ボディーシャンプー

Meaning in English:
英語の意味:

Sounds like a special kind of shampoo for your body
(and potentially different from usual soap or body wash)
体専用の特別なシャンプーのようなものに聞こえる。
いつもの石けんやボディソープとは少し違うタイプかもしれない。

Say Instead:
適切な英語表現:

Body wash, Shower gel

Example Sentences:
例文:

| The _body shampoo_ at the hotel smelled so good! | | The _**body wash**_ at the hotel smelled so good! |

ホテルのボディーシャンプーはとても香りが良かった。

BLOW

Meaning in English:
英語の意味:

1. To make or push air using your mouth or nose
   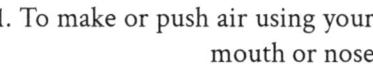 Example: Kids like to *blow* out their birthday candles.

口や鼻を使って空気を出すこと
例：子どもは誕生日ケーキのろうそくを吹き消すのが好きだ。

2. To make something move using air
   ☞ Example: A strong wind might *blow* the sign over.

空気の力で何かを動かすこと
例：強い風で看板が倒れるかもしれない。

Say Instead:
適切な英語表現:

Blow dry

Example Sentences:
例文:

| After my shower, I need to *blow*. | | After my shower, I need to ***blow dry*** my hair. |

シャワーの後は、髪のブローが必要だ。

| In the beauty salon, the hairdresser said, "Now, I'm going to *blow* your hair." | | In the beauty salon, the hairdresser said, "Now, I'm going to ***blow dry*** your hair." |

美容院で、美容師は、私に「髪の毛をブローしていきますね」と言った。

This sounds like the hairdresser is going to blow on your hair like when you blow out a candle.

まるでロウソクを吹き消すように、美容師があなたの髪に息を吹きかけようとしているようだ。

253

CLEANSING

Meaning in English:
英語の意味:

Cleanse (cleansing) - to clean deeply or thoroughly; to purify
深く、または徹底的に洗浄する浄化する・清める・純化する

Say Instead:
適切な英語表現:

Makeup remover

Example Sentences:
例文:

> I hate trying to take off my makeup without _cleansing_.

> I hate trying to take off my makeup without **_makeup remover_**.

クレンジングなしでメイクを落とすのは本当に嫌だ!

 This sounds like you hate taking off your makeup without washing your face!
顔を洗わずにメイクを落とすのが嫌いと言っているようだ。

How English Speakers use "cleansing":
英語話者は(cleansing)をどのように使うか:

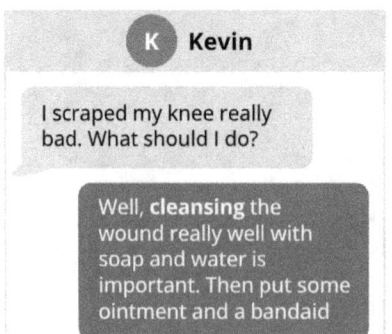

Kevin

I scraped my knee really bad. What should I do?

Well, **cleansing** the wound really well with soap and water is important. Then put some ointment and a bandaid

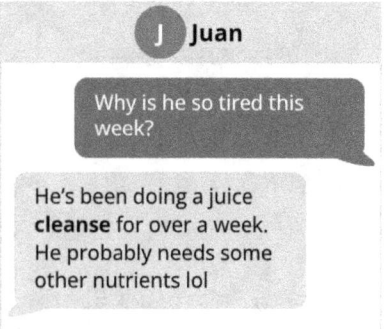

Juan

Why is he so tired this week?

He's been doing a juice **cleanse** for over a week. He probably needs some other nutrients lol

254

ESTE

Meaning in English:
英語の意味:

Doesn't exist
英語には該当する単語がない

Say Instead:
適切な英語表現:

Spa, Med spa, Facial

Example Sentences:
例文:

I'm going to go to _este_ this weekend.	→	I'm going to **_get a facial at a med spa_** this weekend.

今週末エステにいく。

FOUNDATION

ファンデーション

Meaning in English:

英語の意味:

1. Base or most basic part or principle
☞ Example: Math and reading are *foundations* for education.

基礎や基本的な要素(例:数学と読解は教育の基盤となる)

2. The bottom base on which something stands
(e.g., foundation of a building)

物が立つための土台や基盤(例:建物の基礎)

3. Makeup

ファンデーション

Say Instead:

適切な英語表現:

Foundation

Example Sentences:

例文:

I put on my makeup *foundation* ファンデーション and mascara while watching the workers pour the *foundation* 基礎 of my new home.

I put on my makeup ***foundation*** and mascara while watching the workers pour the ***foundation*** of my new home.

私は新居の基礎工事を眺めながら、
ファンデーションとマスカラをつけた。

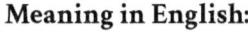

ヘアアイロン

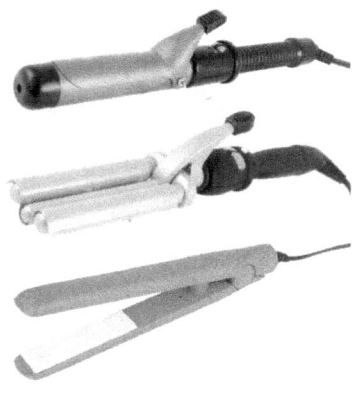

Meaning in English:
英語の意味:

A general word used for any type of device that uses heat to arrange the hair, including curling irons, straighteners, and crimping irons

カーリングアイロン、ストレートア
イロン、波状アイロンなど、熱を
使用して髪を整えるための
一般的な用語

Say Instead:
適切な英語表現:

Hair straightener, Straightener, Flat iron

Example Sentences:
例文:

It seems like girls with straight hair want a curling iron, and girls with curly hair want a _**hair iron**_.

It seems like girls with straight hair want a curling iron, and girls with curly hair want a _**hair straightener**_.

ストレートヘアの女の子はコテを欲しがり、
巻き髪の女の子はヘアアイロンを欲しがるようだ。

LIP / LIP CREAM

Meaning in English:
英語の意味:

Lip - outer part of your mouth
リップ—口の外側

Lip cream - doesn't exist
英語には該当する単語がない

Say Instead:
適切な英語表現:

Lip balm, Chapstick

Example Sentences:
例文:

> Your *lip* smells so good. What kind is it?

> Your ***chapstick***/***lip balm*** smells so good. What kind is it?

あなたのリップ、すごくいい香りがするね。
どんなのをつけてるの?

 This sounds like you are smelling your friend's lips!
友達の唇の匂いを嗅いでいるみたいだ。

How English Speakers use "lip":
英語話者は(lip)をどのように使うか:

B Bobby

At the wedding they had a photobooth with props like funny glasses, mustaches, **lips**, etc.

Oh those are my favorite! Did you get some good pics?

D Daisy

Have you seen the funny videos where they basically do funny bad **lip** reading?

Yes!

MAKE

Meaning in English:
英語の意味:

1. (Verb) To make: build, create, or compose something
(動詞) 作る – 建築する、創造する、または構成する

2. (Noun) A car's vehicle manufacturer
(名詞) 自動車メーカー (車の製造会社)

Say Instead:
適切な英語表現:

Makeup

Example Sentences:
例文:

We love visiting Japan because they have a lot of popular cosme brands with great _make_.

We love visiting Japan because they have a lot of popular makeup brands with great **_makeup_**.

日本に行くのが大好き。
人気のあるコスメブランドがたくさんあるし、
メイクの仕上がりも素晴らしいから。

MAKEUP

Meaning in English:
英語の意味:

Only the noun makeup
メイク(メイクアップの名詞のみ)

Say Instead:
適切な英語表現:

Put on makeup, Wear makeup

Example Sentences:
例文:

Wow, you *made up* today! → Wow, you ***wore makeup*** today!

「まあ!今日は、メイク(メイクアップ)してるんだ!」

How English Speakers use "makeup":
英語話者は(makeup)をどのように使うか:

Helen

What kind of eye **makeup** do you usually wear?

I usually just wear mascara, eyeliner, and a little bit of eyeshadow

Lily

Did you recognize Melinda yesterday?

NO!! She started talking to me, and I was just like omg who is this? She had on so much **makeup** I didn't know it was her at first!

MANICURE

Meaning in English:
英語の意味:

The cosmetic treatment process of getting your nails done, usually at a nail salon. It includes cleaning, trimming, painting, filing, and sometimes massage. It could also include getting fake nails or tips or any other nail art.

ネイルサロンで受けられる美容施術の一環としてのネイルケアには、爪の洗浄、トリミング(整える)、ファイリング(形を整える)、カラーリングやネイルアート(デザインの描画)、時にはマッサージなどが含まれる。また、人工ネイルチップやその他のネイルアートが施されることもある。

Say Instead:
適切な英語表現:

Nail polish

Example Sentences:
例文:

I love your _manicure_ color! I love your **_nail polish_** color!

あなたのマニキュアの色、とても素敵!

How English Speakers use "manicure":
英語話者は(manicure)をどのように使うか:

Manicure & Pedicure
Saturday 9 AM
$50 plus tip
Ask for Betty!!!

D David

What time do you guys want to come over?

The girls have a **manicure** in the morning, so we could go to your house after lunch. Does that work?

NAPKIN

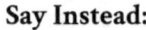

Meaning in English:
英語の意味:

(US) Kitchen napkin
(米) キッチンナプキン
(UK) Sanitary pad
(英) ナプキン

Say Instead:
適切な英語表現:

Feminine product, Sanitary pad

Example Sentences:
例文:

| Is there a conveni where I can buy some *napkins*? | | Is there a convenient store where I can buy some ***feminine products***? |

ナプキンを買えるコンビニはある?

How English Speakers use "napkin":
英語話者は(**napkin**)をどのように使うか:

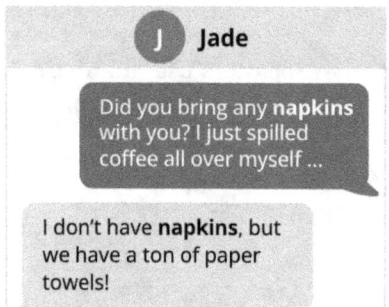

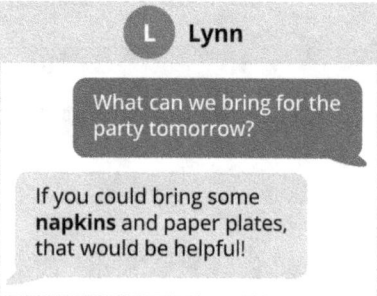

No Make

Meaning in English:
英語の意味:

Doesn't exist
英語には該当する単語がない

Say Instead:
適切な英語表現:

No makeup

Example Sentences:
例文:

I did _no make_ all week, and it was so freeing! I **_didn't wear makeup_** all week, and it was so freeing!

今週ずっと私は、ノーメイクだったんだ。すごく解放感があったわ。

ノーメイク

Pincetto

Meaning in English:
英語の意味:

Doesn't exist
英語には該当する単語がない

Say Instead:
適切な英語表現:

Tweezers

Example Sentences:
例文:

Did you bring the _pincetto_? I think I have a splinter in my foot. Did you bring the **_tweezers_**? I think I have a splinter in my foot.

ピンセットある？足にトゲが刺さったみたいなんだ。

ピンセット

RINSE

リンス

Meaning in English:
英語の意味:

To wash something lightly using only water
☞ Example: *Rinse* the soap off your hands after washing them.
☞ Example: *Rinse* the dishes before you wash them.

水だけを使って軽く洗うこと
例:「手を洗ったあと、石けんをよく洗い流してください」
例:「皿を洗う前に、軽くすすいでください」

Say Instead:
適切な英語表現:

Conditioner, Hair conditioner

Example Sentences:
例文:

| Some men don't use *rinse* for their hair. | | Some men don't use ***conditioner*** for their hair. |

リンスを使わない男性もいる。

How English Speakers use "rinse":
英語話者は(rinse)をどのように使うか:

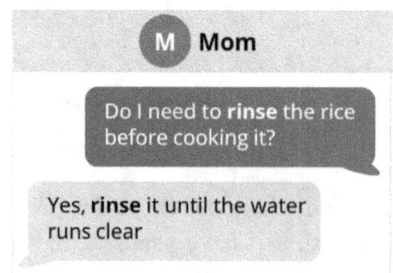

> **M** Mom
>
> Do I need to **rinse** the rice before cooking it?
>
> Yes, **rinse** it until the water runs clear

Make sure you rinse the dishes thoroughly after you wash them to make sure there's no soap left on them!!
THANKS!

KIDS, FAMILY, RELATIONSHIPS

13

子ども・家族・人間関係

Scan for Audio

BABY BED

ベビーベッド

Meaning in English:

英語の意味:

Any bed for a baby, but more general and less common than "crib" or "cot." *Baby bed* could include other types of beds like a bassinet or even a small bed for a toddler.

赤ちゃん用のベッドの総称であり、"crib（ベビーベッド）"や"cot（小型ベッド）"ほど一般的ではなく、バシネットや幼児用の小さなベッドなども含む表現

Say Instead:

適切な英語表現:

Crib (US), Cot (UK)

Example Sentences:

例文:

| Shh. The baby is sleeping on the _baby bed_. | | Shh. The baby is sleeping in the **_crib_**/**_cot_**. |

シ〜！赤ちゃんがベビーベッドで寝ているわ。

BABY CAR

Meaning in English:
英語の意味:

A small toy car for a toddler (like a Little Tikes cozy coupe). It's often pushed by the child's feet or sometimes by a battery-powered pedal.

幼児が足でこいで遊ぶ、小さな乗用おもちゃ（例：リトルタイクスのコージークーペ）。中には電動ペダルで動くものもある。

Say Instead:
適切な英語表現:

Stroller (US), Pushchair (UK), Pram (UK)

Example Sentences:
例文:

You can use our _baby car_ at the zoo tomorrow if you'd like!

You can use our **_stroller_** at the zoo tomorrow if you'd like!

もしよかったら、
明日うちのベビーカーを動物園で使ってもいいよ。

BABYSITTER

Meaning in English:

英語の意味:

Babysitter is usually only used for shorter and less regular periods of time and paid by the hour. (E.g., Parents want to have dinner at a restaurant together without the kids, so they call a *babysitter* for the evening.) A ***nanny*** is usually longer term with a more consistent schedule and more responsibility. (E.g., Mom works four days a week, so the *nanny* does all the childcare responsibilities on those days.)

ベビーシッターは、基本的に短時間で不定期に頼まれることが多く、時給で報酬が支払われる。(例えば、夫婦でレストランに行って夕食を楽しみたいときなどに、夜だけベビーシッターに子どもを預けるケースだ)。ナニーは通常、より長期間にわたって働き、スケジュールも安定しており、任される責任も多い。(例えば、母親が週に4日働いている場合、その間はナニーがすべての育児を担当する)。

Say Instead:

適切な英語表現:

Nanny

Example Sentences:

例文:

The *babysitter* takes care of our toddler every day during the week when I am working. The ***nanny*** takes care of our toddler every day during the week when I am working.

ベビーシッターは、私が仕事をしている間、平日は毎日うちの子の世話をしてくれている。

ベビーシッター

Baby Circle

Meaning in English:
英語の意味:

Doesn't exist
英語には該当する単語がない

Say Instead:
適切な英語表現:

Playpen, Pack and play

Example Sentences:
例文:

A *baby circle* is so helpful when I need to cook dinner. → A **_playpen_** is so helpful when I need to cook dinner.

夕食を作るとき、ベビーサークルがあると本当に助かる。

ベビーサークル

Boy

Meaning in English:
英語の意味:

Young male
若い男性

Say Instead:
適切な英語表現:

Bellboy, Bellhop, Porter

Example Sentences:
例文:

ボーイ

Our hotel was so nice, it even had a *boy*. → Our hotel was so nice, it even had a **_bellhop_**.

泊まったホテルはとても素敵だったよ。
なんとボーイまでいたんだ。

CONSENT

コンセント

Meaning in English:
英語の意味:

To give permission or agree
許可する、または同意する

Say Instead:
適切な英語表現:

Electrical outlet, Socket

Example Sentences:
例文:

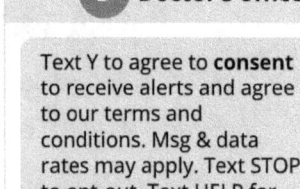

Where is the *consent*? ➞ Where is the *(electrical) outlet*?

コンセントはどこ？

How English Speakers use "consent":
英語話者は（consent）をどのように使うか:

D **Doctor's office**

Text Y to agree to **consent** to receive alerts and agree to our terms and conditions. Msg & data rates may apply. Text STOP to opt-out. Text HELP for Help.

Your appointment on Monday at 8:00pm has been confirmed. You may fill out our confidentiality and **consent** forms online to save time in the office.

J **Jonathan**

I really want to record the phone call next time she calls and threatens us. It would be good evidence if I need to get a lawyer

What are your state's laws about recording **consent**? Do both parties have to **consent** to being recorded or just one?

CRAWL

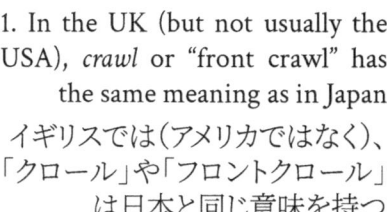

Meaning in English:
英語の意味:

1. In the UK (but not usually the USA), *crawl* or "front crawl" has the same meaning as in Japan

イギリスでは（アメリカではなく）、「クロール」や「フロントクロール」は日本と同じ意味を持つ

2. To use your hands and knees to move around (like a baby)

手と膝を使って移動すること（赤ちゃんのように動き回ること）

Say Instead:
適切な英語表現:

Freestyle (US), Front crawl (UK)

Example Sentences:
例文:

Her son is a really good _crawler_.

→ Her son is really good at **_freestyle stroke_** / **_front crawl_**.

彼女の息子は、本当にクロールが上手い。

This sounds like her son is a baby and is getting pretty good at crawling around. ⚠️
彼女の息子がまだ赤ん坊で、ハイハイがかなり上手になっている、と言っているように聞こえる。

DV

Meaning in English:
英語の意味:

Doesn't exist
英語には該当する単語がない

Say Instead:
適切な英語表現:

Domestic violence

Example Sentences:
例文:

Our non-profit helps provide information to help fight against _DV_.	Our non-profit helps provide information to fight against **_domestic violence_**.

私たちの非営利団体は、
DVに立ち向かうための情報提供を行っている。

Ex

Meaning in English:
英語の意味:

1. Ex-boyfriend, ex-girlfriend, ex- husband, ex-wife
   元彼、元彼女、元夫、元妻
2. Former, but usually with a negative connotation (e.g., ex-boss)

以前の（元の）状態だが、通常は否定的なニュアンスを持つ（例：「元上司」）

Say Instead:
適切な英語表現:

Extract

Example Sentences:
例文:

Applying this herbal _ex_ to the body cures the itching. ➲ Applying this herbal **_extract_** to the body cures the itching.

このハーブエキスを身体に塗ると痒みが治まる。

How English Speakers use "ex":
英語話者は(ex)をどのように使うか:

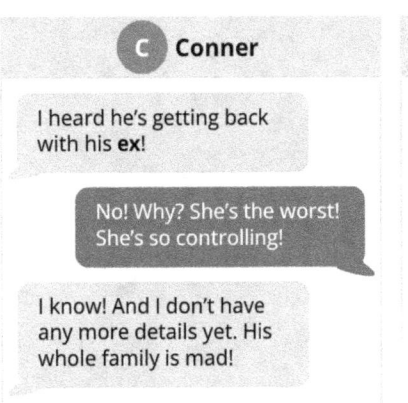

C Conner

I heard he's getting back with his **ex**!

No! Why? She's the worst! She's so controlling!

I know! And I don't have any more details yet. His whole family is mad!

J Jasmine

I saw my **ex** at the store today. I tried to hide, but he saw me and came over to talk. So embarrassing!

That's the worst! What did he say? How did he look?

FAMILY SERVICE

家族サービス

Meaning in English:

英語の意味:

Doesn't exist

英語には該当する単語がない

Say Instead:

適切な英語表現:

Spending time with the kids/family

Example Sentences:

例文:

My husband is doing _family service_ this weekend, so I should be free to meet you for coffee.

My husband is **_spending time with the kids_** this weekend, so I should be free to meet you for coffee.

今週末は夫が家族サービスしてくれるので、
私はコーヒーでも飲みに行けそうよ。

GAL / GIRL

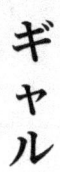

Meaning in English:
英語の意味:

Young girl
若い女性

Say Instead:
適切な英語表現:

Gyaru girl, Into gyaru fashion

Example Sentences:
例文:

SHIBUYA109 is the best place to go if you want to see *gals*!

SHIBUYA109 is the best place to go if you want to see **_gyaru girls_** / **_girls into gyaru fashion_**.

ギャルに会いたいなら、SHIBUYA109が一番のスポットだ!

This sounds like you can see a lot of females at SHIBUYA109.
これは、SHIBUYA109に行けば単にたくさんの女性が見られる、という意味に聞こえる。

How English Speakers use "gal/girl":
英語話者は(gal/girl)をどのように使うか:

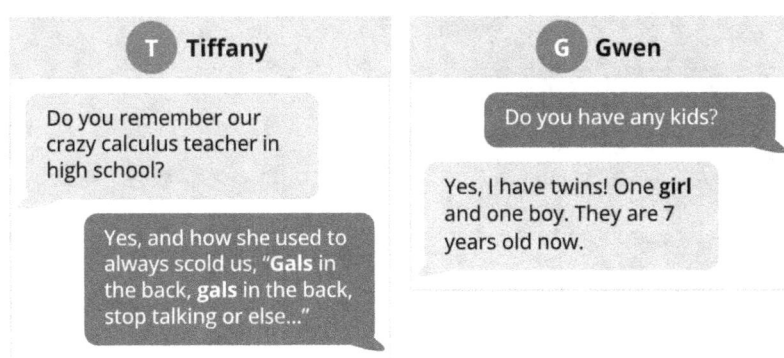

T Tiffany

Do you remember our crazy calculus teacher in high school?

Yes, and how she used to always scold us, "**Gals** in the back, **gals** in the back, stop talking or else..."

G Gwen

Do you have any kids?

Yes, I have twins! One **girl** and one boy. They are 7 years old now.

HOME DRAMA

ホームドラマ

Meaning in English:
英語の意味:

Doesn't exist, but sounds like some type of family drama (drama, conflict, problems between family members in one's home)

英語には、該当する単語はないが、家族間で起こる人間関係のもつれや葛藤などのゴタゴタがテーマのホームドラマのようだ。

Say Instead:
適切な英語表現:

Family friendly TV show

Example Sentences:
例文:

My wife and I watch our favorite _home drama_ every Friday evening.	My wife and I watch our favorite **_family friendly TV show_** every Friday evening.

妻と私は毎週金曜日の夜にお気に入りのホームドラマを見る。

How English Speakers use "home drama":
英語話者は(home drama)をどのように使うか:

C Coworker

That coworker has been so annoying this week - like so rude for no reason!

Yeah, not cool. But I think she has a lot of bad **home drama** going on right now with some stuff with her daughter.

276

HOUSEWIFE

Meaning in English:
英語の意味:

This term is correct and will be understood, but it can have different connotations depending on the person and context. Many people consider it old-fashioned and perhaps even insulting, while others find this term totally normal, even positive. It's generally more common to say "stay at home mom" instead of "housewife."

この言葉は正しいし、理解されるだろうが、人によって異なるニュアンスを持つことがある。多くの人は古臭い、あるいは侮辱的だと感じる一方で、まったく普通の、むしろ肯定的な言葉だと考える人もいる。一般的には、"housewife"よりも"stay-at-home mom"と言うほうが多い。

Say Instead:
適切な英語表現:

Stay at home mom (SAHM) - *(for a woman with kids)*
Stay at home dad (SAHD) - *(for a man with kids)*
I stay at home - *(for a woman or man with or without kids)*

Example Sentences:
例文:

I'm a _housewife_. I'm a **_stay at home mom_**.
I **_stay at home_**.

私は、専業主婦なの。

専業主婦・ハウスワイフ

LOVE LOVE

ラブラブ

Meaning in English:

英語の意味:

Doesn't exist

英語には該当する単語がない

Say Instead:

適切な英語表現:

Head over heels, Passionately in love, All over each other

Example Sentences:

例文:

They are _love love_. I'm so happy they found each other. They are **_head over heels_** for each other. I'm so happy they found each other.

彼らはラブラブだね。
私は、二人が巡り会えたことを心から嬉しく思う 。

They are so _love love_; it's really sweet but also kind of annoying! They are **_all over each other_**; it's really sweet but also kind of annoying!

彼らはすごくラブラブだね。
微笑ましいけど、ちょっと鬱陶しいかもね。

MANNERI

Meaning in English:
英語の意味:

Doesn't exist
英語には該当する単語がない

Say Instead:
適切な英語表現:

Boring, Monotonous, Unexciting, Mundane

Example Sentences:
例文:

Our life has become _manneri_, so we need some kind of change. Maybe I'll do image change!

Our life and relationship has become **_boring and monotonous_**, so we need some kind of change. Maybe I'll change my look and get a new hairstyle!

私たちの生活はマンネリ化しているので、何か変化がいる。
イメージチェンジでもしようかな!

Miss

ミ
ス

Meaning in English:
英語の意味:

1. A title for an unmarried woman. In Japanese, the titles Miss, Ms. and Mrs. all translate to the same word. In English, "Miss" is used for an unmarried woman; "Mrs." is used for a married woman, and "Ms." can be used for either a married or unmarried woman. Nowadays, some women prefer "Ms." in order to avoid being defined by their marriage status. Additionally, "Miss" can sometimes make someone seem young and/or inexperienced.

未婚女性に対する敬称である。日本語ではMiss、Ms.、Mrs.のいずれも同じ語で訳されるが、英語においては「Miss」は未婚女性、「Mrs.」は既婚女性、「Ms.」は既婚・未婚を問わず使用可能である。近年では、結婚の有無により定義されることを避けるため「Ms.」を選ぶ女性もいる。また「Miss」は若さや未熟さを感じさせる場合もある。

2. To arrive too late to experience something or fail to take advantage of an opportunity (e.g., miss a bus because you didn't arrive at the bus stop on time, miss a party because you were sick, miss breakfast at a hotel because you slept too late, miss a good opportunity because you didn't take step towards it)

何かを経験する機会を逃す、あるいはチャンスを活かせないことを指す(例:バス停に間に合わずバスを逃す、病気でパーティーに行けない、寝過ごしてホテルの朝食を逃す、行動を起こさず好機を逸する、など)

3. To not see, hear, or notice something, to overlook it
☞ Example: I'm so sorry I *missed* your previous email!

見逃す、聞き逃す、あるいは気づかずに通り過ぎることを意味する
例:「前回のメールを見落としてしまったことを申し訳なく思っています」

4. To feel sad or longing for a person or thing that is not presently with you
☞ Example: I often ask my students living abroad, 'What do you *miss* most about Japan?'

今そこにいない人や物に対して寂しさや恋しさを感じること
例:海外で暮らしている学生に「日本の何が一番恋しい?」と尋ねることがある。

ミス

5. To not hit something/someone
☞ Example: I tried to shoot my trash into the trash can like a basketball into a goal, but I *missed*, so I had to walk over and pick it up.

目標物に当てることができない、命中しないことを表す
例：「ゴミをゴミ箱へ投げたが外れたため、拾いに行った」

__Note:__ Misutta (page 293) is not a word derived from *Miss* and does not exist in English. It is purely Japanese-English.

※「ミスった」は「Miss」に由来する言葉ではなく、英語には「Misutta」という語は存在しない。和製英語である。

Say Instead:
適切な英語表現:

Miss = [Make a] mistake, error
Careless miss = Careless mistake
Near miss = Run into

Example Sentences:
例文:

| I *had a miss* on the exam. | | I *__made a mistake__* on the exam. |

試験でミスをした。

| I always make *careless miss* on my homework. I need to be more careful! | | I always make *__careless mistakes__* on my homework. I need to be more careful! |

宿題でいつもケアレスミスをしてしまう。もっと気をつけないと！

| I had a *near miss* with Yukiko at the grocery store yesterday! | | I *__ran into__* Yukiko at the grocery store yesterday! |

昨日スーパーでユキコを見かけたけど、ニアミスだった！
昨日スーパーでユキコとニアミスしたんだ。

ONE MAN

ワンマン

Meaning in English:
英語の意味:

Literally, one man

文字通り、一人の男性/ 男性一人/一人の人/人一人

Say Instead:
適切な英語表現:

One-man show, Autocratic, Authoritarian

Example Sentences:
例文:

I worked at that company for 2 years. The owner is _one man_, so the work environment was really unpleasant.

I worked at that company for 2 years, but it's basically a _**one-man show**_. The owner _**makes all the decisions and won't take input or opinions from anyone else**_, so the work environment was really unpleasant.

その会社で2年間働いていた。
オーナーがワンマンな人で、職場環境はすごく悪かった。

⚠️ This sounds like there is only one boss at the company. It sounds like the reason it was an unpleasant work environment could be because it's a small company where everyone, including the boss, was overworked, or perhaps it was unpleasant because there were too few people to interact with!

その会社には社長が1人しかいなくて、それに、職場環境が悪かったのは、小さな会社で社長も含めてみんなが働きすぎていたからかもしれない。あるいは、関わる人が少なすぎて居心地が悪かったのかもしれない。そんな風に聞こえる。

SISTER

シスター

Meaning in English:
英語の意味:

Family member sister
姉／妹

Say Instead:
適切な英語表現:

(Catholic) Nun

Example Sentences:
例文:

She became very religious, and now she's a _sister_.

She became very religious, and now she's a **_nun_**.

彼女は敬虔な信者になり、今ではシスターだ。

How English Speakers use "sister":
英語話者は（sister）をどのように使うか:

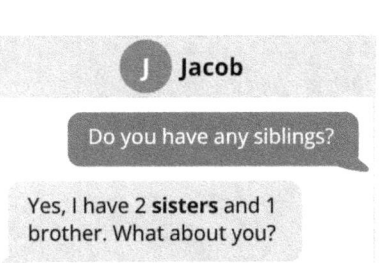

283

SKINSHIP

スキンシップ

Meaning in English:
英語の意味:

Doesn't exist
英語には該当する単語がない

Say Instead:
適切な英語表現:

Physical affection, Physical touch

Example Sentences:
例文:

She's very friendly and does a lot of _skinship_.	She's very friendly and very ***physically affectionate***.

彼女はとてもフレンドリーで、よくスキンシップをする。

You should do more _skinship_ for the dog because he seems really lonely.	You should ***pet*** /***hold*** the dog more because he seems really lonely.

寂しそうだから、もっと犬にスキンシップしてあげた方がいいかも。

TWIN

ツ
イ
ン

Meaning in English:
英語の意味:

1. A child born at the same time as another from the same mother
同じ母親から同時に生まれた子ども

2. Two identical or very similar things, often that pair well together
同じもの、またはよく似たもの同士を組み合わせること

3. (UK) (Verb) To put one thing with another because they make a good pair
(英)[動詞]組み合わせとして相性が良いもの同士を一緒にする（組み合わせる）

Say Instead:
適切な英語表現:

Twin hotel room

Example Sentences:
例文:

Let's see if the hotel has _twins_! Let's see if the hotel has any rooms with **_twin beds_** / **_twin rooms_**.

ホテルにツインルームがあるか見てみよう。

VIRGIN ROAD

ヴァージンロード

Meaning in English:
英語の意味:

Doesn't exist
英語には該当する単語がない

Say Instead:
適切な英語表現:

Walk down the aisle, Wedding aisle

Example Sentences:
例文:

My friend walked with her father on the _virgin road_.

My friend walked with her father _**down the aisle**_.

友達はお父さんと一緒にヴァージンロードを歩いた。

I want to walk the _virgin road_.

I want to _**get married and walk down the aisle**_.

私もヴァージンロードを歩いてみたい。

My best friend fell down on her _virgin road_.

My best friend fell down when she was _**walking down the aisle at her wedding**_.

友だちは、ヴァージンロードで転んだ。

MISCELLANEOUS

その他

14

Scan for Audio

CASE BY CASE

ケースバイケース

Meaning in English:

英語の意味:

In English, *case by case* is used much less frequently. It's usually reserved for situations where you want to consider each situation differently based on its own characteristics and merits rather than apply a general rule.

☞ Example: Doctors should always decide treatment plans on a *case-by-case* basis rather than simply giving exactly the same medicine to all patients with the same diagnosis.

☞ Example: Applications for financial aid will be considered on a *case-by-case* basis.

ケースバイケースと言う表現は、英語ではそれほど頻繁には使われない。すべての状況に一律のルールを当てはめ、十把一絡げに処理するのではなく、それぞれの状況に応じて最適でかつ柔軟な判断をする場面で使われる。

例:医師は、同じ病気の患者全員に全く同じ薬を投与するのではなく、常にケースバイケースで治療方針を決定すべきである。あるいは経済的援助の申請についても、一律の基準で判断するのではなく、個々の事情を踏まえた柔軟な対応(ケースバイケース)が求められる。

Say Instead:

適切な英語表現:

It depends

Example Sentences:

例文:

| - Do you usually drive to work?
- *Case by case*. If my wife needs the car, I take the bus. | ➔ | - Do you usually drive to work?
- ***It depends***. If my wife needs the car, I take the bus. |

「普段は車で通勤するの?」
「ケースバイケースだ。妻が車を使う必要があるときは、バスで行くよ」。

GO SIGN

Meaning in English:
英語の意味:

Doesn't exist
英語には該当する単語がない

Say Instead:
適切な英語表現:

Green light, Go ahead

Example Sentences:
例文:

We got the *go sign* for the project.

We got the **green light** for the project.

そのプロジェクトにゴーサインをもらった。

HAPPENING

ハプニング

Meaning in English:
英語の意味:

Something that has happened, but usually used in plural, not for one singular event

☞ Example: The recent *happenings* have led us to consider stricter security measures.

何かが起こったこと。ただし、通常は複数形で使用され、一つの出来事にはあまり使われない。
例:最近の出来事から、より厳格な安全対策を考えるようになった。

Say Instead:
適切な英語表現:

Something crazy happened, An accident, Unexpected event

Example Sentences:
例文:

| There was a *happening* at my office yesterday. | | ***Something crazy happened*** at my office yesterday. ***There was an accident*** at my office yesterday. |

昨日、私のオフィスでハプニングがあった。

How English Speakers use "happening":
英語話者は(happening)をどのように使うか:

Subscribe to Local L Magazine to be the first to hear about local <u>happenings</u>! Take one for free (below) to check it out!

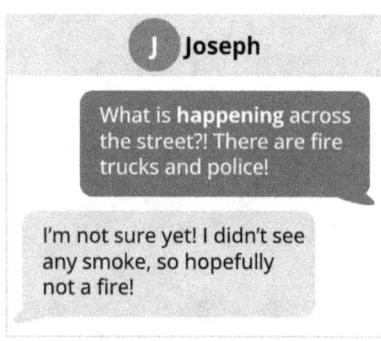

J Joseph

What is **happening** across the street?! There are fire trucks and police!

I'm not sure yet! I didn't see any smoke, so hopefully not a fire!

IMAGE

Meaning in English:
英語の意味:

1. Picture
写真、絵、または画像

2. *Image* often describes how something or someone looks or appears or one's mental picture. *Impression* is usually used to describe your thoughts about something.

☞ Example: She looks different than I *imagined*! In the *image* I had in my head, she was a lot taller.

☞ Example: I only met her once, but my *impression* of her was that she is very honest and takes her job very seriously.

「イメージ」は、物や人の見た目や印象を指すことが多く、特に頭の中で描く姿を表す。一方、「印象・インプレション」は、何かについての考えや感じ方を表すために使われる。

例:「彼女は想像と違う!思い描いていたイメージでは、もっと背が高かった」

例:「彼女には一度しか会っていないが、誠実で仕事に真剣に取り組む人だという印象を受けた」

Say Instead:
適切な英語表現:

Impression

Example Sentences:
例文:

I don't have a good <u>image</u> of that city because the weather was terrible the whole time I was there.	I don't have a good ***impression*** of that city because the weather was terrible the whole time I was there.

滞在中ずっと天気が悪かったので、
あの町にはあまりいいイメージがない。

JUST

ジャスト

Meaning in English:
英語の意味:

As an adverb:
副詞としての用法

1. Only
☞ Example: Oh, don't cry, you'll be okay. It's *just* a small scratch.
ただ/たった〜だけ 例:私は、息子に「泣かないで！大丈夫よ。ちょっとしたかすり傷よ」と言った。

2. (UK only) Now or very soon
☞ Example: I'm *just* cooking dinner.
（イギリスのみ）今／もうすぐ 例:今、夕食を作っている。

3. Very recently
☞ Example: I *just* finished cooking dinner.
ほんの少し前に/ごく最近 例:ちょうど夕食を作り終えた。

4. Exactly
☞ Example: Your daughter looks *just* like you!
まさに/ちょうど　例:「君の娘さんは、君そっくりだね」

As an adjective: fair or related to justice
形容詞としての用法:公正な、または正義に関係する
例:「正当な判断」「公正な社会」

Say Instead:
適切な英語表現:

Exactly

Example Sentences:
例文:

| It's *just* 3 p.m.! | ↗ | It's **_exactly_** 3 p.m.! |

今、3時ジャストだ！

 This sounds like it's only 3 p.m., and it's earlier than expected!
この言い方だと、『まだ午後3時か。思ったよりも早い時間で驚いた』という印象を与える。

JUST TIMING

Meaning in English:
英語の意味:

Doesn't exist
英語には該当する単語がない

Say Instead:
適切な英語表現:

Perfect timing

Example Sentences:
例文:

| *Just timing*! It's just 3 p.m.! | → | ***Perfect timing***! It's exactly 3 p.m.! |

ジャストタイミングだ。ちょうど午後3時だ。

MISUTTA

Meaning in English:
英語の意味:

Doesn't exist
英語には該当する単語がない

Say Instead:
適切な英語表現:

Make a mistake, Mess up, Screw up

Example Sentences:
例文:

| Oh no, I *misutta*! I totally *misutta*! | → | Oh no, I ***messed up***! I totally ***screwed up***! |

ヤバイ、ミスった。完全にミスった。

MY PACE

マ
イ
ペ
ー
ス

Meaning in English:
英語の意味:

Doesn't exist; however, the phrase "work/go at one's own pace" means to work at whatever speed is best for one personally. It does not have the same assumption of being too slow or leisurely.

☞ Example: The school allows students to work *at their own pace*, so high-achieving students are sometimes grade-levels ahead of where they would be in a traditional school environment.

英語には、該当する単語がない。しかし、「work/go at one's own pace」というフレーズは、「自分にとって最適なペースで進める」という意味を持つ。これは、過度に遅い・のんびりしすぎているという前提を含まない。

例:その学校では、生徒が自分のペースで学習できるため、成績優秀な生徒は従来の学校制度よりも学年を先行して進むことがある。

Say Instead:
適切な英語表現:

Slow, Behind, Not punctual, Miss deadlines, Behind on deadlines

Example Sentences:
例文:

> When I started working in the U.S., I was really surprised that a lot of people are _my pace_ at work.

> When I started working in the U.S., I was really surprised that a lot of people are ***slow*** / ***behind*** / ***not very punctual*** / ***behind on deadlines*** at work.

アメリカで働き始めたとき、
多くの人がマイペースで仕事をしていることにとても驚いた。

NG

Meaning in English:
英語の意味:

Doesn't exist
英語には該当する単語がない

Say Instead:
適切な英語表現:

Not good, Not allowed, Unacceptable, Inappropriate, Taboo

Example Sentences:
例文:

Getting out of your seat during takeoff is _NG_ on an airplane.

→ Getting out of your seat during takeoff is **_not allowed_** on an airplane.

飛行機では離陸時の席の移動はNG行動とされている。

Some words are _NG_ on golden time telebi.

→ Some words are **_not allowed_** on prime time TV.

ゴールデンタイムのテレビ番組では、NGとされる言葉もある。

OG

Meaning in English:
英語の意味:

OG is slang meaning "original gangster." This is used to describe the original or first of someone of something.
☞ Example: Many Millennials miss the *OG* social media where you could only share pictures and no political opinions.
☞ Example: You have a Super Nintendo! Whoa, that's *OG*!

"オリジナルギャングスター"を意味するスラングで、何かの「元祖」や「本物」を指す。
例:多くのミレニアル世代は、写真だけを投稿して政治的意見なんてなかった「元祖SNS」が懐かしいと思っている。
例:スーパー任天堂を持ってるんだ。それってOG(元祖)じゃん。

Say Instead:
適切な英語表現:

A female alumna from my university who graduated before me,
She went to the same university as I did

Example Sentences:
例文:

She's an <u>OG</u> from my university. She was part of our business management club and graduated two years before me.	She's an ***alumna from my university***. She was part of the business management club and graduated two years before me.

彼女は私の大学のOGだ。
経営学クラブに入っていて、私より2年早く卒業した。

ON PARADE

Meaning in English:
英語の意味:

Doesn't exist
英語には該当する単語がない

Say Instead:
適切な英語表現:

Continuous, Lineup, Follow suit

Example Sentences:
例文:

The new movie is an
<u>*on parade*</u> of stars.

The new movie has an
all-star cast.

その新作映画は、スターのオンパレードだ。

Company A raised its prices,
and now there's been an
<u>*on parade*</u> of mark up this
month.

Company A raised its prices,
and now many other
businesses have ***followed suit***.

A社が値上げし、今月は他社も次々値上げのオンパレードだ。

PLUS ALPHA

プラスアルファ

Meaning in English:

英語の意味:

Doesn't exist

英語には該当する単語がない。

Say Instead:

適切な英語表現:

A little extra, Additional, Bonus, Other

Example Sentences:

例文:

That international school is so expensive! It's like $20,000 per year *plus alpha*!

→ That international school is so expensive! It's like $20,000 per year ***plus additional fees***!

あのインターナショナルスクール、とても高い！
年間2万ドルで、しかもそれにプラスアルファがあるんだ！

THE NATURAL WORLD

15

自然

Scan for Audio

AMERICAN DOG

アメリカンドッグ

Meaning in English:
英語の意味:

1. A North American dog breed
北米の犬種

2. Possibly a joke about the nationality of a dog
☞ Example: My dog loves American football. He must be an *American dog.*

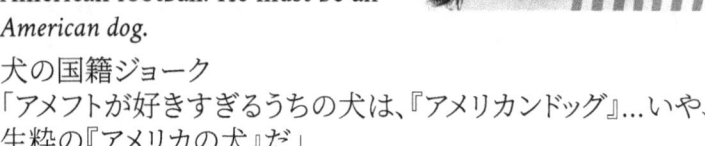

犬の国籍ジョーク
「アメフトが好きすぎるうちの犬は、『アメリカンドッグ』…いや、生粋の『アメリカの犬』だ」

Say Instead:
適切な英語表現:

Corn dog

Example Sentences:
例文:

American dogs are so delicious!

Corn dogs are so delicious!

アメリカンドッグは、とてもおいしい。

 This sentence sounds like you enjoy eating American dogs!
この文だと、アメリカの犬を食べる趣味があるように誤解されるかもしれない。

300

Eco

エ
コ

Meaning in English:
英語の意味:

Sounds like echo
エコーのように聞こえる。

Say Instead:
適切な英語表現:

Environmentally conscious,
Eco-friendly

Example Sentences:
例文:

California is an _eco_ state! → California is so **_eco-friendly_**!

カリフォルニアは、とてもエコな州だ。

How English Speakers use "echo":
英語話者は(echo)をどのように使うか:

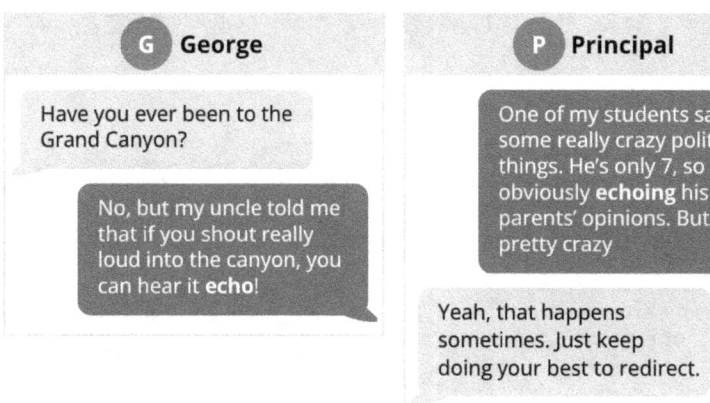

G George

Have you ever been to the Grand Canyon?

No, but my uncle told me that if you shout really loud into the canyon, you can hear it **echo**!

P Principal

One of my students says some really crazy political things. He's only 7, so he's obviously **echoing** his parents' opinions. But it's pretty crazy

Yeah, that happens sometimes. Just keep doing your best to redirect.

GROUND

Meaning in English:
英語の意味:

1. The earth's floor outside
地面

2. The land property of a specific entity or area (e.g., the school grounds)
特定の施設や地域の敷地（例：学校の敷地）

Say Instead:
適切な英語表現:

Field (US), Pitch (UK)
Playground

Example Sentences:
例文:

All students should go to the _ground_ after school today. All students should go to the _**field**_ after school today.

生徒は全員、今日の放課後にグラウンドへ集合すること。

How English Speakers use "ground":
英語話者は（ground）をどのように使うか:

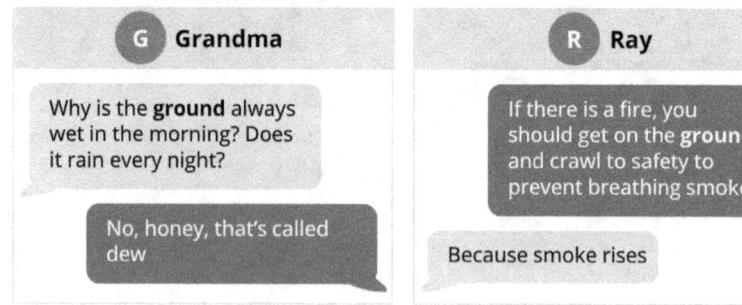

G Grandma

Why is the **ground** always wet in the morning? Does it rain every night?

No, honey, that's called dew

R Ray

If there is a fire, you should get on the **ground** and crawl to safety to prevent breathing smoke

Because smoke rises

HATCHING

Meaning in English:
英語の意味:

1. (Verb) Progressive participle of to hatch (the process of an animal being born from an egg)

（動詞）To hatchの進行形分詞；動物が卵から孵化している最中の状態

2. (Noun) In art, hatching is a technique to create the effect of shading by drawing fine lines close together

（名詞）美術における「ハッチング」は、細い線を密に描くことで陰影を表現する技法

Say Instead:
適切な英語表現:

Highlighted area, Highlighting

Example Sentences:
例文:

Please look at the _hatching_ area on the page.

→

Please look at the **_highlighted_** area on the page.

ページのハッチング部分をご覧ください。

How English Speakers use "hatching":
英語話者は（hatching）をどのように使うか:

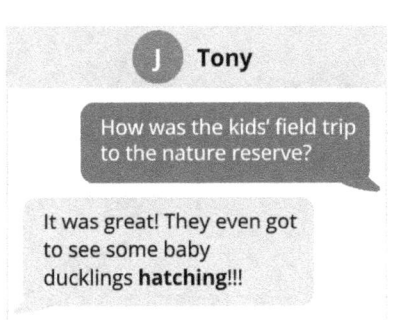

J Tony

How was the kids' field trip to the nature reserve?

It was great! They even got to see some baby ducklings **hatching**!!!

B Hotel Beach

Attention guests: the north part of Sandy Beach will be closed for the rest of the month. Baby turtles will be **hatching** soon and we want to ensure they have privacy and safety!

MARMOT

モルモット

Meaning in English:
英語の意味:

A large rodent similar to a squirrel
リスに似た大型の齧歯類

Say Instead:
適切な英語表現:

Guinea pig

Example Sentences:
例文:

When I was a kid, my best friend had a _marmot_ as a pet.	When I was a kid, my best friend had a **_guinea pig_** as a pet.

子供の頃、親友がモルモットをペットとして飼っていた。

How English Speakers use "marmot":
英語話者は（marmot）をどのように使うか:

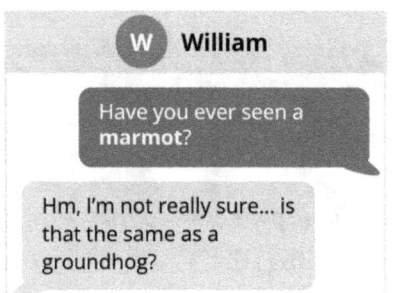

W William

> Have you ever seen a **marmot**?

> Hm, I'm not really sure... is that the same as a groundhog?

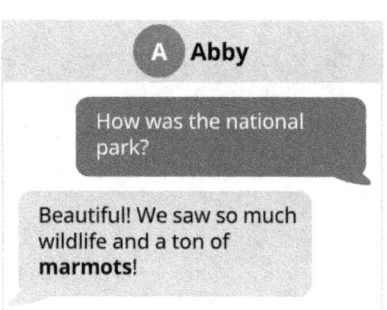

A Abby

> How was the national park?

> Beautiful! We saw so much wildlife and a ton of **marmots**!

MORNING

モーニング

Meaning in English:
英語の意味:

Opposite of night
朝

Say Instead:
適切な英語表現:

Breakfast

Example Sentences:
例文:

That cafe has _morning_ set. That cafe **_serves breakfast_**.

そのカフェには、モーニングセットがある。

How English Speakers use "morning":
英語話者は（morning）をどのように使うか:

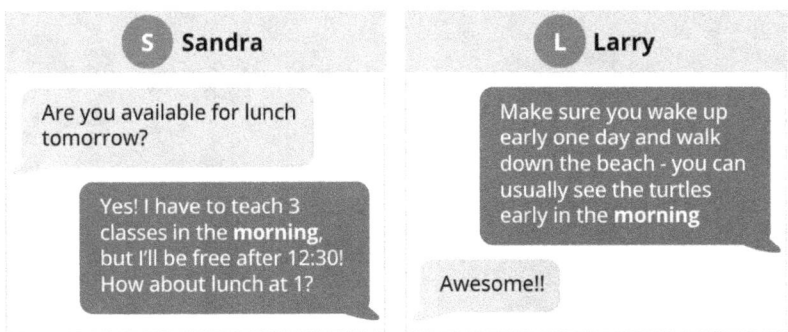

S Sandra

Are you available for lunch tomorrow?

Yes! I have to teach 3 classes in the **morning**, but I'll be free after 12:30! How about lunch at 1?

L Larry

Make sure you wake up early one day and walk down the beach - you can usually see the turtles early in the **morning**

Awesome!!

OPEN SAND

オープンサンド

Meaning in English:
英語の意味:

Doesn't exist
英語には該当する単語がない

Say Instead:
適切な英語表現:

Open face sandwich

Example Sentences:
例文:

| The new cafe has really good *open sands*. | → | The new cafe has really good ***open face sandwiches***. |

新しいカフェのオープンサンドはとてもおいしい。

OUTSIDE

Meaning in English:
英語の意味:

Outdoors
屋外

Say Instead:
適切な英語表現:

Out

Example Sentences:
例文:

アウトサイド

I'm so tired of sitting at home with all the rain this week. Let's eat _outside_ tonight!	I'm so tired of sitting at home with all the rain this week. Let's eat **_out_** tonight!

今週ずっと雨で家にこもりっぱなしで、
もううんざりだ。今夜は外で食べようよ!

This sounds like you want to sit and eat somewhere outdoors even though it's raining!
雨がふっているのに外で食事をしたがっているように聞こえる。

How English Speakers use "outside":
英語話者は(outside)をどのように使うか:

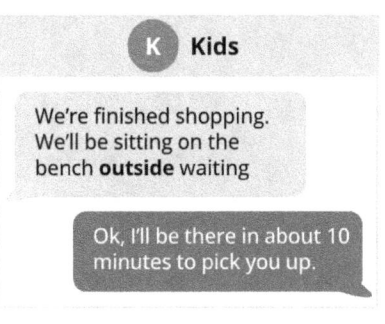

PINE JUICE

Meaning in English:
英語の意味:

Doesn't exist
英語には該当する単語がない

Say Instead:
適切な英語表現:

Pineapple juice, Pineapple soda

Example Sentences:
例文:

I love *pine juice* in the summer! I love ***pineapple juice*** in the summer!

夏は、パインジュースが大好きだ。

 This sounds like maybe you drink some type of exotic juice from an edible variety of pine tree.
まるで食用の松の木から採れたエキゾチックなジュースでも飲んでいるみたいに聞こえる。

POOCHI

Meaning in English:
英語の意味:

Doesn't exist
英語には該当する単語がない

Say Instead:
適切な英語表現:

Small, Petite, Tiny, Short
プチ旅行 = Short trip, Quick trip, Mini getaway
プチ贅沢 = Small treat/indulgence, Guilty pleasure, Treat [yourself]

Example Sentences:
例文:

I'm planning a _poochi_ trip to a hot spring this weekend.	I'm planning a **_short_** trip to a hot spring this weekend.

友達は、「週末は、プチ旅行で温泉に行く予定よ」と言った。

I did _poochi_ luxury today and had two fancy cakes.	I **_treated myself_** today and had two fancy cakes.

「今日はプチ贅沢して、ケーキを2個食べちゃった」

SAND(O)

サンド

Meaning in English:
英語の意味:

Sand (like at the beach)
砂（ビーチにあるような）

Say Instead:
適切な英語表現:

Sandwich, Egg sandwich, Tofu sandwich, Cream sandwich

Example Sentences:
例文:

| At the beach, they sell good egg _sand_. | | At the beach, they sell good egg **_sandwiches_**. |

ビーチでは美味しい卵サンドが売られている。

 This sounds like you can buy a special type of sand at the beach.
ビーチで何か特別な砂を買えると言っているようだ。

How English Speakers use "sand":
英語話者は（sand）をどのように使うか:

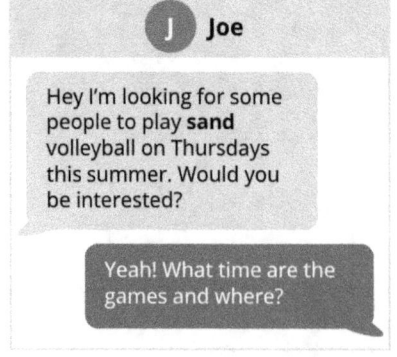

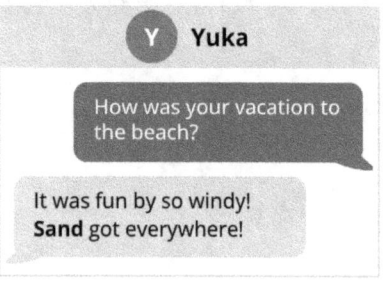

SEAL

Meaning in English:
英語の意味:

1. Animal seal
海に生息する動物のアザラシ

2. A tight and secure closing
(e.g., an airtight food jar,
a sealed envelope)
空気や液体が漏れないように密封されたもの
（例：食品の瓶や閉じられた封筒）

3. An official mark or stamp on a document, often using wax
文書に押される正式な印章やシール（例：蝋で封をするようなもの）

Say Instead:
適切な英語表現:

Sticker

Example Sentences:
例文:

My niece and nephew love to play with _seals_.

My niece and nephew love to play with **_stickers_**.

私の甥と姪は、シールで遊ぶのが好きだ。

This sounds like they enjoy playing with the animal seal.
子どもが動物のアザラシと遊んでいるように聞こえる。

SOLAR SYSTEM

Meaning in English:
英語の意味:

The collection of the planets and stars within our system (our planetary system)
太陽系

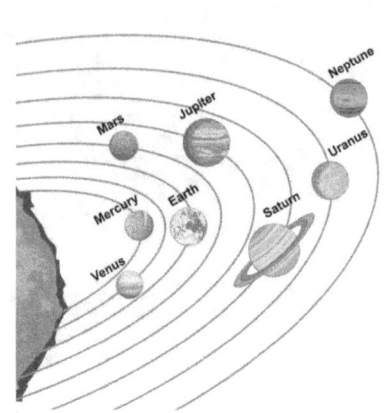

Say Instead:
適切な英語表現:

Solar panels, Solar energy, Solar energy system

Example Sentences:
例文:

Our office recently installed a *solar system*, and it's saving a ton of money on energy costs.		Our office recently installed *solar panels*, and it's saving a ton of money on energy costs.

最近、社内でソーラーシステムを導入したところ、
電気料金の大幅な削減につながっている。

How English Speakers use "solar system":
英語話者は(**solar system**)をどのように使うか:

to: Me <Parent@ElementarySchool.com>
subject: Mr. Blacksmith's 4th Grade Class

Dear Parents:

This coming week, we will be studying the **solar system**. We will read several books about the milky way and the planets. We will study the phases of the moon. At the end of the week, students will do a group project and will create their own **solar system** model. It must include the sun, Mercury, Venus, Earth, Mars, Jupiter, Uranus, Saturn, Neptune, and some asteroids.

SUMMER TIME

サマータイム

Meaning in English:

英語の意味:

(US) Summer (season ranging from around June 20 to September 20)

(米) 夏

(UK) Same as in Japanese

(英) サマータイム

Say Instead:

適切な英語表現:

Daylight Savings Time

Example Sentences:

例文:

Does your state have _summer time_? I heard some states don't have it.		Does your state have **_daylight savings time_**? I heard some states don't have it.

ここの州にはサマータイムってあるの？
ない州もあるって聞いたんだけど。

How English Speakers use "summer time":

英語話者は（**summer time**）をどのように使うか：

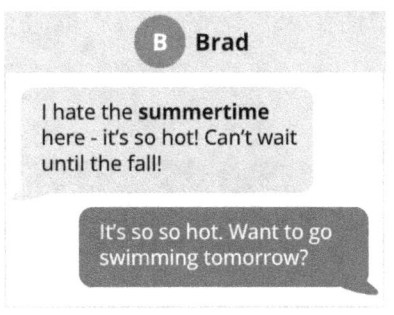

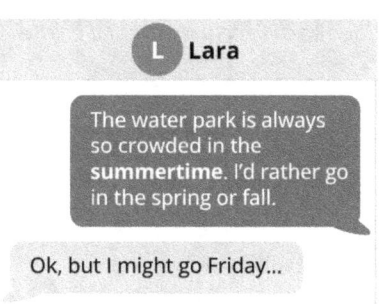

313

SUMMIT

サミット

Meaning in English:
英語の意味:

1. The highest point of a mountain
山の頂上

2. A meeting of government leaders
政府首脳会議

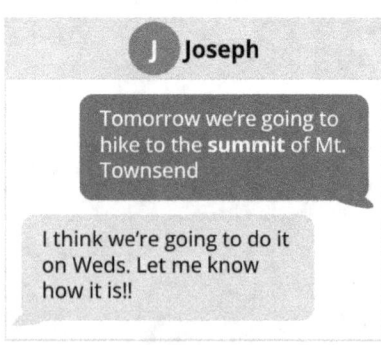

Say Instead:
適切な英語表現:

Summit

Example Sentences:
例文:

The *summit* サミット is in Tokyo, so some of us hope to climb to the *summit* 頂上 of Mt. Fuji in the week afterwards.

The ***summit*** is in Tokyo, so some of us hope to climb to the ***summit*** of Mt. Fuij in the week afterwards.

サミットは東京で開催されるので、その翌週に富士山の頂上まで登りたいと考えている人も何人かいる。

How English Speakers use "summit":
英語話者は(summit)をどのように使うか:

Study for Test:
- 5 Major <u>Summits</u>
- Issues addressed
- Nations attending
- Developments

J Joseph

Tomorrow we're going to hike to the **summit** of Mt. Townsend

I think we're going to do it on Weds. Let me know how it is!!

OFFICE ITEMS

16

オフィス用品

BOND

ボンド

Meaning in English:
英語の意味:

1. (Noun) A relationship or connection
（名詞）関係・つながり

2. (Verb) To connect with someone
（動詞）誰かとつながる、関係を築く

3. (Noun) Two things joined together permanently
（名詞）永久的に結びついたもの

4. (Verb) To join two things together like a chemical bond or adhesive
（動詞）化学結合や接着剤のように二つのものを結びつける

Say Instead:
適切な英語表現:

Glue, (Super)glue

Example Sentences:
例文:

Where did you get that _bond_? Where did you get that **_(super)glue_**?

そのボンド、どこで買った？

How English Speakers use "bond":
英語話者は（**bond**）をどのように使うか:

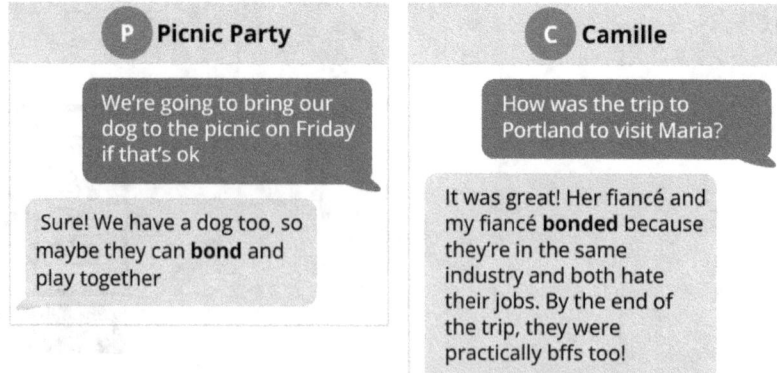

P Picnic Party

We're going to bring our dog to the picnic on Friday if that's ok

Sure! We have a dog too, so maybe they can **bond** and play together

C Camille

How was the trip to Portland to visit Maria?

It was great! Her fiancé and my fiancé **bonded** because they're in the same industry and both hate their jobs. By the end of the trip, they were practically bffs too!

BALL PEN

Meaning in English:
英語の意味:

Doesn't exist
英語には該当する単語がない

Say Instead:
適切な英語表現:

Pen, Ball point pen

Example Sentences:
例文:

Do you have a _ball pen_ I can borrow? ➣ Do you have a **_pen_** I can borrow?

ボールペンを貸してもらえますか？

ボールペン

HOTCHKISS

Meaning in English:
英語の意味:

Doesn't exist
英語には該当する単語がない

Say Instead:
適切な英語表現:

Stapler

Example Sentences:
例文:

Wow, I can't believe your _hotchkiss_ is made of gold. ➣ Wow, I can't believe your **_stapler_** is made of gold.

うわー！君のホチキスは金でできてるなんて信じられない。

ホッチキス

Magic Tape

Meaning in English:

英語の意味:

Doesn't exist, but there is a brand name of clear tape with this product name

英語には、該当する単語がないが、この名前の透明テープのブランドが実在する

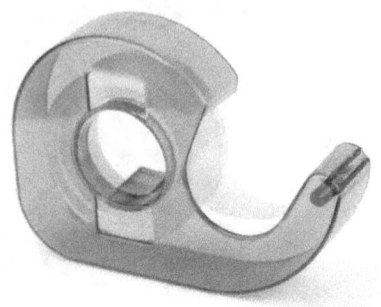

Say Instead:

適切な英語表現:

Hook and loop, Velcro

Example Sentences:

例文:

My son loves _magic tape_ shoes. → My son loves **_Velcro_** shoes.

私の息子は、マジックテープの靴が好きだ。

MAIL

Meaning in English:
英語の意味:

Postal mail
郵便

メール

Say Instead:
適切な英語表現:

E-mail

Example Sentences:
例文:

When I came back to my office after a 2-week vacation, I had so much *mail*.

→

When I came back to my office after a 2-week vacation, I had so many *e-mails*!

2週間の休暇からオフィスに戻ったら、
多量のメールが届いていた。

This sounds like you had a lot of letters and envelopes to open.
たくさんの手紙や封筒を開けることになったようだ。

How English Speakers use "mail":
英語話者は(mail)をどのように使うか:

to: Me <Resident@OurApartments.com>

subject: Residents at Apartment Green

Attention All Residents:

Our **mail** carrier has requested that we remind you to check your mailbox often. If a mailbox becomes too full, the carrier will return the **mail** to the post office. We have been having some issues with overflowing mailboxes, so please make sure to check your mailbox. We have placed recycling bins in the **mail** room for your convenience if you wish to throw away any spam **mail** or newspapers.

MAIL AD / MAIL ADDRESS

メルアド・メールアドレス

Meaning in English:
英語の意味:

Mail ad doesn't exist
英語には該当する単語がない

Mail address doesn't exist, but sounds like a mailing address
英語には、該当する単語がない が、郵送先住所に聞こえる

Say Instead:
適切な英語表現:

E-mail address, E-mail

Example Sentences:
例文:

> I still use the *mail ad* that I used when I was in middle school.

> I still use the ***e-mail address*** that I used when I was in middle school.

私は、中学の時に使っていたメルアドを今でも使っている。

> I still use the *mail address* that I used when I was in middle school.

> I still use the ***e-mail address*** that I used when I was in middle school.

私は、中学の時に使っていたメールアドレスを 今でも使っている。

⚠ This sounds like you use the same home mailing address and have lived in the same place since middle school.
中学校の頃からずっと同じ住所に住んでいて、郵便物の宛先も 変わっていないようだ。

MAIL MAGAZINE

Meaning in English:
英語の意味:

Doesn't exist
英語には該当する単語がない

Say Instead:
適切な英語表現:

Newsletter, E-mail newsletter

Example Sentences:
例文:

メールマガジン

I receive their _mail maga_
every week. I receive their **_newsletter_**
every week.

私は、毎週メールマガジン（メルマガ）を受け取っている。

MEMO

Meaning in English:
英語の意味:

Memorandum
覚書や備忘録

Say Instead:
適切な英語表現:

Note

Example Sentences:
例文:

メモ

I wrote some _memos_ from the
class in my note. I wrote some **_notes_** from the
class in my notebook.

授業でノートにいくつかのメモを書き留めた。

NOTE

ノート

Meaning in English:
英語の意味:

1. A short piece of information or message written down somewhere
メモ帳などに書かれた短い情報やメッセージ

2. A music note
音符

Say Instead:
適切な英語表現:

Notebook

Example Sentences:
例文:

Let me write this in my _note_. → Let me write this in my **_notebook_**.

これを私のノートに書かせてください。

How English Speakers use "note":
英語話者は(note)をどのように使うか:

U **Uncle Steve**

Did you talk to the airlines to see about changing his flight?

They said they might be able to waive the change fee if he submits a doctor's **note** by tomorrow

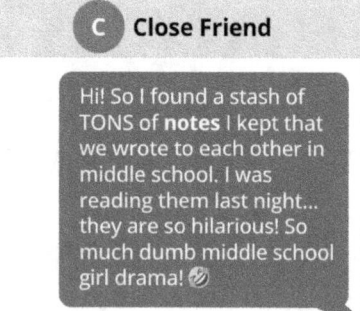

C **Close Friend**

Hi! So I found a stash of TONS of **notes** I kept that we wrote to each other in middle school. I was reading them last night... they are so hilarious! So much dumb middle school girl drama! 🤣

PRINT

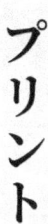

Meaning in English:
英語の意味:

(Verb) To make copies of something like text or pictures onto paper
文字や絵などを紙にコピーする
こと

Say Instead:
適切な英語表現:

Printout, Handout

Example Sentences:
例文:

He brought _prints_ for everyone at the meeting.

→ He brought **_handouts/printouts_** for everyone at the meeting.

彼はミーティングでみんなにプリントを配った。

How English Speakers use "print":
英語話者は(print)をどのように使うか:

Diana

Do you by chance have a working printer I could use? I have an interview this afternoon and need to **print** out a copy of my resume, but our printer isn't working

Yes! I can **print** it for you!

SCHEDULER

スケジューラ

Meaning in English:
英語の意味:

A person whose job it is to create the schedule, usually in a complicated system (e.g., a scheduler for the hospital, a schedule for a channel's TV programming)
複雑なシステム内でスケジュールの作成を担う職業の人
（例：病院やテレビ番組のスケジューラー）

Say Instead:
適切な英語表現:

Calendar, Planner (US), Schedule book, Diary (UK)

Example Sentences:
例文:

I can't meet you on Monday. I have a schedule. Let me look in my _scheduler_ to see some other options.		I can't meet you on Monday. I have plans. Let me look at my **_planner_** to see some other options.

月曜は予定があるので会えないんだ。
他の日で都合がつくかスケジュール帳で確認してみるよ。

How English Speakers use "scheduler":
英語話者は（scheduler）をどのように使うか:

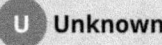 **Unknown**

Thank you for trying our new automated meeting **scheduler**. Would you be willing to share your feedback in a quick survey? Please reply Y for Yes or N for No.

 City Hospital

We have received your doctor's orders for your upcoming surgery. Our hospital **scheduler** will get in touch with you this week for further details.

SHARP PEN

Meaning in English:
英語の意味:

Doesn't exist
英語には該当する単語がない

シャーペン

Say Instead:
適切な英語表現:

Mechanical pencil

Example Sentences:
例文:

I asked my students to use _sharp pens_ for their math assignments.

I asked my students to use **_mechanical pencils_** for their math assignments.

私は、生徒たちに数学の課題には、
シャーペンを使うように伝えた。

This sounds like you asked them to use a pen (instead of a pencil) to do math. It also causes some confusion: how can a pen be sharp? Do you mean a fine-tipped pen that writes in very thin lines?

この表現は、数学の作業に鉛筆ではなくペンを使用するよう促しているように受け取れる。また、「ペンが尖っている」という表現も少し分かりにくく、細字のペン、つまり細い線が書けるタイプのペンのことを指してるのかと思う。

SIGN PEN

サインペン

Meaning in English:
英語の意味:

Doesn't exist
英語には該当する単語がない

Say Instead:
適切な英語表現:

Thin felt-tipped permanent marker, Sharpie

Example Sentences:
例文:

The city clerk said, "Please put your sign here with your *sign pen*."

The city clerk said, "Please put your signature here with a ***felt-tipped pen***."

市役所の人は私に「サインペンでこちらに署名をお願いします」と言った。

スパム

Meaning in English:
英語の意味:

Inbox (8)

Spam (99)

Trash (3)

1. Undesired or unsolicited phone calls, or mail, usually e-mail, including advertisements or newsletters that are harmless but still annoying

通常、電子メールで送られてくるダイレクトメールやニュースレターなど、受信者が望んでいないのに届く、煩わしく感じられる宣伝メールまたは、電話

2. A canned meat product
肉の缶詰

Say Instead:
適切な英語表現:

Phishing, Scam, Junk mail

Example Sentences:
例文:

He went to jail for _spam_. → He went to jail for **_phishing_**.

彼は迷惑メール（スパム）を送信したことで刑務所に入った。

How English Speakers use "spam":
英語話者は（spam）をどのように使うか:

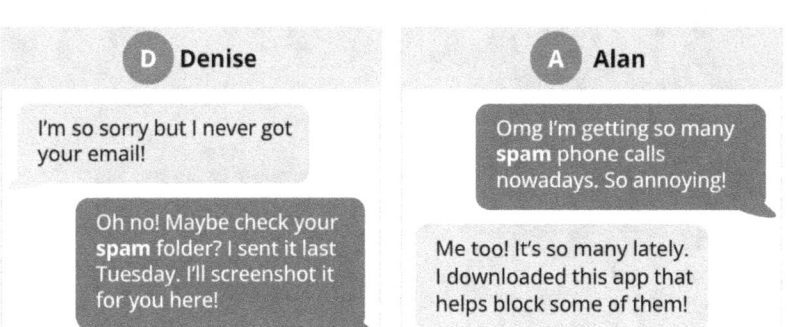

STAMP

スタンプ

Meaning in English:
英語の意味:

1. Postage sticker
郵便切手

2. A stamp made on paper using a tool and ink

インクと道具を使って紙に押す印

3. Stamp tool used with ink (both for art or official purposes)

インクを使って図柄や印を紙などに押す道具(芸術目的や公式用途の両方に用いられる)

Say Instead:
適切な英語表現:

Postmark, Postmark stamp

Example Sentences:
例文:

> We need to see the *postmark stamp* 消印 to verify when this mail was sent. It has a *postage stamp* 切手, but I can't find the *stamp with the date* 日付印.

> We need to see the postmark ***stamp*** to verify when this mail was sent. It has a postage ***stamp***, but I can't find the ***stamp with the date***.

この郵便物がいつ送られたかを確認するには消印を見る必要がある。切手は貼られているが、日付印が見つからない。

SHOPPING

17

ショッピング

AFTER SERVICE

アフターサービス

Meaning in English:

英語の意味:

Doesn't exist

英語には該当する単語がない

Say Instead:

適切な英語表現:

Warranty, Customer support, Customer service, After-sales service, After-sales support

Example Sentences:

例文:

I'm thinking of buying a TV, but if it breaks, I'll be in trouble. Do you know any electronics stores with good _after service_ you could recommend?

I'm planning to buy a TV, but if it breaks, I'll be in trouble. Do you have any recommendations for an electronics store with good **_customer support_**?

「テレビを買おうと思っているんだけど。もし壊れたら困るし、アフターサービスがしっかりしてるおすすめの電気屋さんって、どこか知ってる?」

I just bought a phone a week ago, but it's been acting up a bit. Do they offer any _after service_?

I just bought a phone one week ago, but it's been acting up a bit. Do they offer any **_after-sales support_**?

「1週間前にスマホを買ったばかりなんだけど、なんだか調子が悪くて。アフターサービスってあるのかな」。

ANTENNA SHOP

Meaning in English:
英語の意味:

Doesn't exist
英語には該当する単語がない

Say Instead:
適切な英語表現:

A store that sells specialties from another region, area, city
(A store in Tokyo that sells specialties from Hokkaido)

Example Sentences:
例文:

Since you don't have time to visit Hokkaido, let me take you to an _antenna shop_ in Tokyo!

Since you don't have time to visit Hokkaido, let me take you to _**a shop in Tokyo that sells authentic specialties from Hokkaido**_!

北海道に行く時間がないなら、
東京のアンテナショップに連れていってあげるよ。

アンテナショップ

BARGAIN

バーゲン

Meaning in English:
英語の意味:

1. (Verb) To negotiate
(動詞)交渉する

2. (Noun) Something that is cheaper or a better deal than usual
(名詞)通常より安いもの/お得なもの

Say Instead:
適切な英語表現:

Sale

Example Sentences:
例文:

| That store is having a _bargain_ this weekend. | ➤ | That store is having a **_sale_** this weekend. |

その店は、今週末バーゲンだ。

How English Speakers use "bargain":
英語話者は(bargain)をどのように使うか:

Monica

How much did you get your new speakers for? They seem really good!

It was such a **bargain**! They were on sale for only $300 - that's more than 50% off!

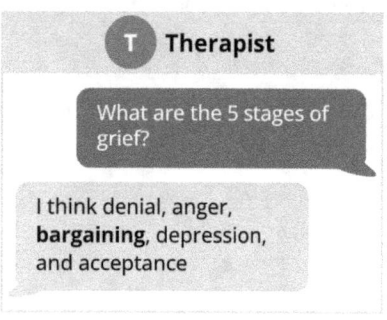

Therapist

What are the 5 stages of grief?

I think denial, anger, **bargaining**, depression, and acceptance

キャッシング

Meaning in English:
英語の意味:

In English, *cashing* primarily means "to exchange for cash" or "to convert into money." *To cash a check* is to take it to the bank and get it exchanged into (cash) money.

換金する、現金化することを指す。"To cash a check"とは、小切手を銀行に持って行き、現金に換えてもらうこと

Say Instead:
適切な英語表現:

Cash advance (on a credit card)

Example Sentences:
例文:

I don't like *cashing*. There's too much interest.

I don't like taking out a ***cash advance*** with my credit card. There's too much interest.

キャッシング/カードローンは好きじゃない。
利息が高すぎる。

How English Speakers use "cashing":
英語話者は(cashing)をどのように使うか:

to: Me <JoeSchmo@MyLife.com>
subject: LL Banking New Policy Update

Attention Bank Account Holder:

We wanted to inform you of our new policy that will go into effect as of 10 December 2029.

All clients, including current account holders, will now be required to show two valid forms of ID when **cashing** a check in any amount exceeding $100 USD.

CONVENI

コンビニ

Meaning in English:
英語の意味:

Doesn't exist
英語には該当する単語がない

Say Instead:
適切な英語表現:

Convenience store

Example Sentences:
例文:

In Japan, _conveni_ has everything! You can pay utility bills, send and receive packages, use ATM machines, make copies, print documents, and much more!	In Japan, **_convenience stores_** have everything! You can pay utility bills, send and receive packages, use ATM machines, make copies, print documents, and much more!

日本では、コンビニで何でもできる。
公共料金の支払い、宅配便の発送・受け取り、ATMの利用、
コピーやプリントサービスなど。

Doz

ダース

Meaning in English:
英語の意味:

Doesn't exist, but sounds like "does"
"does"に聞こえるが、英語に存在しない。

Say Instead:
適切な英語表現:

A dozen

Example Sentences:
例文:

How many donuts do you want? A *doz*.

How many donuts do you want? A ***dozen***.

何個ドーナツが欲しい?1ダース。

Eco (Echo) Bag

エコバッグ

Meaning in English:
英語の意味:

Doesn't exist
英語には該当する単語がない

Say Instead:
適切な英語表現:

Reusable shopping bag, Eco-friendly shopping bag

Example Sentences:
例文:

Eco bags are really popular in Japan.

Reusable shopping bags are really popular in Japan.

エコバッグは日本でとても人気がある。

HANDMADE

Meaning in English:
英語の意味:

Handmade is usually used for crafted items (e.g., handmade jewelry)
通常、工芸品や手作りのアイテムを指す（例：手作りのジュエリー）

Homemade is usually for any item made at home (e.g., homemade pie)
通常、家庭で作られたあらゆる物に使われる（例：ホームメイドの パイ）

Made from scratch is usually for food made from fresh ingredients
通常、新鮮な材料から作った料理に使われる（例：素材から手作 りした料理）

Say Instead:
適切な英語表現:

Handmade, Homemade, Made from scratch

Example Sentences:
例文:

Our soup is *handmade*. → Our soup is ***made from scratch***.

私たちのスープは、すべてハンドメイドだ。

⚠ This sounds like you prepared the soup using your hands.
手を使ってスープを作ったように聞こえる。

How English Speakers use "handmade":
英語話者は（handmade）をどのように使うか:

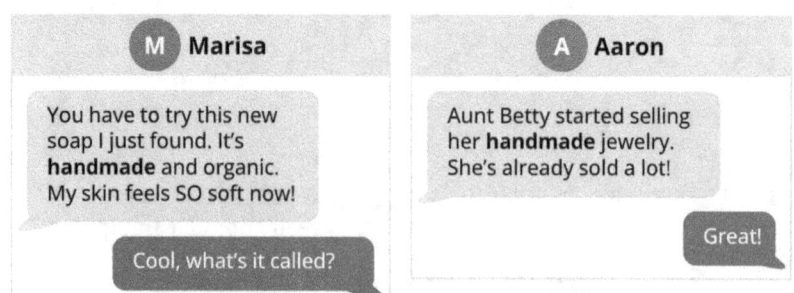

336

HIGH GRADE

Meaning in English:
英語の意味:

High grade is used to indicate that something is pure or of good quality, but it's typically only used when discussing materials from which something is made.

☞ Example: Our *high grade* stainless steel products are safe to use with food and free from additives.

ハイグレードは、純度が高いことや品質が優れていることを示すときに使われるが、一般的には、素材や原料について説明するときにのみ使われる

例:当社のハイグレードステンレススチール製品は、食品に使用しても安全で、添加物を含まない

Say Instead:
適切な英語表現:

High-quality, Good quality

Example Sentences:
例文:

The new grocery store is really *high grade*. ↝ The new grocery store is really ***good quality***.

新しい食料品店はとても高級(ハイグレード)だ。

How English Speakers use "high grade":
英語話者は(high grade)をどのように使うか:

to:　Me <Buyer@SteelBuyer.com>

subject:　Information Inquiry Regarding Steel Products and Composition

Dear Mr. Steel Buyer,

Thank you so much for your inquiry and interest in our products. I'd be happy to share a little more information and address all your questions.

First, for our Group 1 steel products, we utilize **high-grade** carbon steel, giving it highly corrosion-resistant properties.

Kiosk

キオスク

Meaning in English:
英語の意味:

1. An open stand or machine with things for sale or a small building where things are sold through a window

商品を販売するためのオープンなスタンドや自動販売機、または窓口を通じて販売が行われる小さな建物。

2. In the UK, *kiosk* may mean a telephone booth (telephone box)

(英) 電話ボックス

Say Instead:
適切な英語表現:

A convenience store called Kiosk

Example Sentences:
例文:

Nearly every train station in Japan has <u>kiosk</u>. Nearly every train station in Japan has ***a small convenience store called Kiosk***.

日本のほとんどの駅にはキオスクがある。

How English Speakers use "kiosk":
英語話者は(kiosk)をどのように使うか:

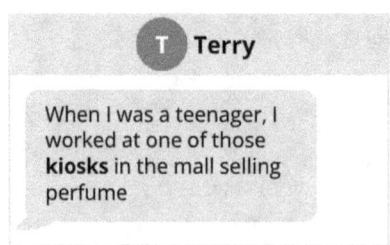

Terry: When I was a teenager, I worked at one of those **kiosks** in the mall selling perfume

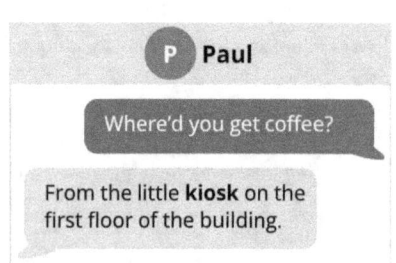

Paul: Where'd you get coffee?

From the little **kiosk** on the first floor of the building.

MY BAG

Meaning in English:
英語の意味:

A bag that is mine or in my possession
私のバッグ

Say Instead:
適切な英語表現:

Reusable shopping bag, Eco-friendly shopping bag

Example Sentences:
例文:

I prefer to bring _my bag_ to the store; it's better for the environment.

I prefer to bring a **_reusable shopping bag_** to the store; it's better for the environment.

私は、マイバッグを店に持って行くほうが好きなんだ。
環境に良いからね。

How English Speakers use "my bag":
英語話者は(my bag)をどのように使うか:

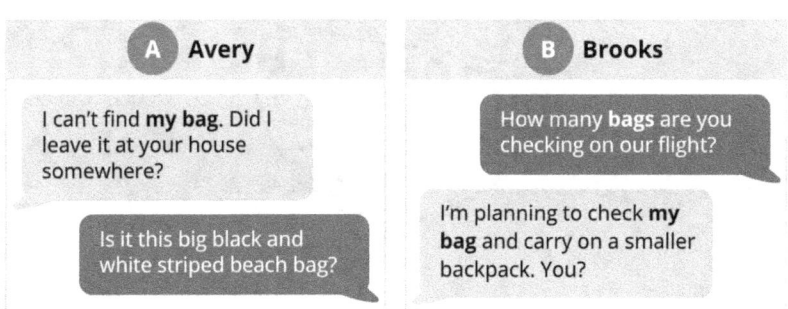

A Avery

I can't find **my bag**. Did I leave it at your house somewhere?

Is it this big black and white striped beach bag?

B Brooks

How many **bags** are you checking on our flight?

I'm planning to check **my bag** and carry on a smaller backpack. You?

ORDER MADE

オーダーメイド

Meaning in English:
英語の意味:

Doesn't exist
英語には該当する単語がない

Say Instead:
適切な英語表現:

Custom-made

Example Sentences:
例文:

My dream is to have an _order made_ suit someday. My dream is to have a **_custom-made_** suit someday.

いつかオーダーメイドのスーツを作るのが夢だ。

RECYCLE SHOP

Meaning in English:
英語の意味:

Doesn't exist
英語には該当する単語がない

Say Instead:
適切な英語表現:

Second hand store, Thrift store, Resale shop

Example Sentences:
例文:

リサイクルショップ

Look what I found at the
recycle shop! Look what I found at the
thrift store!

リサイクルショップでこんなものを見つけたよ!

This sounds like you found something
interesting at the recycling depository.
リサイクル回収所で何か見つけたみたいに聞こえる。

REGI

レジ

Meaning in English:
英語の意味:

Doesn't exist
英語には該当する単語がない

Say Instead:
適切な英語表現:

Cash register (US), Till (UK)

Example Sentences:
例文:

You can ask for the tickets at the _regi_. You can ask for the tickets at the _**(cash) register**_.

レジでチケットのことを聞いてみて。

SELF-REGI

セルフレジ

Meaning in English:
英語の意味:

Doesn't exist
英語には該当する単語がない

Say Instead:
適切な英語表現:

Self-checkout

Example Sentences:
例文:

Some convenis have _self-reji_ now. Some convenient stores have _**self-checkout**_ now.

一部のコンビニにはセルフレジがある。

SERVICE

サービス

Meaning in English:
英語の意味:

1. The act of helping, serving, or assisting someone
(e.g., community service)

誰かを助けたり、奉仕したり、支援する行為
（例：地域奉仕活動）→ 社会的・人道的な支援の意味で使われる「サービス」

2. Work, help, or assistance provided for a customer
(e.g., customer service)

顧客に対して提供される仕事・支援・援助
（例：カスタマーサービス）→ 接客や顧客対応に関する「サービス」

3. Jobs that provide a skilled service, rather than a good
(e.g., accountant, lawyer, language school)

モノではなく、専門的な技術や知識を提供する職業
（例：会計士、弁護士、語学教室）→ 有形の商品ではなく、技術・知識という「サービス」を提供する職種のこと

Say Instead:
適切な英語表現:

Complimentary, Free, On the house

Example Sentences:
例文:

These appetizers are from our _service_. These appetizers are ***on the house*** / ***complimentary***.

こちらは、サービスでお出ししています。

343

TIME SALE

タイムセール

Meaning in English:
英語の意味:

Doesn't exist
英語には該当する単語がない

Say Instead:
適切な英語表現:

Limited time offer

Example Sentences:
例文:

The cafe is having a _time sale_ this week and offering free coffee refills all week.

The cafe is having a **_limited time offer_** this week and offering free coffee refills all week.

今週、カフェがタイムセールをやっていて、
コーヒーのおかわりが無料なんだ。

SOCIAL LIFE & LOCAL COMMUNITY

18

社会生活・地域生活

Scan for Audio

BARTEN

バーテン

Meaning in English:
英語の意味:

Doesn't exist
英語には該当する単語がない

Say Instead:
適切な英語表現:

Bartender

Example Sentences:
例文:

| We can ask *barten* for some limes. | | We can ask the ***bartender*** for some limes. |

バーテンに頼めば、ライムをもらえるよ。

Boom

Meaning in English:
英語の意味:

1. A loud, deep sound (e.g., sound of thunder)
大きくて低い音（例：雷の音）

2. Period of sudden growth or success in business/economy
ビジネスや経済の急成長・成功の時期

Say Instead:
適切な英語表現:

Trend, Fad

Example Sentences:
例文:

| J-pop is a big _boom_ right now. | ➤ | J-pop is a huge **_trend_** right now. |

今、J-popは大ブームだ。

How English Speakers use "boom":
英語話者は（boom）をどのように使うか:

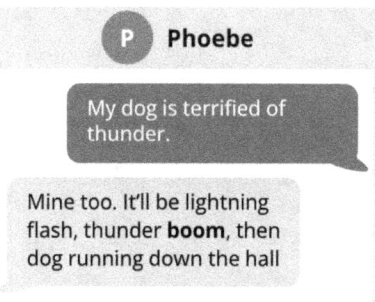

Ross

Business is **booming** right now! We just had to hire 3 additional salesmen!

That's so great to hear! All your hard work is paying off!

Phoebe

My dog is terrified of thunder.

Mine too. It'll be lightning flash, thunder **boom**, then dog running down the hall

BOTTLE KEEP

ボトルキープ

Meaning in English:

英語の意味:

Doesn't exist

英語には該当する単語がない

Say Instead:

適切な英語表現:

Ask the bar to save our bottle of alcohol so we can come back and finish it later at another time

Example Sentences:

例文:

I don't think we will drink this whole bottle of sake tonight. Let's do *bottle keep* and come back and finish it another night this week.

I don't think we will drink this whole bottle of sake tonight. Let's ***ask the bar to save it for us***, and we can come back and finish it another night this week.

今夜はこの日本酒を飲みきれないと思うから、
ボトルキープして、今週中にまた来て飲み切ろう。

CORNER

コーナー

Meaning in English:

英語の意味:

Most commonly, a place where two sides, edges, streets, etc., meet

一般的には、二つの側面、端、通りなどが交わる場所で、
角や隅を指す

Say Instead:

適切な英語表現:

Time, Space, Place, Area

Example Sentences:

例文:

| After the lecture, we'll have a _corner_ for questions. | → | After the lecture, we'll have a _**time**_ for questions / Q&A. |

講義の後、質問コーナーがある。

| At the festival, they have a _corner_ for petting zoo and also pig races! | → | After the festival, they have an _**area**_ with a petting zoo and another _**area**_ for pig races! |

そのフェスティバルでは、
ふれあい動物園とピッグレースのコーナーがある。

CULTURE CENTER

カルチャーセンター

Meaning in English:

英語の意味:

A center that focuses on a specific culture. For example, you might find a Japanese *culture center* in a major city in the USA where people can learn about Japanese culture, take Japanese lessons, watch a drumming performance, or have their name written in traditional calligraphy. These types of *culture centers* in the USA also usually offer services to people of that culture. For example, Japanese people could take English lessons or find resources to help them find a job locally or learn about how the American school system works, etc.

特定の文化に焦点を当てたセンター。例えば、アメリカの大都市には「日本文化センター」があり、アメリカ人が日本文化を学んだり、日本語のレッスンを受けたり、和太鼓の演奏を鑑賞したり、伝統的な書道で自分の名前を書いてもらったりすることができる。また、アメリカにあるこうした文化センターでは、その文化に属する人々向けのサービスも提供されることが多い。例えば、日本人が英語のレッスンを受けたり、地元での仕事探しに役立つ情報を得たり、アメリカの学校制度について学んだりするための資料を見つけることができる。

Say Instead:

適切な英語表現:

Community center, Adult education center, Community arts center

Example Sentences:

例文:

My aunt has been going to a *culture center* recently and started learning knitting and flower arrangement.	My aunt has been going to a ***community center*** recently and started learning knitting and flower arrangement.

私のおばは、最近カルチャーセンターに行って、編み物とフラワーアレンジメントを習っている。

 This sounds like she has been going to a center that teaches activities from a foreign culture.

外国の文化を学べるセンターに通っているようだ。

DOME

Meaning in English:
英語の意味:

Anything dome-shaped
ドーム型の

Say Instead:
適切な英語表現:

Stadium

Example Sentences:
例文:

Our school festival will be held at the _dome_.		Our school festival will be held at the **_stadium_**.

私たちの学校の文化祭は、ドームで行われる。

How English Speakers use "dome":
英語話者は(dome)をどのように使うか:

 Lucy

Here's our plan for Friday in Rome:
7am. - St. Peter's Basilica
8am - climb the stairs to the **dome**
11am - Colosseum tour
I hope you can meet up with us!

 Andrew

Why is it so hot? It's extra hot... this isn't normal...

I read there's something called a heat **dome** - the heat basically gets trapped above us

EVENT

イベント

Meaning in English:

英語の意味:

Event is typically only used for bigger events that require a lot of planning and organization beforehand and usually include a lot of people. This can't be used for small things like a birthday party or dinner, unless it is a large, extravagant *event*. Some examples of *events* are a wedding, a large party, a festival, a service. Most people will use the specific name of the event, "I went to a wedding this weekend." "The school had a festival."

"Event"（イベント）は、事前に多くの計画や準備が必要で、通常は大勢の人が関わる大規模な催しを指す。誕生日パーティーや食事会などの小さな集まりには通常使われず、それが豪華で規模の大きいものである場合に限られる。イベントの例としては、結婚式、大規模なパーティー、フェスティバル、式典などが挙げられる。ほとんどの場合、人々はイベントの具体的な名称を使う。（例：「週末に結婚式に行った」「学校でフェスティバルが開催された」）

If you don't know what kind of event it is or it isn't relevant, then you can call it an event.

☞ Example: The hotel was really crowded this weekend because they had a special *event*.

☞ Example: I'm sorry, the restaurant isn't taking any reservations this weekend because they are booked for an *event*.

イベントの種類が分からない場合や、詳しい説明が不要な場合は「イベント」と呼ぶことができる。例えば、「この週末、ホテルは特別なイベントがあったため、とても混雑していた」。
「申し訳ありませんが、この週末はレストランがイベントの予約で埋まっているため、予約を受け付けておりません」。

Say Instead:

適切な英語表現:

Sale

イ
ベ
ン
ト

Example Sentences:

例文:

> The store is having an _event_.   The store is having a **_sale_**.

> 店で、イベントがある。

This sounds like the store is hosting a community event like a festival or a party.

そのお店は、フェスティバルやパーティーのような地域イベントを開催しているようだ。

How English Speakers use "event":

英語話者は(event)をどのように使うか:

B Bella

> I should be able to drop by this weekend for the going away party!

> Great! It's an open house **event**, so a come and go visit is awesome!

B Best Friend

> When should we plan our trip? I'm flexible on dates!

> Well, a lot of **events** happen from October 31 to February 14. Then there's a little lull until the end of May... so maybe April?

Fami Res

ファミレス

Meaning in English:
英語の意味:

Doesn't exist
英語には該当する単語がない

Say Instead:
適切な英語表現:

Casual dining restaurant, Fast casual restaurant

Example Sentences:
例文:

My family usually goes to *fami res* on Saturdays together. My family usually goes to a ***casual dining restaurant*** on Saturdays together.

私の家族は、毎週土曜日にファミレスに行く。

Missa

ミサ

Meaning in English:
英語の意味:

Doesn't exist
英語には該当する単語がない

Say Instead:
適切な英語表現:

(Catholic) Mass

Example Sentences:
例文:

They joined the Christmas *missa*. They went to the Christmas ***mass***.

彼らは、クリスマスのミサに参加した。

MAN TO MAN

Meaning in English:
英語の意味:

1. This term is usually used to mean an honest and usually serious conversation that two people (usually men) have face to face.
☞ Example: Bob's comments and behavior were making some of the women in our group uncomfortable, but I know he is a good guy who doesn't intend to disrespect women. So I talked to him *man to man* and explained how some of the women were perceiving his comments. Ever since then, he's been more careful about his words and actions.

この表現は、通常、2人（特に男性同士）が向かい合って、誠実かつ真剣に話し合うことを意味する。
例: ボブの言動がグループ内の女性の一部を不快にさせていたが、私は、彼は悪気があるわけではなく、女性を軽視するつもりもないことを知っていた。だから、彼と男同士で率直に話をし、彼の発言を女性がどう受け止めているかを説明した。それ以来、彼は言動に気をつけるようになった。

2. In team sports, the defense strategy where one player is supposed to mark or guard another specific player from the opposing team
☞ Example: In basketball, some teams play more of a *man-to-man* defense; whereas, others play more of a zone defense.

チームスポーツにおいて、一人の選手が相手チームの特定の選手をマークしたり守ったりすることを指す。
例: バスケットボールでは、チームによって、マンツーマンディフェンスを採用する場合と、ゾーンディフェンスを採用する場合がある。

Say Instead:
適切な英語表現:

One on one, Private

Example Sentences:
例文:

| I'd like to study English *man to man*. | | I'd like to study English **one on one**. |

私は、マンツーマンで英語を勉強したい。

MORNING SERVICE

Meaning in English:
英語の意味:

A service (most likely religious) that takes place in the morning ☞ Example: They usually attend the church's *morning service* at 9 a.m.
朝に行われる礼拝（主に宗教的な儀式）（例：彼らは通常、午前9時に教会の朝の礼拝に参加する）

Say Instead:
適切な英語表現:

Breakfast room service, Room service breakfast

Example Sentences:
例文:

The hotel offers nice *morning service*.	The hotel offers a nice ***room service breakfast***.

ホテルは、素敵なモーニングサービスを提供している。

How English Speakers use "morning service":
英語話者は（**morning service**）をどのように使うか:

N Noah

We're going to go to the **morning service** at 9am, then we are gonna get brunch at Pickles if you want to come!

M Meredith

Did you go to church today?

Yes, we went to the **morning service**. You?

MY BOOM

マイブーム

Meaning in English:
英語の意味:

Doesn't exist
英語には該当する単語がない

Say Instead:
適切な英語表現:

What I'm into right now

Example Sentences:
例文:

Now, J-pop is _my boom_.	⟿	I'm **_really into_** J-pop **_right now_**.

今、J-pop がマイブームなんだ。

STARBU

スタバ

Meaning in English:
英語の意味:

Doesn't exist
英語には該当する単語がない

Say Instead:
適切な英語表現:

Starbucks

Example Sentences:
例文:

Starbu in Japan has a really delicious matcha latte.	⟿	**_Starbucks_** in Japan has a really delicious matcha latte.

日本のスタバには、すごく美味しい抹茶ラテがある。

TERRACE

テラス

Meaning in English:
英語の意味:

1. A flat, often raised area, typically along the ground
地面に沿っているが、しばしば少し高くなっている平らな場所

2. A flat rooftop
平らな屋根

3. A balcony or patio on an apartment, especially on top of a living area rather than a true "balcony" which hangs from the side of a building
テラスとは、アパートの居住スペースの上に設けられるバルコニーやパティオであり、建物の側面に張り出すタイプの「バルコニー」とは区別される。

4. (UK) A row of identical townhouses
(英)同じ外観のタウンハウスが並んだ列（連棟式住宅）

Say Instead:
適切な英語表現:

Balcony, Patio, Deck

Example Sentences:
例文:

Let's sit on the _terrace_ at the restaurant; I prefer to be up high rather than on ground level.	Let's sit on the **_balcony_** at the restaurant; I prefer to be up high rather than on ground level.

レストランではテラス席に座ろうよ。
地上階よりも高いところの方が好きなんだ。

SPORTS & EXERCISE

スポーツ・運動

Scan for Audio

AEROBIKE

エアロバイク

Meaning in English:
英語の意味:

Doesn't exist
英語には該当する単語がない

Say Instead:
適切な英語表現:

Stationary bike, Exercise bike

Example Sentences:
例文:

We recently got an _aerobike_, so we don't have to go to the gym.

We recently go an **_exercise bike_**, so we don't have to go to the gym.

最近エアロバイクを購入したので、ジムに行く必要がなくなった。

AME FOOT

アメフト

Meaning in English:
英語の意味:

Doesn't exist
英語には該当する単語がない

Say Instead:
適切な英語表現:

Football (US), American football (everywhere else)

Example Sentences:
例文:

Ame foot seems so dangerous!

American football seems so dangerous!

アメフトはとても危なそう!

BACK NET

バックネット

Meaning in English:
英語の意味:

Doesn't exist
英語には該当する単語がない

Say Instead:
適切な英語表現:

Backstop

Example Sentences:
例文:

The _back net_ protected the
fans from the foul ball.

The _**backstop**_ protected the
fans from the foul ball.

バックネットのおかげでファウルボールが観客に当たらずに済んだ。

BODY BUIL

ボディビル

Meaning in English:
英語の意味:

Doesn't exist
英語には該当する単語がない

Say Instead:
適切な英語表現:

Body building

Example Sentences:
例文:

After college, she got
interested in _body buil_.

After college, she got
interested in _**body building**_.

大学卒業後、彼女はボディビルに興味を持つようになった。

BATON TOUCH

バトンタッチ

Meaning in English:
英語の意味:

Doesn't exist
英語には該当する単語がない

Say Instead:
適切な英語表現:

Hand over, Hand off [to someone else]

Example Sentences:
例文:

I have an important task to finish at work before my vacation, but I think I can do _baton touch_ if I need to since it's a team project.

I have an important task to finish at work before my vacation, but I think I can **_hand it over/off to someone else_** if I need to since it's a team project.

休暇前に終わらせないといけない重要な仕事があるんだけど、
チームで進めている案件だから、
必要なら他のメンバーにバトンタッチできると思う。

Body Check

Meaning in English:
英語の意味:

When a person uses their whole body to run into, hit, knock over, or block another person, often in sports
☞ Example: The football player *body checked* his opponent.

人が全身を使って相手に突進したり、ぶつかったり、
ブロックしたりする行為。スポーツでよく使われる。
例：そのフットボール選手は相手にボディーチェックをした。

Say Instead:
適切な英語表現:

Frisk, Search, Pat-down, Randomly selected for screening

Example Sentences:
例文:

We almost missed our flight because we had to do *body check*.

We almost missed our flight because we got ***searched/ frisked/randomly selected***.

ボディーチェックが必要だったせいで、
危うく飛行機に乗り遅れるところだった。

How English Speakers use "body check":
英語話者は（body check）をどのように使うか:

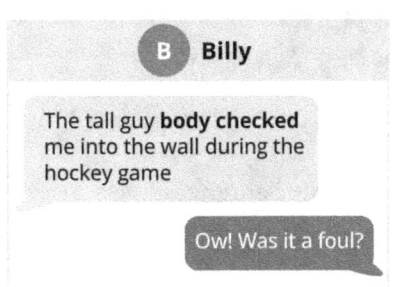

363

BOUND

Meaning in English:
英語の意味:

To run, jump, or leap in a fast (often excited) way
素早く(しばしば興奮して)走る、跳ぶ、または飛び跳ねること

Say Instead:
適切な英語表現:

Bounce

Example Sentences:
例文:

Kids, don't _bound_ the ball in the house.

Kids, don't **_bounce_** the ball in the house.

子どもたち、家の中でボールをつかない!

CATCH BALL

Meaning in English:
英語の意味:

Doesn't exist
英語には該当する単語がない

Say Instead:
適切な英語表現:

(Play) catch, Throw the ball back and forth

Example Sentences:
例文:

My kids like to play _catch ball_ outside with their dad.

My kids like to play **_catch_** outside with their dad.

うち子は、お父さんとキャッチボールをするのが好きなのよ。

CHEER DANCE

Meaning in English:
英語の意味:

Sounds like a combination of cheerleading and dancing
チアリーディングとダンスを組み合わせたようなもの。

Say Instead:
適切な英語表現:

Cheerleading, Cheer

Example Sentences:
例文:

| The cheer girls did *cheer dance* at the ame foot game. | | The cheerleaders **cheered** at the football game. |

チアガールたちは、アメフトの試合でチアダンスをした。

CHEER GIRL

Meaning in English:
英語の意味:

Doesn't exist
英語には該当する単語がない

Say Instead:
適切な英語表現:

Cheerleader

Example Sentences:
例文:

| The *cheer girls* did cheer dance at the ame foot game. | | The **cheerleaders** cheered at the football game. |

チアガールたちは、アメフトの試合でチアダンスをした。

DEAD BALL

Meaning in English:

英語の意味:

Used generally in many sports when the ball is out of play and there is a break in play until restarted in the correct way depending on the rules/officials (For example, in soccer, if a ball goes out of bounds, players cannot continue playing it. It is *dead* and needs to be thrown back in via a throw in.)

一般的に多くのスポーツで使用される用語であり、ボールがコートやフィールドの外に出たときに適用される。試合は一時中断され、ルールや審判の判断に従って正しい方法で再開される
(例: サッカーでは、ボールがラインを越えてアウトになった場合、プレーを続行することはできず、スローインによって試合が再開される)

Say Instead:

適切な英語表現:

Hit-by-pitch, The pitcher hit the batter with the ball

Example Sentences:

例文:

The game was crazy! There were three *dead balls*!		The game was crazy! There were three ***hit-by-pitches***!

試合は、めちゃくちゃだったよ。デッドボールが3回もあったんだ。

FLYING (START)

Meaning in English:
英語の意味:

Doesn't exist
英語には該当する単語がない

Say Instead:
適切な英語表現:

False start

Example Sentences:
例文:

She was disqualified from the race for a *flying start*.

→ She was disqualified from the race for a ***false start***.

彼女はフライングスタートで失格になった。

FOUR BALL

Meaning in English:
英語の意味:

Doesn't exist
英語には該当する単語がない

Say Instead:
適切な英語表現:

Walk, Base on balls

Example Sentences:
例文:

The baseball game was kind of boring and slow. There were a lot of *four balls*.

→ The baseball game was kind of boring and slow. There were a lot of ***walks***.

フォアボールが多くて、試合の流れがゆっくりでちょっと退屈だった。

FULL BASE

フルベース

Meaning in English:
英語の意味:

Doesn't exist
英語には該当する単語がない

Say Instead:
適切な英語表現:

Bases are loaded

Example Sentences:
例文:

> It's *full base*! Can he hit a grand slam?!

> The ***bases are loaded***! Can he hit a grand slam?!

満塁だ！彼はグランドスラムを打てるのか？！

GAME SET

ゲームセット

Meaning in English:
英語の意味:

Doesn't exist
英語には該当する単語がない

Say Instead:
適切な英語表現:

Game, set, match!

Example Sentences:
例文:

> *Game set*! That was the last inning! Let's go home!

> ***Game, set, match***! That was the last inning! Let's go home!

ゲームセット！今のが最終回だったね。家に帰ろう。

GERENDE

ゲレンデ

Meaning in English:
英語の意味:

Doesn't exist
英語には該当する単語がない

Say Instead:
適切な英語表現:

Ski slopes

Example Sentences:
例文:

We love going to _gerende_ in the winter.		We love going to the **_ski slopes_** in the winter.

冬にゲレンデに行くのが大好きだ。

The _gerende_ is illuminated at night, creating a truly magical atmosphere.		The **_ski slopes_** are lit up at night, creating a truly magical atmosphere.

夜のゲレンデはライトアップされていて、とても幻想的だ。

GOAL

ゴール

Meaning in English:
英語の意味:

1. The place to score points in sports with a ball
ボールを使うスポーツで得点を決める場所

2. Aim or objective
目標や目的

Say Instead:
適切な英語表現:

Finish line

Example Sentences:
例文:

> When he ran across the _goal_, the crowd cheered. It was the first time he had ever gotten first place in a race.

> When he ran across the **_finish line_**, the crowd cheered. It was the first time he had ever gotten first place in a race.

彼がゴールラインを越えたとき、観客は歓声を上げた。
彼にとってレースで初めての優勝だった。

How English Speakers use "goal":
英語話者は(goal)をどのように使うか:

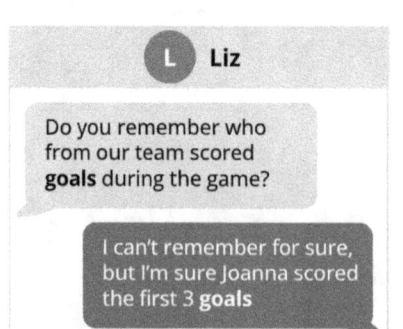

Liz

Do you remember who from our team scored **goals** during the game?

I can't remember for sure, but I'm sure Joanna scored the first 3 **goals**

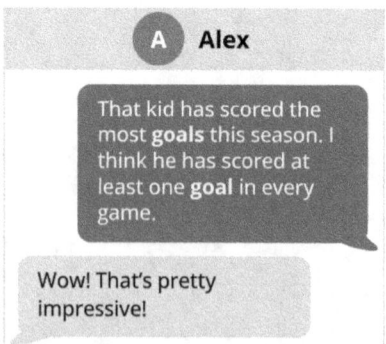

Alex

That kid has scored the most **goals** this season. I think he has scored at least one **goal** in every game.

Wow! That's pretty impressive!

GOAL IN

Meaning in English:
英語の意味:

Doesn't exist
英語には該当する単語がない

Say Instead:
適切な英語表現:

Finally get married, Tie the knot

Example Sentences:
例文:

Mary and Mike did _goal in_ this weekend! They dated for five years and finally got married!

Mary and Mike **_finally tied the knot_** this weekend! They dated for five years and finally got married!

メアリーとマイクは今週末ついにゴールインした！
5年間付き合って、ついに結婚したんだ。

JOCKEY

ジョッキ

Meaning in English:
英語の意味:

A professional horse rider in horse races
騎手

Say Instead:
適切な英語表現:

Beer mug

Example Sentences:
例文:

I love drinking beer from a _jockey_.

I love drinking beer from a **_beer mug_**.

私はジョッキでビールを飲むのが大好きだ。

 This sounds like you enjoy drinking beer from a professional horse rider.
この文の感じだと、あなたは騎手(ジョッキー)からビールを飲むのが好きみたいだ。

How English Speakers use "jockey":
英語話者は(jockey)をどのように使うか:

KICKBOARD

Meaning in English:
英語の意味:

A board to hold onto and kick while swimming
泳ぐ際につかんでキックするためのボード
ビートバン・ビートボード

Say Instead:
適切な英語表現:

Scooter

Example Sentences:
例文:

My kids ride their *kickboards* to their friend's house.

My kids ride their **scooters** to their friend's house.

私の子供たちはキックボードに乗って友達の家へ行く。

How English Speakers use "kickboard":
英語話者は（kickboard）をどのように使うか:

Mia

Are you bringing anything to the beach?

The kids want to bring their **kickboards** and boogie boards.

Chris

In swimming class today, the kids practiced blowing bubbles with their faces in the water and then practiced kicking hard with a **kickboard**

Loss Time

ロスタイム

Meaning in English:
英語の意味:

Doesn't exist
英語には該当する単語がない

Say Instead:
適切な英語表現:

Stoppage time, Added time, Injury time, Extra time

Example Sentences:
例文:

The referee added 5 minutes _loss time_ at the end of the game.

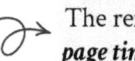

The ref added 5 minutes of _**stoppage time**_ at the end of the game.

審判は試合終了時に5分のロスタイムを追加した。

No Count

ノーカウント

Meaning in English:
英語の意味:

Doesn't exist
英語には該当する単語がない

Say Instead:
適切な英語表現:

No goal

Example Sentences:
例文:

The soccer player scored a beautiful goal, but the referee said it was _no count_ since she was slightly offside.

The soccer player scored a beautiful goal, but the referee said it was a _**no goal**_ since she was slightly offside.

そのサッカー選手がきれいなゴールを決めたけど、
審判はオフサイドでノーカウントにした。

ONE TEAM

ワンチーム

Meaning in English:
英語の意味:

Literally, one team
文字通り、一つのチーム/チーム一つ

Say Instead:
適切な英語表現:

Work together as a team, Work in sync

Example Sentences:
例文:

The game started off poorly in the first half, but in the second half, we did *one team* and were able to come back and win the game.

➤

The game started off poorly in the first half, but in the second half, we started ***working together as a team*** and were able to come back and win the game.

試合の前半はあまり良くなかったけれど、
後半はワンチームになって逆転し、勝つことができた。

*****Note:*** "One team" is a newer phrase used in Japan, similar in meaning to the traditional concept of "working together as one."

注: ワンチーム（最近になって使われるようになった）になって
＝チーム一丸となって（昔から使われていた表現）

PUNCH

パンチ

Meaning in English:
英語の意味:

1. (Verb) To hit someone with a closed fist
（動詞）握った拳で人を殴ること
2. (Noun) A hit with a closed fist
（名詞）握った拳での打撃、パンチ
3. (Noun) Force or effectiveness
（名詞）力強さ、迫力、効果

Say Instead:
適切な英語表現:

Hole punch
Spicy, Has a kick
Bold, Bright

Example Sentences:
例文:

Do we have a _punch_ here? Do we have a **_hole punch_** here?

ここにパンチがあるかな。

This food has _punch_. This food is **_spicy_**.

この料理、パンチが効いてるね。

Your dress really has _punch_! Your dress has really **_bold colors_**!

そのドレス、パンチが効いててかっこいい!

RUGGER

Meaning in English:
英語の意味:

Rugby (less common in the USA)
ラグビー

Say Instead:
適切な英語表現:

Lager, Rugby player, Rugger (UK)

Example Sentences:
例文:

The famous _ruggers_ always drink _ruggers_ after the game at the bar I often go to.

The famous **_rugby players_** always drink **_lager_** after the game at the bar I often go to.

試合のあと、有名なラガーマンたちは、
私がよく行くバーでラガー（ビール）を飲む。

ラガー

RUNNING SHIRT

Meaning in English:
英語の意味:

Doesn't exist
英語には該当する単語がない

Say Instead:
適切な英語表現:

Sleeveless shirt, Tank top,
Muscle shirt

Example Sentences:
例文:

I got a sunburn because I wore a *running shirt* to do yard work.

I got a sunburn because I wore a ***tank top*** to do yard work.

ランニングシャツを着て庭仕事をしたから、日焼けした。

How English Speakers use "running shirt":
英語話者は(**running shirt**)をどのように使うか:

Danielle

Have you seen my new **running shirt** anywhere?

Which one?

The blue one with long sleeves

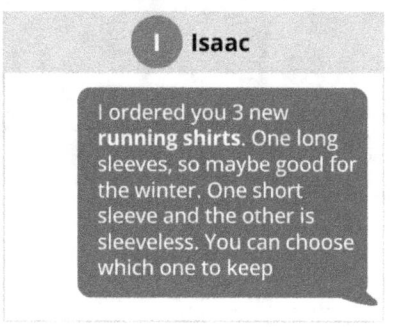

Isaac

I ordered you 3 new **running shirts**. One long sleeves, so maybe good for the winter. One short sleeve and the other is sleeveless. You can choose which one to keep

ランニングシャツ

RUNNING HOME RUN

Meaning in English:
英語の意味:

Doesn't exist
英語には該当する単語がない

Say Instead:
適切な英語表現:

Inside-the-park home run

Example Sentences:
例文:

In the last inning, he hit a _running home run_ and tied the game.

→ In the last inning, he hit an **_inside-the-park home run_** and tied the game.

最終回、彼がランニングホームランを打って同点に追いついた。

ランニングホームラン

SAYONARA HIT

さよならヒット

Meaning in English:
英語の意味:

Doesn't exist
英語には該当する単語がない

Say Instead:
適切な英語表現:

Game-winning hit, Walk-off

Example Sentences:
例文:

They were behind, but the star player had a _sayonara hit_ in the last inning.

They were behind, but the star player had a **_walk-off_** in the last inning!

負けていたが、最終回にスター選手がサヨナラヒットを打って、逆転勝利した！

SEASON OFF

シーズンオフ

Meaning in English:
英語の意味:

Doesn't exist
英語には該当する単語がない

Say Instead:
適切な英語表現:

Off-season

Example Sentences:
例文:

It's _season off_, so I don't have basketball practice after school.

➤ It's the **_off-season_**, so I don't have basketball practice after school.

今はシーズンオフなので、放課後のバスケ練習はない。

TOUCH OUT

タッチアウト

Meaning in English:
英語の意味:

Doesn't exist
英語には該当する単語がない

Say Instead:
適切な英語表現:

Force out

Example Sentences:
例文:

The outfielder threw the ball to second base for the _touch out_.

➤ The outfielder threw the ball to second base for the **_force out_**.

外野手はセカンドベースにボールを投げて、タッチアウトになった。

TOUCH UP

タッチアップ

Meaning in English:
英語の意味:

To make small changes to something to improve it
何かを改善するために、対象に対して小さな変更を加えること。

Say Instead:
適切な英語表現:

Tag up (on the base)

Example Sentences:
例文:

The player forgot to *touch up first base* after the fly ball. So the outfielder threw the ball to the first baseman, and they got an out.	The player forgot to ***tag up on first base*** after the fly ball. So the outfielder threw the ball to the first baseman, and they got an out.

選手はフライを取ったあと、
ファーストベースにタッチアップするのを忘れて、
外野手がファーストに投げてアウトになった。

How English Speakers use "touch up":
英語話者は(**touch up**)をどのように使うか:

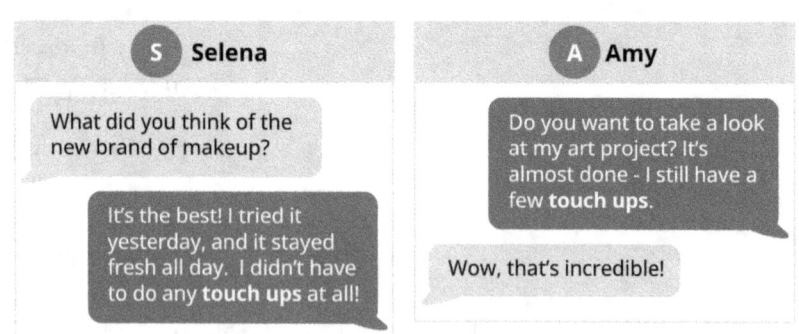

S Selena

What did you think of the new brand of makeup?

It's the best! I tried it yesterday, and it stayed fresh all day. I didn't have to do any **touch ups** at all!

A Amy

Do you want to take a look at my art project? It's almost done - I still have a few **touch ups**.

Wow, that's incredible!

VOLLEY

バレー

Meaning in English:
英語の意味:

(Verb) To return a ball before it touches the ground
(動詞) ボールが地面に触れる前に打ち返す

Say Instead:
適切な英語表現:

Volleyball

Example Sentences:
例文:

| Do you know where we can play _volley_? | Do you know where we can play **_volleyball_**? |

バレーできる所、どこか知ってる?

How English Speakers use "volley":
英語話者は(volley)をどのように使うか:

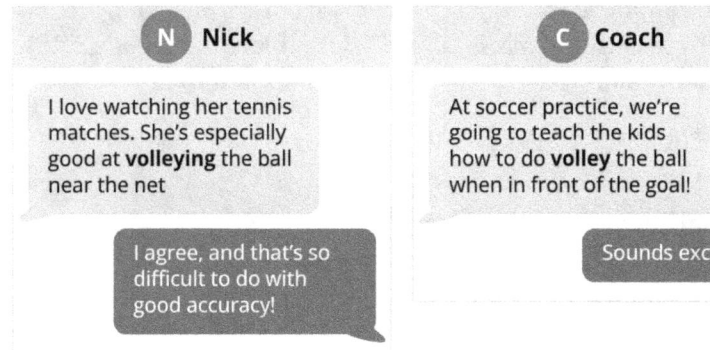

N Nick

I love watching her tennis matches. She's especially good at **volleying** the ball near the net

I agree, and that's so difficult to do with good accuracy!

C Coach

At soccer practice, we're going to teach the kids how to do **volley** the ball when in front of the goal!

Sounds exciting!

YACHT

ヨット

Meaning in English:
英語の意味:

Typically a larger sail boat that can accommodate overnight use. Yachts are commonly privately owned and used for luxury or racing and typically have connotations of a luxurious, super-rich lifestyle

ヨットとは、通常、大型で宿泊も可能な帆船。一般的に個人所有で、贅沢な遊びやレースなどに使われることが多く、豪華で贅沢なライフスタイルの意味合いを持つ。

Say Instead:
適切な英語表現:

Sailboat, Windsail, Windsurf, Yacht

Example Sentences:
例文:

We took a _yacht_ lesson at the lake this weekend. It was so fun!

We took a **_windsurfing_** lesson at the lake this weekend. It was so fun!

今週末は湖でヨットのレッスンを受けてきた。すごく楽しかった！

How English Speakers use "yacht":
英語話者は（yacht）をどのように使うか:

Cynthia

The bay in that city has a ton of **yachts**. The super rich go there to vacation

Justin

OMG, my boss owns a **yacht** with a private chef and just invited us for the weekend!

TECHNOLOGY

20

テクノロジー

Scan for Audio

APPLI

アプリ

Meaning in English:
英語の意味:

Doesn't exist
英語には該当する単語がない

Say Instead:
適切な英語表現:

App, Application

Example Sentences:
例文:

Their new *appli* is terrible. Their new **app** is terrible.

新しいアプリは、ひどい。

BS

アプリ

Meaning in English:
英語の意味:

Rubbish, Nonsense, Lies
でたらめ、無意味

Say Instead:
適切な英語表現:

Satellite TV

Example Sentences:
例文:

Do you have *BS*? I do! Do you have **satellite TV**? I do!

BS持ってる?私は、持ってる。

DM

Meaning in English:
英語の意味:

"Direct message" on social media
「ダイレクトメッセージ（DM）」

Say Instead:
適切な英語表現:

Junk mail, Spam

Example Sentences:
例文:

I'm getting so many <u>*DM*</u>s this week in my e-mail!

I'm getting so much **<u>*spam*</u>/<u>*junk mail*</u>** this week in my e-mail!

今週、私のメールにたくさんディーエムが届いてる。

This sounds like you are getting a lot of private messages on your social media accounts!

これは、ソーシャルメディアでたくさんのプライベートメッセージを受け取っているように聞こえる。

How English Speakers use "DM":
英語話者は（DM）をどのように使うか:

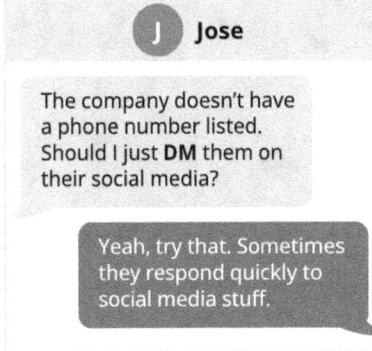

Diji Came

デジカメ

Meaning in English:

英語の意味:

Doesn't exist

英語には該当する単語がない

Say Instead:

適切な英語表現:

Digital camera

Example Sentences:

例文:

I still like using my *diji came* even though most people just use their phones now.

I still like using my ***digital camera*** even though most people just use their phones now.

ほとんどの人が、スマホで写真を撮っているけれど、私は、まだ、デジカメが好きだ。

FREE DIAL

フリーダイヤル

Meaning in English:
英語の意味:

Doesn't exist
英語には該当する単語がない

Say Instead:
適切な英語表現:

Toll-free number

Example Sentences:
例文:

They should have a *free dial* you can call. They should have a ***toll-free number*** you can call.

問い合わせ用のフリーダイヤルが設置されているはずだ。

HANDLE NAME

ハンドルネーム

Meaning in English:
英語の意味:

Doesn't exist
英語には該当する単語がない

Say Instead:
適切な英語表現:

Screenname, Username, Handle, Profile name

Example Sentences:
例文:

What's your *handle name* for social media? What's your ***username/handle*** for social media?

SNSのハンドルネームは何?

INPUT

インプット

Meaning in English:
英語の意味:

1. (Noun) Information or data entered into a computer
☞ Example: Did you give Bob the new *inputs*? They need to be entered today.
(名詞) コンピューターに入力された情報やデータ
例:「ボブに新しい入力データを渡した？今日中に入力する必要があるんだ」

2. (Noun) Help, ideas, opinions, energy given to a situation or project for consideration
☞ Example: We would love your *input* if you have any thoughts on how we can improve our program for the future."
☞ Example: Thanks so much for your *input* yesterday on how to handle our tricky family situation. It was really helpful for us to consider.
(名詞) ある状況やプロジェクトに対して提供される助言、アイデア、意見、エネルギー 例:「今後のプログラム改善について何か考えがあれば、ぜひご意見をいただきたい」例:「昨日は家族のこと、いろいろアドバイスをくれてありがとう。本当に参考になったわ」

3. (Verb) To put information or data into a computer
☞ Example: I *input* the data into the new system, and it immediately gave me an updated list of all of our clients.
(動詞) コンピューターに情報やデータを入力する
例: 「新しいシステムにデータを入力したら、すぐに最新の顧客リストが表示された」

Say Instead:
適切な英語表現:

Listening, Reading, Studying [language]

Example Sentences:
例文:

> I didn't <u>*input*</u> anything this weekend; I only did output. I feel so empty and need to start doing input again.

> I didn't do *any English **reading or listening practice*** this weekend; I only spoke a little bit. I feel so drained and need to start studying again.

今週末は何もインプットせず、アウトプットばかりだった。とても空虚な気分なので、またインプットを始めたい。

HIGH VISION TV

Meaning in English:
英語の意味:

Doesn't exist
英語には該当する単語がない

Say Instead:
適切な英語表現:

HDTV

Example Sentences:
例文:

ハイビジョンテレビ

Do you have _high vision TV_? Do you have **_HDTV_**?

ハイビジョンテレビをもってる?

MISHIN

Meaning in English:
英語の意味:

Doesn't exist
英語には該当する単語がない

Say Instead:
適切な英語表現:

Sewing machine

Example Sentences:
例文:

ミシン

Do you have a _mishin_? I have a rip in my pants that I need to fix. Do you have a **_sewing machine_**? I have a rip in my pants that I need to fix.

ミシンを持ってる?ズボンが破れたので、直したいんだ。

MANNER MODE

マナーモード

Meaning in English:
英語の意味:

Doesn't exist
英語には該当する単語がない

Say Instead:
適切な英語表現:

Silent, Vibrate

Example Sentences:
例文:

Please put your phone on _manner mode_. Please put your phones on **_silent_**.

携帯電話をマナーモードにしてください。

NAVI

ナビ

Meaning in English:
英語の意味:

Doesn't exist
英語には該当する単語がない

Say Instead:
適切な英語表現:

Car GPS, Navigational system

Example Sentences:
例文:

Does your car have _navi_? Does your car have a **_navigational system_**?

君の車、ナビついてる？

NOTE PERSON COM

Meaning in English:
英語の意味:

Doesn't exist
英語には該当する単語がない

Say Instead:
適切な英語表現:

Laptop, Computer

Example Sentences:
例文:

ノートパソコン

Some of the newest
note perso coms are so
lightweight compared to the
ones from 10 years ago.

Some of the newest **_laptops_**
are so lightweight compared
to the ones from 10 years ago.

最新のノートパソコンの中には、
10年前のものと比べて非常に軽量なものもある。

REMO CON

リモコン

Meaning in English:
英語の意味:

Doesn't exist
英語には該当する単語がない

Say Instead:
適切な英語表現:

Remote, Remote control

Example Sentences:
例文:

Can you pass me the _remo con_? Can you pass me the **_remote_**?

リモコンをとってくれる。

SNS

エスエヌエス

Meaning in English:
英語の意味:

Doesn't exist
英語には該当する単語がない

Say Instead:
適切な英語表現:

Social media

Example Sentences:
例文:

Let's follow each other on _SNS_. → Let's follow each other on **_social media_**.

お互いにSNSでフォローしようよ。

SUKSHO

スクショ

Meaning in English:
英語の意味:

Doesn't exist
英語には該当する単語がない

Say Instead:
適切な英語表現:

Screenshot

Example Sentences:
例文:

| Please take a _suksho_ of what I sent you. | | Please take a **_screenshot_** of what I sent you. |

私が送ったものをスクショに撮っておいて。

TELEBI

テレビ

Meaning in English:
英語の意味:

Doesn't exist
英語には該当する単語がない

Say Instead:
適切な英語表現:

TV, Television

Example Sentences:
例文:

| My hobby is watching _telebi_. | | My hobby is watching **_TV_**. |

趣味はテレビを見ることだ。

TELEBI GAME

テレビゲーム

Meaning in English:
英語の意味:

Doesn't exist
英語には該当する単語がない

Say Instead:
適切な英語表現:

Video game

Example Sentences:
例文:

| My sister broke up with her boyfriend because all he wanted to do was play *telebi games*. | | My sister broke up with her boyfriend because all he wanted to do was play *video games*. |

妹は彼氏と別れたんだ。
彼がテレビゲームばっかりやってたから。

TELOP

テロップ

Meaning in English:
英語の意味:

Doesn't exist
英語には該当する単語がない

Say Instead:
適切な英語表現:

Text and graphics over a video

Example Sentences:
例文:

Many social media personalities use _telop_ to show funny comments during their videos.

Many social media personalities use **_graphics and text over their videos_** to show funny comments during their posts.

SNSでバズってる人たちは、
動画の中で面白いコメントをテロップで出してるよね。

VERSION UP

バージョンアップ

Meaning in English:
英語の意味:

Doesn't exist
英語には該当する単語がない

Say Instead:
適切な英語表現:

Update (to the latest software)

Example Sentences:
例文:

I need to *version up* my computer operating system. I need to ***update*** my computer operating system.

コンピューターのOSをバージョンアップする必要がある。

My phone does *version up* automatically. My phone ***updates*** automatically.

私の携帯は、自動的にバージョンアップしてくれる。

Tools & Useful Items

21

道具・便利グッズ

Scan for Audio

ALUMI

アルミ

Meaning in English:
英語の意味:

Doesn't exist
英語には該当する単語がない

Say Instead:
適切な英語表現:

Aluminum (US), Aluminium (UK)

Example Sentences:
例文:

| Our research will look for more efficient ways to recycle _alumi_. | | Our research will look for more efficient ways to recycle **_aluminum_**. |

私たちの研究は、
アルミをより効率的にリサイクルする方法を探ることを目的としている。

ALUMI FOIL

アルミホイル

Meaning in English:
英語の意味:

Doesn't exist
英語には該当する単語がない

Say Instead:
適切な英語表現:

Aluminum foil (US), Aluminium foil (UK)

Example Sentences:
例文:

| I don't have a to-go box, but you can use _alumi foil_. | | I don't have a to-go box, but you can use **_aluminum foil_**. |

テイクアウト用の箱はないけれど、アルミホイルならつかえるよ。

CONTAINER

Meaning in English:
英語の意味:

Anything (usually box-like) that contains (holds) something else, often for transportation or storage

輸送や保管のために、他の何かを収納（保持）するもの（通常は箱状のもの）

Say Instead:
適切な英語表現:

Shipping container

Example Sentences:
例文:

コンテナ・コンテナー

We need to use a _container_ to bring our items from Japan to Canada.

We need to use a **_shipping container_** to bring our belongings from Japan to Canada.

日本からカナダへ荷物をコンテナで運ぶ必要がある。

This sounds like you will be bringing your items in a Tupperware container or closet storage container!
物をタッパーや蓋つきの保存容器に入れて持っていくように聞こえる。

How English Speakers use "container":
英語話者は（container）をどのように使うか:

R **Roommate**

Hey! I already left but there are some dumplings in the fridge! There is also sauce to go with them - it's in a small **container**

Wow! Thanks! That sounds amazing!

D **Diana**

Do you have any extra storage **containers**?

Yes! We have several of those large plastic **containers**, but I'm not sure if they all have lids!

COOLER

クーラー

Meaning in English:
英語の意味:

An insulated box or bag that keeps things cool
保冷ボックス

Say Instead:
適切な英語表現:

Air conditioner

Example Sentences:
例文:

It's so hot today! Do you have a _cooler_ in your apart?

It's so hot today! Do you have an **_air conditioner_** in your apartment?

今日は、とっても暑いね。アパートには、クーラーがついてるの?

⚠ This sounds like you are asking if there is an ice chest inside the apartment!
これは、クーラーボックス(またはアイスチェスト)があるか尋ねているように聞こえる。

How English Speakers use "cooler":
英語話者は(cooler)をどのように使うか:

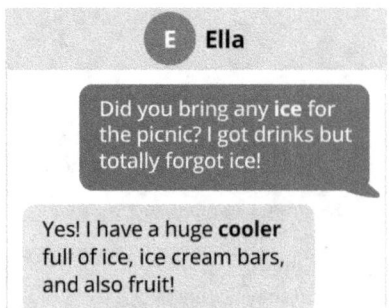

Ella

Did you bring any **ice** for the picnic? I got drinks but totally forgot ice!

Yes! I have a huge **cooler** full of ice, ice cream bars, and also fruit!

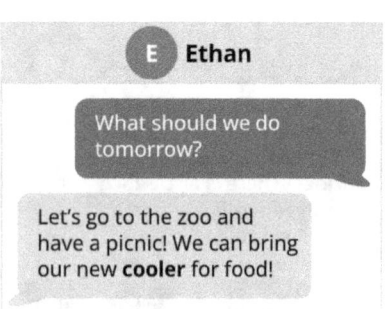

Ethan

What should we do tomorrow?

Let's go to the zoo and have a picnic! We can bring our new **cooler** for food!

CUTTER

カッター

Meaning in English:
英語の意味:

1. A general word for anything that cuts. *Cutter* is usually not used alone and has a descriptive adjective in front (paper cutter, metal cutter, glass cutter, etc.)

何かを切るための一般的な言葉。単独で使われることは少なく、通常は前に説明的な形容詞が付く。(紙用カッター、金属用カッター、ガラス用カッターなど)

2. A specific type of baseball pitch
野球の投球の特定の種類

Say Instead:
適切な英語表現:

Utility knife, X-acto knife

Example Sentences:
例文:

I need a *cutter* for my school project.

I need a ***utility knife*** for my school project.

学校のプロジェクトでカッターがいる。

How English Speakers use "cutter":
英語話者は(cutter)をどのように使うか:

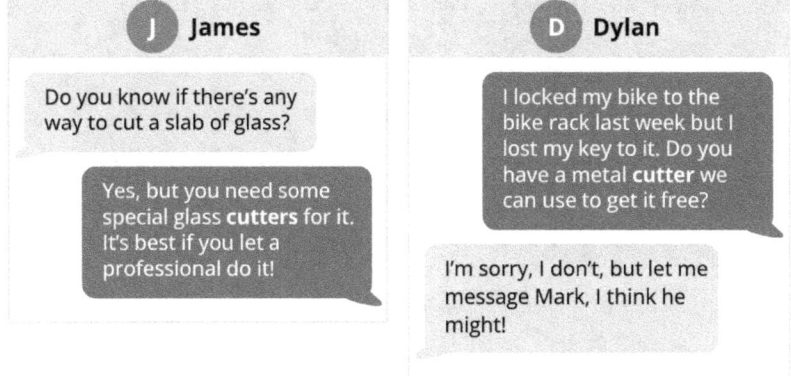

James

Do you know if there's any way to cut a slab of glass?

Yes, but you need some special glass **cutters** for it. It's best if you let a professional do it!

Dylan

I locked my bike to the bike rack last week but I lost my key to it. Do you have a metal **cutter** we can use to get it free?

I'm sorry, I don't, but let me message Mark, I think he might!

Danboru

段ボール

Meaning in English:
英語の意味:

Doesn't exist, but sounds like Dumbo, which means:
英語には該当する単語がないが、「ダンボ」に似た響きの名前
ちなみに「ダンボ」には次のような意味がある:

1. An area or neighborhood within the New York City borough, Brooklyn, that stands for Down Under the Manhattan Bridge Overpass (DUMBO)
ニューヨーク市ブルックリン区にある地区の名称で、「マンハッタン橋の高架下（Down Under the Manhattan Bridge Overpass）」の略称

2. An animated movie about an elephant with giant ears with this name
巨大な耳を持つ象のダンボが主人公の、ディズニーによるアニメ映画

Say Instead:
適切な英語表現:

Cardboard box

Example Sentences:
例文:

We need some _danboru_ to fill our container for the move overseas.

We need some **_cardboard boxes_** to fill our shipping container for the move overseas.

海外への引っ越しに使うコンテナに詰めるために、
ダンボが必要だ。

JAR

Meaning in English:
英語の意味:

A container usually made of glass or clay
通常、ガラスや陶器で作られた容器

Say Instead:
適切な英語表現:

Rice cooker

Example Sentences:
例文:

I always make rice in my _jar_. I always make rice in my ***rice cooker***.

私は、いつも炊飯ジャーでお米を炊く。

This sounds confusing... how can you make rice in a jar?
これは、混乱するね。どうやって瓶の中でご飯を作ることができるんだ？

How English Speakers use "jar":
英語話者は(jar)をどのように使うか:

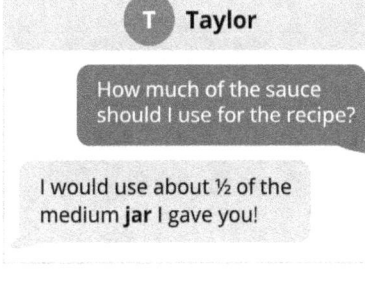

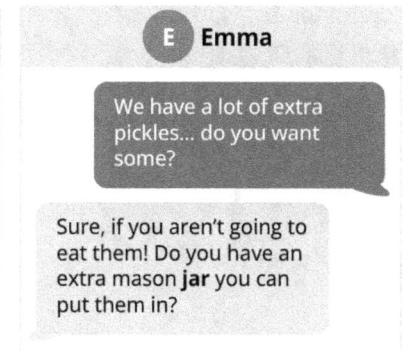

405

HANDI / HANDY

ハンディ・ハンディー

Meaning in English:
英語の意味:

Handy is always used as an adjective in English and never as a noun (which can have an inappropriate meaning). As an adjective, *handy* can mean the following:

"Handy"は英語では常に形容詞として使われ、名詞としては不適切な意味を持つことがある。形容詞としての意味は次の通り。

1. Convenient, easy to use, close by, useful
☞ Example: Wow, this kitchen gadget is really *handy*! I use it all the time!

便利な、使いやすい、近くにある、有用な
例:「このキッチン用品は本当に便利だね！いつも使ってるよ！」

2. A person who is good at fixing things
☞ Example: In Western culture, it's often considered attractive for a man to be *handy* around the house.

物を修理するのが得意な人
例:「西洋文化では、家の中で修理やDIYが得意な男性は魅力的だと考えられることが多い」

3. Nearby, ready to use, easily accessible
☞ Example: Let's keep these snacks *handy*; I think we'll want them during our hike tomorrow.

すぐ手に取れる、準備ができている、アクセスしやすい
例:「このお菓子、明日のハイキングで食べたくなると思うから、すぐ取れるところに置いておこう」

Say Instead:
適切な英語表現:

Handicap *(disability)*
Hand-held
Handicap *(in golf)*

Example Sentences:
例文:

| She has a <u>handi</u>. | | She has a ***disability***. |

彼女にはハンディがある。

HANDI / HANDY

I want a *handy-size* dictionary. I want a **hand-held** dictionary.

私は、ハンディーサイズの辞書が欲しい。

He has a golf *handi* of 7. He has a golf **handicap** of 7.

彼のゴルフのハンディは、7だ。

How English Speakers use "handy":
英語話者は（handy）をどのように使うか：

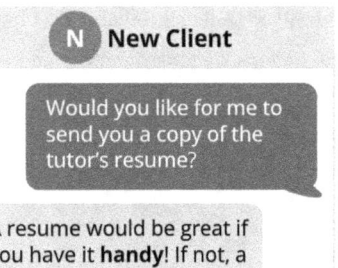

KITCHEN PAPER

キッチンペーパー

Meaning in English:

英語の意味:

Doesn't exist

英語には該当する単語がない

Say Instead:

適切な英語表現:

Paper towels (US), Kitchen roll (UK)

Example Sentences:

例文:

I noticed that Americans use a lot of _kitchen paper_, even for cleaning!

I noticed that Americans use a lot of **_paper towels_**, even for cleaning!

アメリカ人はキッチンペーパーをたくさん使うことに気づいたよ。掃除にまで使うんだね!

KNIFE

ナイフ

Meaning in English:
英語の意味:

Any kind of knife, including cutlery, kitchen tools, pocket knives, weapons, etc.

カトラリー(ステーキなどを切るナイフ)、調理器具、折りたたみナイフ、武器など、あらゆる種類のナイフ

Say Instead:
適切な英語表現:

Knife

Example Sentences:
例文:

A chef can't just use a _knife_ ナイフ. He needs a _chef's knife_ 包丁 for chopping. A chef can't just use a steak **_knife_**, he needs a chef's **_knife_** for chopping.

シェフは普通のナイフだけではなく、
シェフナイフ(包丁)が必要だ。

How English Speakers use "knife":
英語話者は(knife)をどのように使うか:

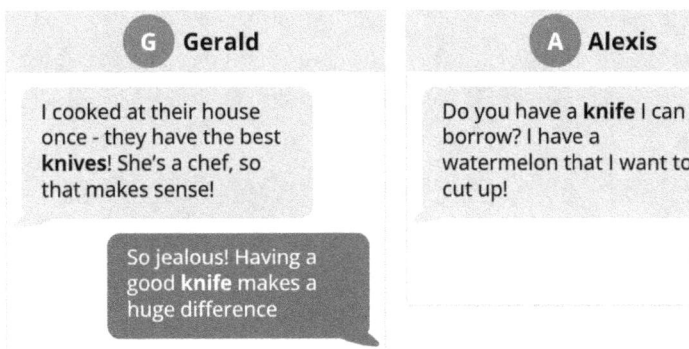

G **Gerald**

I cooked at their house once - they have the best **knives**! She's a chef, so that makes sense!

So jealous! Having a good **knife** makes a huge difference

A **Alexis**

Do you have a **knife** I can borrow? I have a watermelon that I want to cut up!

Yes!

MINUS DRIVER

Meaning in English:
英語の意味:

Doesn't exist
英語には該当する単語がない

Say Instead:
適切な英語表現:

Flathead screwdriver

Example Sentences:
例文:

I think I know how to fix the problem with the sink, but first I need to get a *minus driver*.

I think I know how to fix the problem with the sink, but first I need to get a ***flathead screwdriver***.

シンクは、修理できると思うけれど、
まずはマイナスドライバーを手に入れないといけない。

MUG CUP

Meaning in English:
英語の意味:

Doesn't exist
英語には該当する単語がない

Say Instead:
適切な英語表現:

Mug, Coffee cup, Coffee mug

Example Sentences:
例文:

That cafe has really cool *mug cups*. → That cafe has really cool **_mugs_**.

あのカフェには、本当に素敵なマグカップがある。

PAN

パ
ン

Meaning in English:
英語の意味:

Pan for cooking
フライパン

Say Instead:
適切な英語表現:

Bread, Pastries

Example Sentences:
例文:

> Cafes in Japan have really good *pans*. Melon pan is my favorite!

> Cafes in Japan have really good ***bread*** and ***pastries***. Melon bread is my favorite!

日本のカフェは、美味しいパンが多い。
私はメロンパンが一番好き！

⚠️ This sounds like cafes have good pans for cooking and baking.
カフェには料理やお菓子作りにとても良いフライパンがあるように聞こえる。

How English Speakers use "pan":
英語話者は（pan）をどのように使うか:

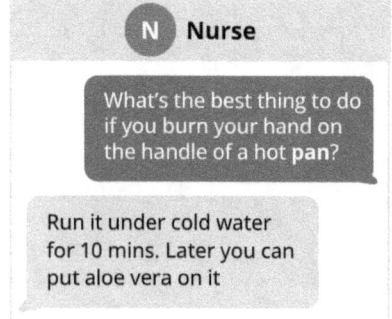

N Nurse

What's the best thing to do if you burn your hand on the handle of a hot **pan**?

Run it under cold water for 10 mins. Later you can put aloe vera on it

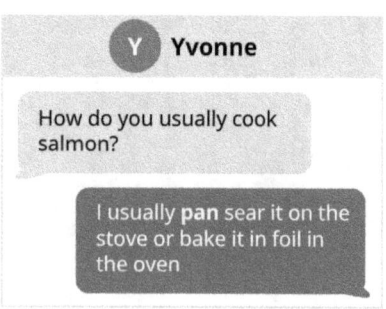

Y Yvonne

How do you usually cook salmon?

I usually **pan** sear it on the stove or bake it in foil in the oven

PENCHI

ペンチ

Meaning in English:
英語の意味:

Doesn't exist
英語には該当する単語がない

Say Instead:
適切な英語表現:

Pliers

Example Sentences:
例文:

I need a hammer and some _penchi_ to fix this pipe.		I need a hammer and some **_pliers_** to fix this pipe.

このパイプを直すのに、ハンマーとペンチが要るよ。

PET BOTTLE

ペットボトル

Meaning in English:
英語の意味:

Doesn't exist
英語には該当する単語がない

Say Instead:
適切な英語表現:

Disposable plastic bottle

Example Sentences:
例文:

The Japanese company has proposed a new eco design for their _PET bottles_.	→	The Japanese company has proposed a new eco-friendly design for their **_plastic bottles_**.

その日本企業は、ペットボトルの新しいエコデザインを提案している。

PLUS DRIVER

プラスドライバー

Meaning in English:

英語の意味:

Doesn't exist
英語には該当する単語がない

Say Instead:

適切な英語表現:

Phillips screwdriver, Phillips-head screwdriver

Example Sentences:

例文:

I think I know how to fix the problem with the sink, but first I need to get a _plus driver_.

I think I know how to fix the problem with the sink, but first I need to get a **_Phillips screwdriver_**.

シンクは修理できると思うけれど、
まずはプラスドライバーを手に入れないといけない。

POT

Meaning in English:
英語の意味:

1. Pot for cooking
   鍋・片手鍋

2. A container for growing plants
   植物を育てる鉢やプランター

Say Instead:
適切な英語表現:

Electric kettle

Example Sentences:
例文:

My parents gave me a _pot_ when I went to college, and it was the best gift ever!

My parents gave me an _**electric kettle**_ when I went to college, and it was the best gift ever!

大学に入るときに両親がポットをくれて、
それが本当に最高のプレゼントだった！

This sounds like your parents gave you a pot for cooking.
両親が料理用の鍋をくれたと言っているように聞こえる。

How English Speakers use "pot":
英語話者は(pot)をどのように使うか:

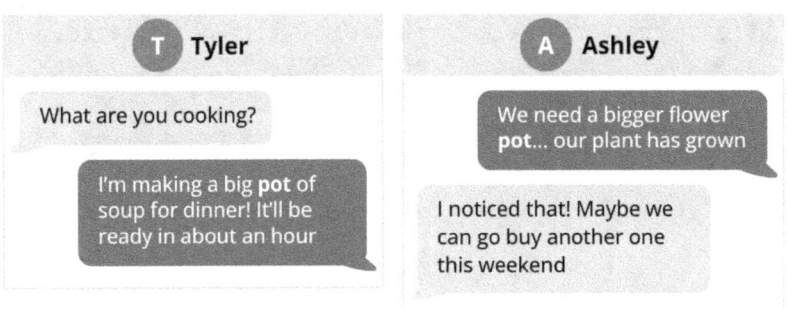

Tyler

What are you cooking?

I'm making a big **pot** of soup for dinner! It'll be ready in about an hour

Ashley

We need a bigger flower **pot**... our plant has grown

I noticed that! Maybe we can go buy another one this weekend

SAND BAG

サンドバッグ

Meaning in English:
英語の意味:

A bag filled with sand, often used for temporary walls or to prevent and lessen water damage from flooding

砂を詰めた袋のことで、仮設の壁に使ったり、洪水による水害を防いだり軽減したりするためによく使われる。

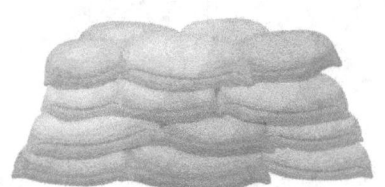

Say Instead:
適切な英語表現:

Punching bag, Boxing bag

Example Sentences:
例文:

They have *sand bags* at my gym.

They have ***punching/boxing bags*** at my gym.

ジムにはサンドバッグがある。

⚠ This sounds like they have bags of sand, maybe to prevent water coming inside the building if it floods, or maybe it's a new exercise trend: lift sand bags instead of weights.

そこに砂袋が置いてあるのは、洪水の際に建物の中に水が入るのを防ぐためなのか、それとも最近流行りの「ウエートの代わりに砂袋を使う」エクササイズの一環なのかもしれないと思われる。

TUPPA

タッパー

Meaning in English:
英語の意味:

Doesn't exist
英語には該当する単語がない

Say Instead:
適切な英語表現:

Tupperware

Example Sentences:
例文:

I like the water bottles made from _tuppa_. → I like the **_Tupperware_** bottles.

私はタッパー製の水筒が好きだ。

Vinyl

Meaning in English:

英語の意味:

1. Vinyl record

ビニールレコード
（アナログレコード）

2. Specific material made from PVC or polyvinyl chloride. (This can be used to make certain things like rain boots, vinyl clothing, vinyl flooring, vinyl siding, etc.)

PVC（ポリ塩化ビニル）で作られた特定の素材（レインブーツ、ビニール製の衣類、ビニール床材、外壁材などの製造に使用される）

Say Instead:

適切な英語表現:

Plastic (bag)

Example Sentences:

例文:

We need to stop using *vinyl bags* to save our environment. To save the environment, we need to stop using ***plastic bags***.

私たちは、環境を守るために、
ビニール袋の使用をやめる必要がある。

 This sounds like many people are using bags made of vinyl material.

これは、多くの人がビニール素材のバッグを使っているように聞こえる。

TRAVEL & TOURISM

22

旅行・観光

BUSINESS HOTEL

ビジネスホテル

Meaning in English:

英語の意味:

Any hotel that commonly caters to businesses or businesspeople. These are usually high quality (even luxurious) and nicer than a typical hotel. They may offer discounted corporate rates and high quality conference rooms and amenities catered towards businesses and business travelers.

一般的にビジネスやビジネスパーソン向けのサービスを提供するホテル。通常、高品質（時には豪華）で、一般的なホテルよりもグレードが高いことが多い。企業向けの割引料金や、ビジネストラベラー向けの高品質な会議室や設備を備えている場合がある。

Say Instead:

適切な英語表現:

No-frills hotel, Budget hotel

Example Sentences:

例文:

| I don't like traveling for work because we usually stay at _business hotels_, and the rooms are so small. | | I don't like traveling for work because we usually stay at **_no-frills budget hotels_**, and the rooms are so small. |

私は出張での旅行があまり好きじゃない。
というのも、たいていビジネスホテルに泊まることになり、
部屋がとても狭いからだ。

CA / CABIN ATTENDANT

Meaning in English:
英語の意味:

Doesn't exist
英語には該当する単語がない

Say Instead:
適切な英語表現:

Flight attendant

Example Sentences:
例文:

キャビンアテンダント

She easily found a job as a _CA_ because she speaks four languages and likes to travel.

➜

She easily found a job as a **_flight attendant_** because she speaks four languages and likes to travel.

彼女は4か国語を話し、旅行が好きなので、
CAの仕事を簡単に見つけた。

CHECKPOINT

チェックポイント

Meaning in English:
英語の意味:

The most common meaning is a place or point blocked off (often by authorities) so that people passing through can be checked for some purpose such as security. For example, a large event might have a security *checkpoint* that individuals have to walk through, or a road *checkpoint* might be set
up if trying to catch a criminal who may be driving through the area. A border *checkpoint* might exist at the line between two countries.

「チェックポイント」の一般的な意味は、通行する人を検査するために（多くの場合、当局によって）封鎖された場所やポイントを指す。例えば:
大規模なイベントでは、セキュリティチェックポイントが設置され、参加者が通過する際に検査を受けることがある。
犯罪者がその地域を通過する可能性がある場合、道路に検問所（チェックポイント）が設置されることがある。
国境には、2つの国の間で出入国審査を行う『国境検問所（ボーダーチェックポイント）』が設置されている場合がある。

Say Instead:
適切な英語表現:

Something to check/review

Example Sentences:
例文:

| Our project is almost complete, but we have three major *checkpoints*. | ↝ | Our project is almost complete, but we have three major ***things to review and potentially revise***. |

私たちのプロジェクトはほぼ完了しているが、重要なチェックポイントが3つある。

DEPART

Meaning in English:
英語の意味:

(Verb) To leave
出発する

Say Instead:
適切な英語表現:

Department store

Example Sentences:
例文:

デ
パ
ー
ト

Some _departs_ in Japan are 10 floors high!　　Some **_department stores_** in Japan are 10 floors high!

日本のデパートの中には、10階建てのものもある。

How English Speakers use "depart":
英語話者は(depart)をどのように使うか:

C Chelsea

What time are you planning to get to the airport? Our flight **departs** at 5 PM.

I'm not sure yet, but our flight leaves a little after yours!

L LY Airlines

LY Airlines Alert: Your flight now **departs** at 9:50 AM from gate C15.

Form / Home

フォーム・ホーム

Meaning in English:
英語の意味:

Form has meaning meanings, but when used as a noun, it most commonly means:

「フォーム/form」には多くの意味があるが、名詞として使われるとき下記の意味が最も一般的だ。

1. A document that needs to be filled out
☞ Example: Please fill out this *form*.
記入すべき書類
例:「このフォームに記入してください」

2. A figure or shape
☞ Example: The bush was cut into the *form* of a dog.
形や姿
例:その低木は犬の形に刈り込まれていた。

3. A type of something
☞ Example: Running is a good *form* of exercise.
種類や形式
例:ランニングは良い運動だ。

Home means the place where you live
ホームは、「家」

Say Instead:
適切な英語表現:

Platform, Train platform

424

FORM / HOME

Example Sentences:
例文:

I was waiting at *home* for the train, and I saw Bob with his new girlfriend.		I was waiting on the ***platform*** for the train, and I saw Bob with his new girlfriend.

ホームで電車を待っていたら、
ボブが新しい彼女といるのを見た。

This sounds like you were at your house waiting for the train.
これは、あなたが自分の家で電車を待っていたように聞こえる。

How English Speakers use "form":
英語話者は(form)をどのように使うか:

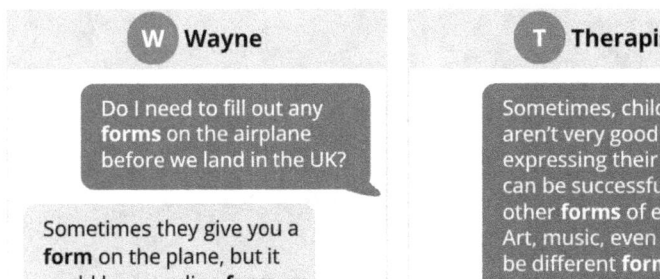

W Wayne

Do I need to fill out any **forms** on the airplane before we land in the UK?

Sometimes they give you a **form** on the plane, but it could be an online **form**, or maybe nothing...

T Therapist

Sometimes, children who aren't very good at expressing their emotions can be successful using other **forms** of expression. Art, music, even dance can be different **forms** of showing their feelings.

How English Speakers use "home":
英語話者は(home)をどのように使うか:

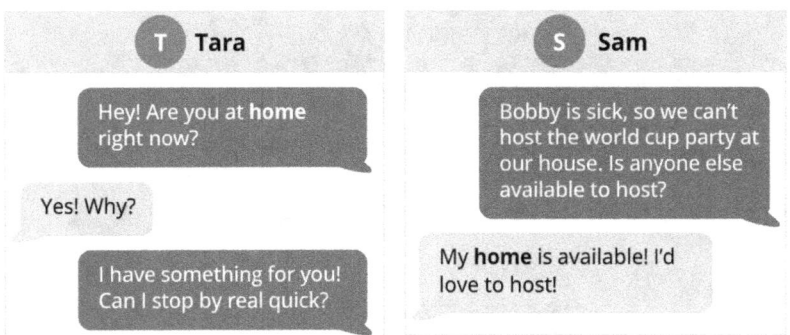

T Tara

Hey! Are you at **home** right now?

Yes! Why?

I have something for you! Can I stop by real quick?

S Sam

Bobby is sick, so we can't host the world cup party at our house. Is anyone else available to host?

My **home** is available! I'd love to host!

FRANKFURT

Meaning in English:
英語の意味:

1. The city in Germany
ドイツにある町の名前

2. *Frankfurter* can mean boiled sausage or hot dog, but this seems to be much less common
「フランクフルター」は、茹でたソーセージやホットドッグを指すこともあるが、それほど一般的ではない。

Say Instead:
適切な英語表現:

Sausage, Sausage on a stick

Example Sentences:
例文:

Let's eat *Frankfurt* for dinner! ⟶ Let's eat ***sausage*** for dinner!

晩ごはんにフランクフルトを食べよう。

How English Speakers use "Frankfurt":
英語話者は（Frankfurt）をどのように使うか:

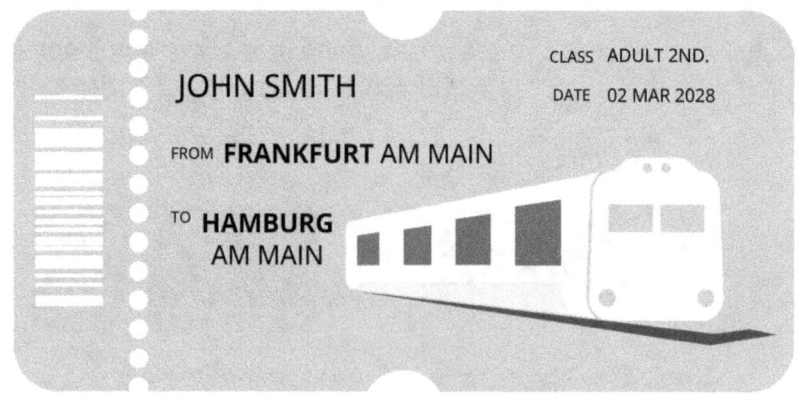

FRONT

OPPOSITES

Front　Back

Meaning in English:
英語の意味:

The forward-most part
☞ Example: The *front* of my
house is blue.

最も前方の部分
例：私の家の正面は青い

Say Instead:
適切な英語表現:

Front desk, Reception

Example Sentences:
例文:

You can ask for towels at *front*. You can ask for towels at the
front desk / at **_reception_**.

フロントに頼めば、タオルもらえるよ。

How English Speakers use "front":
英語話者は（front）をどのように使うか:

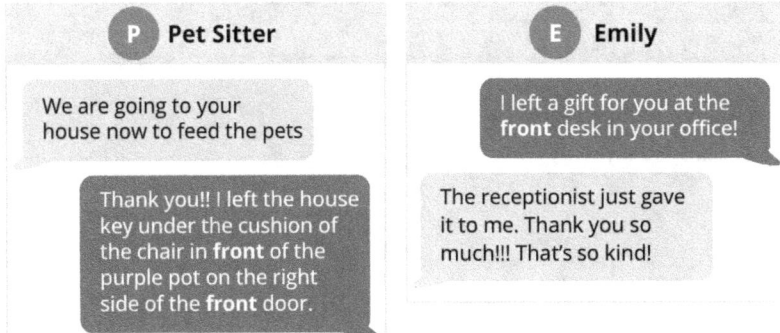

P Pet Sitter

We are going to your
house now to feed the pets

Thank you!! I left the house
key under the cushion of
the chair in **front** of the
purple pot on the right
side of the **front** door.

E Emily

I left a gift for you at the
front desk in your office!

The receptionist just gave
it to me. Thank you so
much!!! That's so kind!

GONDOLA

ゴンドラ

Meaning in English:
英語の意味:

1. Cable car, aerial tram
   ケーブルカー、ロープウェー
2. Narrow boat used in the canals of Venice, Italy
   ゴンドラ（イタリア・ヴェネツィアの運河で使われる細長い船）

Say Instead:
適切な英語表現:

Ferris wheel

Example Sentences:
例文:

We rode in the *gondola* in Singapore.	We rode the ***Ferris wheel*** in Singapore.

私たちは、シンガポールでゴンドラに乗った。

⚠ This sounds like you rode in a cable car or in a traditional Venetian boat from Venice, Italy.

これは、ロープウェイ（ケーブルカー）や伝統的なヴェネツィアの船に乗ったように聞こえる。

How English Speakers use "gondola":
英語話者は（gondola）をどのように使うか:

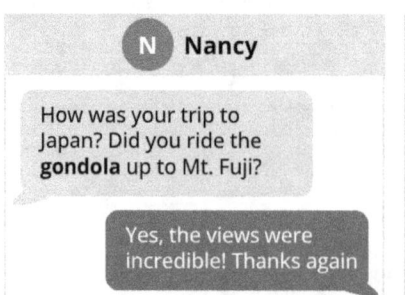

N **Nancy**

How was your trip to Japan? Did you ride the **gondola** up to Mt. Fuji?

Yes, the views were incredible! Thanks again

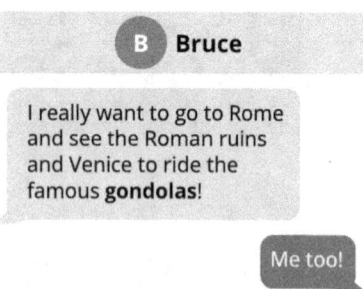

B **Bruce**

I really want to go to Rome and see the Roman ruins and Venice to ride the famous **gondolas**!

Me too!

HAMBURG

Meaning in English:
英語の意味:

The city in Germany
ドイツの町の名前

Say Instead:
適切な英語表現:

Hamburger steak, Salisbury steak

Example Sentences:
例文:

My cousin lives in Hawaii and told me that _hamburg_ is popular there too!	My cousin lives in Hawaii and told me **_hamburger steak_** is popular there too!

私のいとこはハワイに住んでいるが、そこでもハンバーグは人気 があると言っていた!

How English Speakers use "Hamburg":
英語話者は(Hamburg)をどのように使うか:

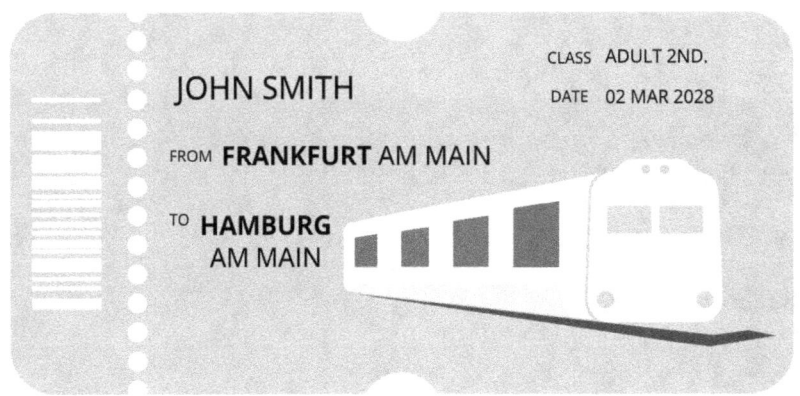

JOHN SMITH

CLASS ADULT 2ND.
DATE 02 MAR 2028

FROM **FRANKFURT** AM MAIN

TO **HAMBURG** AM MAIN

Jet Coaster

ジェットコースター

Meaning in English:
英語の意味:

Doesn't exist
英語には該当する単語がない

Say Instead:
適切な英語表現:

Roller coaster

Example Sentences:
例文:

Do you like *jet coasters*? → Do you like ***roller coasters***?

「ジェットコースターは好き?」

Kenta

ケンタ

Meaning in English:
英語の意味:

Doesn't exist
英語には該当する単語がない

Say Instead:
適切な英語表現:

KFC, Kentucky Fried Chicken

Example Sentences:
例文:

Japanese people love *Kenta* at Christmas time! → Japanese people love ***KFC*** at Christmas time!

日本人はクリスマスの時期にケンタ(ケンタッキー・フライドチキン)を食べるのが大好きだ

KENTUCKY

ケンタッキー

Meaning in English:
英語の意味:

The American state Kentucky
ケンタッキー州

Say Instead:
適切な英語表現:

KFC, Kentucky Fried Chicken

Example Sentences:
例文:

Japanese people love *Kentucky* at Christmas time! → Japanese people love **_KFC_** at Christmas time!

日本人はクリスマスの時期、ケンタッキーが大好きだ!

This sounds like Japanese people love to visit the state of Kentucky at Christmas time!

この文の感じだと、日本人はクリスマスの時期にケンタッキー州を訪れるのが大好きなように聞こえる。

How English Speakers use "Kentucky":
英語話者は(Kentucky)をどのように使うか:

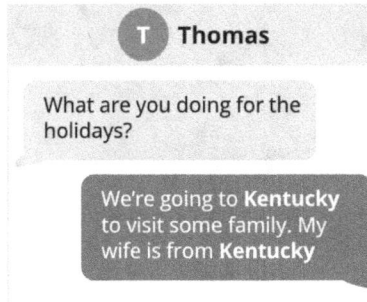

Thomas

What are you doing for the holidays?

We're going to **Kentucky** to visit some family. My wife is from **Kentucky**

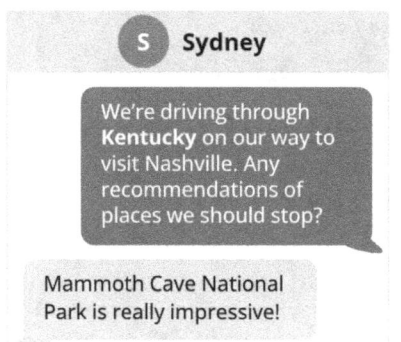

Sydney

We're driving through **Kentucky** on our way to visit Nashville. Any recommendations of places we should stop?

Mammoth Cave National Park is really impressive!

Los

ロス

Meaning in English:
英語の意味:

Doesn't exist
英語には該当する単語がない

Say Instead:
適切な英語表現:

Los Angeles, LA

Example Sentences:
例文:

Let's go to _Los_ this weekend!

Let's go to **_Los Angeles_** this weekend!

今週末はロスへ行こう！

MORNING CALL

モーニングコール

Meaning in English:
英語の意味:

Doesn't exist
英語には該当する単語がない

Say Instead:
適切な英語表現:

Wake-up call

Example Sentences:
例文:

Can I get a _morning call_ at 7 a.m.?

Can I get a **_wake-up call_** at 7 a.m.?

午前7時にモーニングコールをしてもらえますか。

PACK

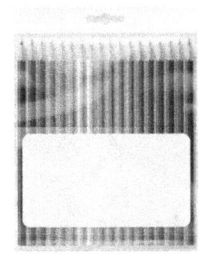

パック

Meaning in English:
英語の意味:

1. To put your things in boxes or suitcases for a move or trip

引っ越しや旅行のために、自分の物を箱やスーツケースに詰めること

2. A group of products sold together in bulk (e.g., a pack of cigarettes, a pack of pencils, a pack of tissues)

複数の商品がまとめてひと組で販売されているもの(例:1箱のたばこ、1セットの鉛筆、1袋のティッシュなど)

Say Instead:
適切な英語表現:

Facial mask; Do a facial mask; Pre-packaged food

Example Sentences:
例文:

That brand sells really good _packs_.

That brand sells really good **_facial masks_**.

あのブランドのパック製品はとても質がいい。

My friend and I _packed_ our faces last night.

My friend and I **_did facial masks_** last night.

昨日の夜、友達と一緒に顔にパックした。

Most grocery stores around here sell some really good _packed_ food like _packed_ salads.

Most grocery stores around here sell some really good **_pre-packaged_** food like salads.

このあたりのスーパーでは、パック入りのサラダとか、美味しい惣菜がたくさん売っている。

ROPEWAY

ロープウェー

Meaning in English:
英語の意味:

Doesn't exist
英語には該当する単語がない

Say Instead:
適切な英語表現:

Cable car, Gondola, Tramway

Example Sentences:
例文:

My Fuji has a really scenic _ropeway_ with fantastic views!

Mt. Fuji has a really scenic **_gondola_**/**_cable car_**/**_tramway_** with fantastic views!

富士山には景色のいいロープウェイがあって、
眺めが本当にすばらしいよ!

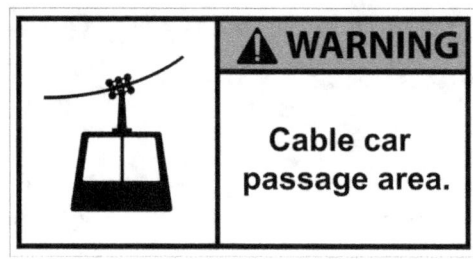

WARNING

Cable car passage area.

SF

SAN FRANCISCO

Meaning in English:
英語の意味:

SF is not a widely used or recognized abbreviation but often means San Francisco. *SF* can sometimes be used for a variety of very specific abbreviations in unique fields. For example, *sf* can mean "square feet" in measurements of area when written; however, people would still say "square feet" when speaking. There are some very small groups of people who use *SF* in written English online in science fiction fan groups, but this is a very small minority of people. I have never personally come across any English speaker using the letters "SF" in spoken English to mean "science fiction."

"SF"は広く使われている略語ではないが、一般的には「サンフランシスコ」を意味することが多い。"SF"は特定の分野では非常に限定的な略語として使われることがある。例えば、"sf"は面積の測定において「平方フィート(square feet)」を意味し、会話では"square feet"とそのまま使われる。オンラインのSFファンのグループなど、非常に限られたコミュニティでは"SF"が「サイエンス・フィクション「science fiction」を指すこともあるが、これはごく少数派にとどまる。筆者自身、英語話者の会話の中で"SF"と言って「サイエンス・フィクション」を意味しているのを聞いたことはない。

Say Instead:
適切な英語表現:

Sci-fi, Science fiction

Example Sentences:
例文:

I love *SF* novels! → I love *science fiction* / *sci-fi* novels!

SF小説が大好きだ。

SILVER SEAT

シルバーシート

Meaning in English:
英語の意味:

Doesn't exist
英語には該当する単語がない

Say Instead:
適切な英語表現:

Priority seat (for the elderly)

Example Sentences:
例文:

The bus driver said, "Please save the _silver seat_ for any passengers who may need it."

The bus driver said, "Please save the **_priority seat for any elderly passengers_** who may need it."

「優先席(シルバーシート)は、
必要とする方のために空けておいてください。」
とバスの運転手は言った。

TICKET

チケット

Meaning in English:

英語の意味：

1. Any proof of permission to enter an event, transportation, location (e.g., train ticket, plane ticket, museum ticket, performance ticket)

イベント、交通機関、施設などの利用や入場の権利を証明する券（例：電車の切符、航空券、美術館のチケット、公演の入場券など）

2. A fine for a small infraction (e.g., a parking ticket, a speeding ticket)

軽微な違反に対して科される罰金や違反切符（例：駐車違反、スピード違反の反則金など）

Say Instead:

適切な英語表現：

Ticket

Example Sentences:

例文：

Does everyone have their _tickets チケット_? You need your _plane ticket 搭乗券_, _bus ticket 乗車券_, _ticket 入館券_ to the museum, and _ticket 入場券_ to the concert.

Does everyone have their **_tickets_**? You need your plane **_ticket_**, bus **_ticket_**, **_ticket_** to the museum, and **_ticket_** to the concert.

ガイドは、「みなさん、チケットは揃っていますか？飛行機の搭乗券、バスの乗車券、美術館の入館券、そしてコンサートの入場券が必要です」と言った。

Our bus drivers will drive safely to avoid _speeding tickets 切符_.

Our bus drivers will drive safely to avoid **_speeding tickets_**.

バスの運転手は、スピード違反の切符を切られないためにも、安全運転を心がけている。

TOURING

ツーリング

Meaning in English:
英語の意味:

1. Taking a tour of an area

「地域を巡ること」「観光すること」「見学すること」など

2. When a musician or other celebrity goes to different cities to perform as part of their circuit

「（アーティストなどが）ツアーで各地を回ること」「巡業すること」「公演ツアーに出ること」など

Say Instead:
適切な英語表現:

Ride a motorcycle around a scenic area

Example Sentences:
例文:

| My friends and I love to go _touring_ on the weekends through the national park. | | My friends and I love to _**ride motorcycles together**_ on the weekends through the national park. |

週末は友達と一緒に国立公園をツーリングするのが好きなんだ。

TV, Music, Movies, Entertainment

23

映画・テレビ・音楽・エンタメ

Scan for Audio

ANIME

アニメ

Meaning in English:
英語の意味:

Only refers to Japanese-style animation
特に日本風のアニメーションを指す

Say Instead:
適切な英語表現:

Animation, Animated film/movie, Cartoon

Example Sentences:
例文:

My kids love American _anime_. My kids love American **_animated movies_**.

私の子どもは、アメリカのアニメが好きだ。

 This sounds like there is a special American style of anime that is different from cartoon animation but inspired by traditional Japanese anime.

これは、特別なアメリカスタイルのアニメ、つまり『伝統的な日本のアニメに影響を受けつつも、カートゥーンとは違うもの』があるように聞こえる。

AF RECO (AFREKO)

アフレコ

Meaning in English:
英語の意味:

Doesn't exist
英語には該当する単語がない

Say Instead:
適切な英語表現:

Dubbing, Voice-over

Example Sentences:
例文:

The voice actors did the *af reco* for the movie. → The voice actors did **_the voice-over for the dubbed version of the film_**.

声優たちは吹き替え版のアフレコをした。

BACK DANCER

バックダンサー

Meaning in English:
英語の意味:

Doesn't exist
英語には該当する単語がない

Say Instead:
適切な英語表現:

Backup dancer

Example Sentences:
例文:

That singer has good *back dancers*. The singer has good **_backup dancers_**.

その歌手には、良いバックダンサーがついている。

Back Music (BGM)

バックミュージック

Meaning in English:
英語の意味:

Doesn't exist
英語には該当する単語がない

Say Instead:
適切な英語表現:

Animation, Animated film/movie, Cartoon

Example Sentences:
例文:

| That CM is famous for its _BGM_/_back music_. | → | That commercial is famous for its **_background music_**. |

そのCMはBGM（バックミュージック）で有名だ。

Back Singer

バックシンガー

Meaning in English:
英語の意味:

Doesn't exist
英語には該当する単語がない

Say Instead:
適切な英語表現:

Backup singer

Example Sentences:
例文:

| The _back singers_ make the music better. | | The **_backup singers_** make the music better. |

バックシンガーで音楽がさらに良くなるね。

BACK NUMBER

Meaning in English:
英語の意味:

Doesn't exist
英語には該当する単語がない

Say Instead:
適切な英語表現:

Old famous hits
Back issue, Old issue
License plate number (US), Registration number (UK)

Example Sentences:
例文:

I love that singer's _back numbers_ so much! Let's sing them tonight at karaoke!	I love that singer's **_old famous hits_** so much! Let's sing them tonight at karaoke!

あの歌手のバックナンバーが大好き！今夜カラオケで歌おう！

There's a really good _back number_ of L Magazine from last December.	There's a really good **_back issue_** of L Magazine from last December.

Ｌマガジンの昨年12月号のバックナンバーは本当に良い内容だ。

What's our _back number_? I can't see our number plate.	What's our **_license plate number_**? I can't see our license plate number.

私たちの車のナンバーって何だったっけ？
ナンバープレートが見えない。

BAND MAN

バンドマン

Meaning in English:
英語の意味:

Doesn't really exist; it could be a man who is really interested in bands
英語には該当する単語がない
バンドに非常に興味を持っている男性と言うことかもしれない。

Say Instead:
適切な英語表現:

In a band

Example Sentences:
例文:

My boyfriend is a _band man_. My boyfriend is **_in a band_**.

私の彼は、バンドマンだ。

BRI CHAN

ブリちゃん

Meaning in English:
英語の意味:

Doesn't exist
英語には該当する単語がない

Say Instead:
適切な英語表現:

Britney Spears

Example Sentences:
例文:

It's amazing that _Bri Chan_ is still popular. It's amazing that **_Britney Spears_** is still popular.

ブリちゃんがまだ人気なのはすごいね。

Bra Pi / Bla Pi

ブ
ラ
ピ

Meaning in English:

英語の意味:

Doesn't exist

英語には該当する単語がない

Say Instead:

適切な英語表現:

Brad Pitt
BLACKPINK

Example Sentences:

例文:

I think _Bra Pi_ is in that movie. I think **_Brad Pitt_** is in that movie.

あの映画にブラピが出てると思う。

Bla Pi is cool but getting kind of old now. **BLACKPINK** is cool but getting kind of old now.

ブラックピンクは、素敵だけど、ちょっと最近年をとってきたね。

CAMERAMAN

カメラマン

Meaning in English:
英語の意味:

Someone who operates a video camera, usually for TV or movies

テレビ番組や映画の撮影で、ビデオカメラを扱う人

Say Instead:
適切な英語表現:

Photographer
Cameraman
Videographer

Example Sentences:
例文:

He's a _cameraman_ for weddings.

He's a wedding **_photographer_**.

彼は、結婚式のカメラマンだ。

How English Speakers use "cameraman":
英語話者は（cameraman）をどのように使うか:

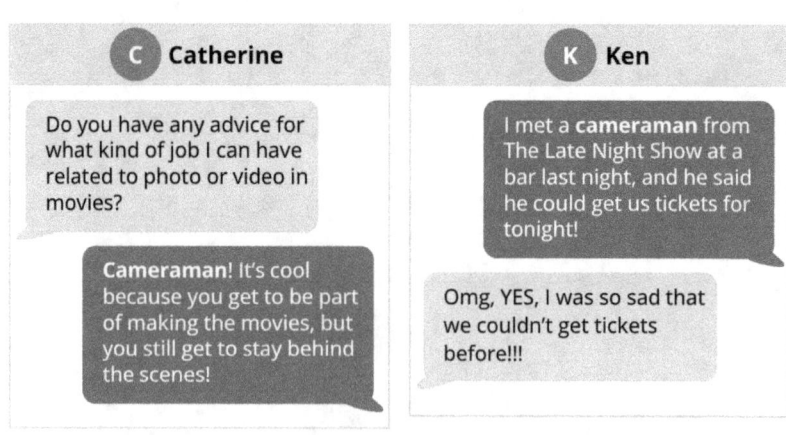

C Catherine

Do you have any advice for what kind of job I can have related to photo or video in movies?

Cameraman! It's cool because you get to be part of making the movies, but you still get to stay behind the scenes!

K Ken

I met a **cameraman** from The Late Night Show at a bar last night, and he said he could get us tickets for tonight!

Omg, YES, I was so sad that we couldn't get tickets before!!!

CATCHPHRASE

Meaning in English:
英語の意味:

A short phrase or expression that a character or famous person is known for saying or repeating.
☞ Example: 'How you doin'?' is Joey's *catchphrase* in the show *Friends*.

「キャッチフレーズ」とは、キャラクターや有名人がよく言う決まり文句やおなじみのフレーズのことである。'How you doin'?'は、テレビドラマ『フレンズ』のジョーイのキャッチフレーズだ。

Say Instead:
適切な英語表現:

Tagline

Example Sentences:
例文:

The company's <u>catchphrase</u> is "Just go with it." ➘ The company's **tagline** is "Just go with it."

会社のキャッチフレーズは、
「Just go with it / 流れに乗ろう」だ。

CHORUS

コーラス

Meaning in English:
英語の意味:

1. The main (often repeated) part of a song
歌の主要部分(よく繰り返される部分)

2. A group of singers like a choir but often including dancing and often accompanied by instrumental music like an orchestra
合唱団に似たグループで、ダンスなどの演出が加わることもあり、オーケストラなどの伴奏が付く場合もある。

3. Sometimes an extremely large choir
非常に大規模な合唱団のこともある。

Say Instead:
適切な英語表現:

Choir

Example Sentences:
例文:

In high school, I was a member of the _chorus_ club. ⟿ I was in the high school _**choir**_.

高校ではコーラス部に所属していた。

How English Speakers use "chorus":
英語話者は(**chorus**)をどのように使うか:

O Ollie

What was the song we kept singing last night?

Ummm, I don't know the name. It's the **chorus** of that famous song that they always play on the radio

B Becca

Did you hear all the frogs and cicadas last night?

Yes, they were so loud! It was like a **chorus** of nature singing it's night song!

CM

Meaning in English:
英語の意味:

Doesn't exist
英語には該当する単語がない

Say Instead:
適切な英語表現:

Commercial (US), TV ad (UK), Advert (UK)

Example Sentences:
例文:

Did you see that _CM_?
It was so weird!

Did you see that **_commercial_**?
It was so weird!

あのCM 見た?すごく変だったね。

CM SONG

Meaning in English:
英語の意味:

Doesn't exist
英語には該当する単語がない

Say Instead:
適切な英語表現:

Jingle

Example Sentences:
例文:

That brand is famous for its
CM song.

That brand is famous for its
jingle.

あのブランドは、CMソングで有名だ。

COMBI

コンビ

Meaning in English:
英語の意味:

Doesn't exist
英語には該当する単語がない

Say Instead:
適切な英語表現:

Pair, Comedy duo

Example Sentences:
例文:

| They're a really good comedy _combi_. | | They're a really good comedy _**duo**_. |

彼らは、とても良いお笑いコンビだ。

CONTO

コント

Meaning in English:
英語の意味:

Doesn't exist
英語には該当する単語がない

Say Instead:
適切な英語表現:

Skit

Example Sentences:
例文:

| _Conto_ is really popular in Japanese comedy. | | _**Skits**_ are really popular in Japanese comedy. |

コントは、日本のお笑いでとても人気がある。

CRANK IN

クランクイン

Meaning in English:
英語の意味:

Doesn't exist
英語には該当する単語がない

Say Instead:
適切な英語表現:

Start filming (a movie)
The start of filming (a movie)

Example Sentences:
例文:

It took a full year from the decision to produce to the _crank in_.

It took a full year from the greenlighting of the film to the **_start of filming_**.

製作が決まってクランクインまで、丸1年かかった。

DRAMA

ドラマ

Meaning in English:
英語の意味:

A specific genre of show, like comedy or horror or drama
コメディやホラー、ドラマのような特定のジャンルの番組

Say Instead:
適切な英語表現:

Show, TV show, TV series

Example Sentences:
例文:

What kind of *dramas* do you watch? I enjoy comedies. What kind of *shows* do you watch? I enjoy comedies.

どんなドラマを見るの。私は、コメディーがすき。

How English Speakers use "drama":
英語話者は(drama)をどのように使うか:

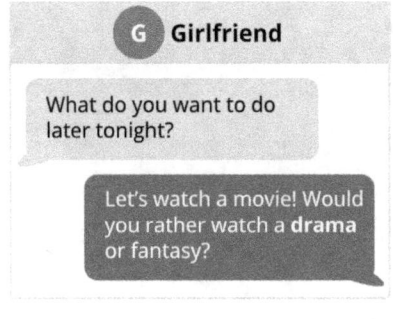

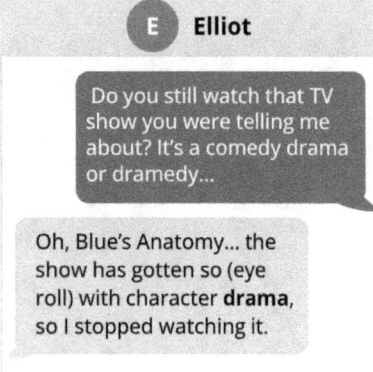

DUBBING

Meaning in English:
英語の意味:

To add in a different soundtrack to a recording after it's been filmed, often with a different language

☞ Example: Old Godzilla movies were often *dubbed* over into English for American movie fans.

録画された映像に、後から別の音声トラック(しばしば別の言語)を追加すること

例:昔のゴジラ映画は、アメリカの映画ファン向けに英語で吹き替えられることがよくあった。

Say Instead:
適切な英語表現:

Ripping, Burning

Example Sentences:
例文:

Dubbing could be illegal copyright infringement if you don't have the permission of the copyright holder.

↱

Ripping DVDs or CDs could be illegal copyright infringement if you don't have the permission of the copyright holder.

著作権者の許可がない場合、
ダビングは違法な著作権侵害となる可能性がある。

How English Speakers use "dubbing":
英語話者は(dubbing)をどのように使うか:

A Actor's Alliance

The voice actor audition for the **dubbed** version of the film has been rescheduled to Tuesday.

B Brenda

I was really impressed with the quality of the **dubbing** of the Japanese film. It's really well done!

453

EPISODE

Meaning in English:

英語の意味:

1. One episode of a TV show or podcast with many episodes

連続ドラマやシリーズ作品の1つのエピソード（話）

2. Psychological terminology that may refer to a temporary change in mental state or seizure, as in a depressive episode or an episode of mental breakdown.

心理学用語　うつ病のエピソードや精神的な崩壊のエピソードというように、一時的な精神状態の変化や発作を指す場合がある

NEXT EPISODE

Episode Name

SATURDAY | 16:00

Say Instead:

適切な英語表現:

A story, Something that happened, What happened

Example Sentences:

例文:

I have to tell you an _episode_ that happened yesterday!

I have to tell you **_a story about what happened_** yesterday!

昨日あったエピソードを話しておかないといけない。

⚠ This sounds like you watched a new episode of a show that came out yesterday that you are excited to talk about.

昨日放送されたテレビ番組の新しいエピソードを観て、それについて話したくて仕方がないようだ。

FILM

Meaning in English:
英語の意味:

1. Film for photography
写真撮影用のフィルム
2. Film for making a movie
映画制作のためのフィルム
3. A movie
映画(作品)

Say Instead:
適切な英語表現:

Film

Example Sentences:
例文:

The new MovieTown museum is really cool! You can see how to process _film フィルム_ for photos, how they use _film 映画フィルム_ to make a movie reel, and how they eventually moved from silent _films 映画_ to modern _films 映画_ with sound.

The new MovieTown museum is really cool! You can see how to process **_film_** for photos, how they use **_film_** to make a movie reel, and how they eventually moved from silent **_films_** to modern **_films_** with sound.

新しいMovieTown博物館はとても魅力的だ!
ここでは、昔ながらの写真用フィルムの現像方法や、
映画のフィルムをリールにする仕組み、そして無声映画から音声
付き映画への移り変わりを学ぶことができるんだ。

Golden Time/Hour

ゴールデンタイム

Meaning in English:
英語の意味:

Doesn't exist
英語には該当する単語がない

Say Instead:
適切な英語表現:

Prime time TV

Example Sentences:
例文:

My interview is supposed to show tomorrow during *golden time*! ➔ My interview is supposed to show tomorrow during ***prime time TV***!

私のインタビューは、ゴールデンタイムに放送される予定だ。

Guara

ギャラ

Meaning in English:
英語の意味:

Doesn't exist
英語には該当する単語がない

Say Instead:
適切な英語表現:

Performance fee, Appearance fee

Example Sentences:
例文:

The singer's *guara* is $500; do you think we can afford it? The singer's ***performance fee*** is $500; do you think we can afford it?

その歌手のギャラは500ドルなんだよ。私たちに払えると思う？
と学園祭実行委員長は、私に言った。

IDOL

アイドル

Meaning in English:
英語の意味:

1. A person who is admired or respected greatly as a hero or role model
英雄や模範として深く尊敬・賞賛される人物

2. A person or thing that you worship as part of a religion or lifestyle
宗教的に崇拝される人物やモノ

Say Instead:
適切な英語表現:

Celebrity, Star

Example Sentences:
例文:

He's my favorite _idol_! He's my favorite **_celebrity_**!

彼は、私の好きなアイドルだ。

The tiger is the _idol_ in this zoo. The tiger is the **_star of_** / **_most popular animal_** in this zoo.

この動物園ではトラがアイドルだ。

If a person has a religious background, this might sound like the tiger is worshiped as part of a religion or like the zoo may have a tiger statue that people come to worship.

宗教的な背景を持つ人にとっては、この文は、虎が宗教の一部として崇拝されている、または人々が崇拝する虎の像があるように聞こえるかもしれない。

LIVE

ライブ

Meaning in English:
英語の意味:

1. Alive
生きている

2. For a performance, while it is happening; not pre-recorded
(E.g., A *live-recording* is one that is happening at that moment and has not been pre-recorded.)
(公演・放送など)リアルタイムで行われる、録音・録画ではないもの
例: ライブ録音は、その瞬間に録音されており、事前に録音されたものではない。

Say Instead:
適切な英語表現:

Concert

Example Sentences:
例文:

> We're going to a *live* of our favorite J-pop group.

→

> We're going to a ***concert*** of our favorite J-pop group.

私たちはお気に入りのJ-popバンドのライブに行く。

How English Speakers use "live":
英語話者は(live)をどのように使うか:

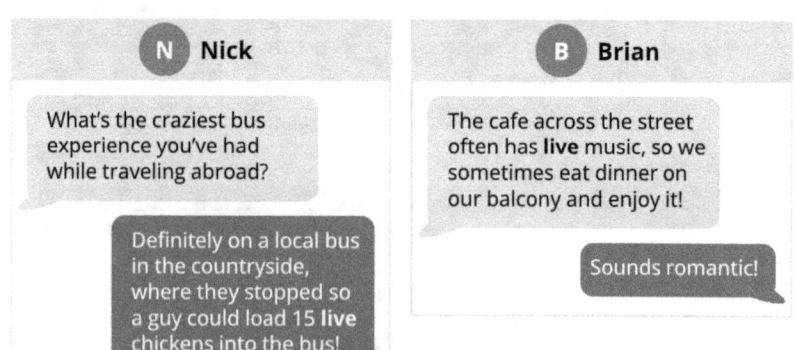

N Nick

What's the craziest bus experience you've had while traveling abroad?

Definitely on a local bus in the countryside, where they stopped so a guy could load 15 **live** chickens into the bus!

B Brian

The cafe across the street often has **live** music, so we sometimes eat dinner on our balcony and enjoy it!

Sounds romantic!

LIVE HOUSE

ライブハウス

Meaning in English:
英語の意味:

Doesn't exist
英語には該当する単語がない

Say Instead:
適切な英語表現:

Live music venue, Music venue

Example Sentences:
例文:

There's a _live house_ next to where we live, so we can hear a free live every weekend.

There's a **_live music venue_** next to where we live, so we can hear a free concert every weekend.

私たちの家の近くにライブハウスがあるので、
毎週末無料でライブを聞けるんだ。

LOKE

ロ
ケ

Meaning in English:
英語の意味:

Doesn't exist
英語には該当する単語がない

Say Instead:
適切な英語表現:

Filming location

Example Sentences:
例文:

The _loke_ of the new movie is really close to my hometown! The **_filming location_** of the new movie is close to my hometown!

新しい映画のロケ地は、私の故郷のすぐ近くなんだ!

In Hawaii, you can visit the _loke_ of many famous movies. In Hawaii, you can visit the **_filming locations_** of many famous movies.

ハワイでは、多くの有名映画のロケ地を訪れることができる。

LOVE COMEDY

ラ
ブ
コ
メ
デ
ィ
ー

Meaning in English:
英語の意味:

Doesn't exist
英語には該当する単語がない

Say Instead:
適切な英語表現:

Romantic comedy

Example Sentences:
例文:

My boyfriend hates it when I make him watch *love comedies* with me. He says they're so predictable.

My boyfriend hates it when I make him watch *romantic comedies* with me. He says they're so predictable.

彼は、私がラブコメ(ラブコメディー)を一緒に見ようとするとすごく嫌がるの。展開が読めすぎるって言うのよ。

MELODRAMA

メロドラマ

Meaning in English:

英語の意味:

Drama - a specific genre of TV show or movie that emphasizes storytelling and character emotions. It often portrays realistic human relationships and social themes.

ドラマ – 特定のジャンルのテレビ番組や映画。物語の展開や登場人物の感情表現を重視し、リアルな人間関係や社会的テーマを描くことが多い。

Melodrama - An exaggerated form of drama where emotions are highly intensified, and characters' struggles and conflicts are shown in an overly dramatic manner

メロドラマ – 極端に誇張されたドラマ。感情表現が非常に強調され、登場人物の苦悩や対立が劇的に描かれる。

Say Instead:

適切な英語表現:

Romantic drama

Example Sentences:

例文:

She really likes to watch <u>*melodramas*</u>. She really likes to watch <u>***romantic dramas***</u>.

彼女は、本当にメロドラマを見るのが好きだ。

 This sounds like she likes to watch overly dramatic or exaggerated shows like soap operas.

昼ドラのような大げさなドラマを見るのが好きな人みたいだ。

MULTI TALENT

Meaning in English:

英語の意味:

Doesn't exist, but *multi-talented* means having many talents

英語には該当する単語がないが、マルチタレントとは多くの才能を持つことを意味する

Say Instead:

適切な英語表現:

Actress and singer, Actor and singer

Example Sentences:

例文:

She's an actress and a singer; she's a *multi talent*!　⤳　She's an ***actress and a singer***!

彼女は、女優であり歌手だ。彼女は、マルチタレントだ。

MV

Meaning in English:
英語の意味:

Doesn't exist
英語には該当する単語がない

Say Instead:
適切な英語表現:

Music video

Example Sentences:
例文:

My high school students love to watch _MV_ of their favorite idols. My students love to watch _**music videos**_ from their favorite idols.

私の高校生の生徒たちは、好きなアイドルのMV（ミュージックビデオ）を見るのが大好きだ。

No Cut

Meaning in English:
英語の意味:

Doesn't exist
英語には該当する単語がない

Say Instead:
適切な英語表現:

Uncut

Example Sentences:
例文:

This is a _no cut_ movie. This is the _**uncut version**_ of the movie.

これは、ノーカット版の映画だ。

OPEN STAGE

オープンステージ

Meaning in English:
英語の意味:

Doesn't exist
英語には該当する単語がない

Say Instead:
適切な英語表現:

Outdoor stage

Example Sentences:
例文:

They're going to perform the play at the park on the _open stage_.	They're going to perform the play at the park on the **_outdoor stage_**.

その劇は公園のオープンステージで上演される予定だ。

 This sounds like the stage may be open to anyone who wants to perform on it.
誰でもそのステージに立ってパフォーマンスができるように聞こえる。

OFF RECO

オフレコ

Meaning in English:
英語の意味:

Doesn't exist
英語には該当する単語がない

Say Instead:
適切な英語表現:

Off the record, Secret, Confidential

Example Sentences:
例文:

It's a secret. Don't tell. This is _off reco_! → It's a secret. Don't tell. This is **_confidential_ / _off the record_**!

これは、内緒だよ。言わないで。オフレコだよ。

PIERROT

ピエロ

Meaning in English:
英語の意味:

Doesn't exist
英語には該当する単語がない

Say Instead:
適切な英語表現:

Clown

Example Sentences:
例文:

I worked part time wearing a _pierrot_ costume. → I worked part time wearing a **_clown_** costume.

私は、ピエロの衣装を着て、パートをしていた。

POPS

ポップス

Meaning in English:
英語の意味:

1. An extremely casual name for a dad or grandfather
父親や祖父のとてもカジュアルな呼び名
2. To pop is when something breaks with a popping sound (e.g., a balloon)
「ポン!」という音を立てて何かが破裂すること(例: 風船)

Say Instead:
適切な英語表現:

Pop music, J-pop

Example Sentences:
例文:

I love it when _pops_ comes on the radio.

I love it when **_J-pop_** comes on the radio.

ラジオでポップスが流れると、気分が上がる。

This sounds like your dad or grandpa sometimes comes on the radio; (maybe he has a song, or maybe he's a radio host, or maybe he has a commercial)!

貴方のお父さんかおじいさんがときどきラジオに出てくるみたいに聞こえる。(彼の曲が流れるとか、ラジオのDJをやってるとか、CMに出てるとか)!

PUNC / PUNK

パンク

Meaning in English:
英語の意味:

1. *Punk* can mean an inexperienced trouble-maker (often youth causing trouble - this can range from something harmless like someone with a bad attitude to something more serious and dangerous like criminal-behavior).

"punk"は、未熟で問題を起こしがちな若者を指すことがある。これは、態度が悪いだけでそれほど害のない者から犯罪を犯すような危険で深刻な人物まで、幅広い意味がある。

2. *Punk* can also mean a small piece of wood used to help start a fire or light something on fire like fireworks.

火をつけるときや、花火などに点火するときに使われる小さな木片を指すこともある。

3. *Punk* (rock) is a style of music

パンク(ロック)は音楽のスタイルの一つである。

Say Instead:
適切な英語表現:

Flat tire (US), Flat tyre (UK), Puncture (UK)

Example Sentences:
例文:

She had a _punc_ this morning, so she'll be late to class today. She had a **_flat tire_** this morning, so she'll be late to class today.

今朝、タイヤがパンクしたので、彼女は、授業に遅れる。

VOICE DRAMA

ボイスドラマ

Meaning in English:
英語の意味:

Doesn't exist
英語には該当する単語がない

Say Instead:
適切な英語表現:

Audio play, Audio drama, Audio theater

Example Sentences:
例文:

I'm sorry I missed your phone call earlier. I was listening to a new *voice drama*.

I'm sorry I missed your phone call earlier. I was listening to a new ***audio play***.

さっき電話に出られなくてごめんね。
新しいボイスドラマを聴いてたんだ。

WIDE SHOW

ワイドショー

Meaning in English:
英語の意味:

Doesn't exist
英語には該当する単語がない

Say Instead:
適切な英語表現:

Late night entertainment show, Variety show, Talk show, Celebrity gossip show

Example Sentences:
例文:

My coworker loves watching _wide shows_ every night.

My coworker loves watching _**late night entertainment shows**_ every night.

同僚は、毎晩ワイドショーを見るのが好きだ。

WORK, OFFICE, JOBS

24

仕事・オフィス・職業

ARBEIT(O) / BEIT(O)

アルバイト・バイト

Meaning in English:
英語の意味:

Doesn't exist
英語には該当する単語がない

Say Instead:
適切な英語表現:

Part-time job

Example Sentences:
例文:

Some high schools in Japan prohibit students from getting *arbeito* after school.	Some high schools in Japan prohibit students from getting a ***part-time job*** after school.

日本の一部の高校では、
学生が放課後にアルバイトをすることを禁止している。

BLANK

Meaning in English:
英語の意味:

Empty, bare, empty space
空の、何もない、むき出しの、
飾り気のない、空間、余白

Say Instead:
適切な英語表現:

Gap in your resume
A break from, An absence from, A hiatus

Example Sentences:
例文:

I have a few years <u>blank</u> for piano because I wanted to try the saxophone instead.

I ***took a break from*** playing the piano for a few years because I wanted to try the saxophone instead.

まずは、サックスに挑戦したかったので、
ピアノには数年間のブランクがある。

It can be difficult to find a job with a <u>blank</u>.

It can be difficult to find a job with a ***gap in your resume***.

履歴書にブランクがあると、
仕事探しが難しくなる場合がある。

This sounds like you forgot a word... a blank what?
言葉を忘れたの?ブランクって何?。

Buil

ビル

Meaning in English:
英語の意味:

Sounds like bill

bill (請求書・紙幣の意) に聞こえる。

Say Instead:
適切な英語表現:

Office building

Example Sentences:
例文:

My *bill* is really big. → My ***office building*** is really big.

私のビルは、本当に大きい。

This sounds like you owe a lot of money for a bill.

これは、請求書の支払いで多額の借金を抱えているように聞こえる。

How English Speakers use "bill":
英語話者は (bill) をどのように使うか:

Joe: My dad told everyone that you paid for the whole **bill** at dinner. He was really impressed. When did you even pay?

Joe: I "went to the bathroom" but was actually paying the **bill**

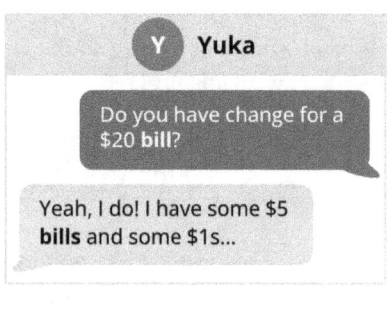

Yuka: Do you have change for a $20 **bill**?

Yuka: Yeah, I do! I have some $5 **bills** and some $1s...

CAREER UP

Meaning in English:
英語の意味:

Doesn't exist
英語には該当する単語がない

Say Instead:
適切な英語表現:

Advance your career, Improve your career,
Improve/strengthen your resume, Beef up your resume

Example Sentences:
例文:

This certification course will be good for your *career up*, especially if you plan to work in Europe or North America.

This certification course will be good for *advancing your career* / *beefing up your resume*, especially if you plan to work in Europe or North America.

この認定コースは、あなたのキャリアアップに役立つ。
特に、ヨーロッパや北米での就職を目指しているなら、
より大きなメリットになる。

キャリアアップ

CONNE

コ
ネ

Meaning in English:
英語の意味:

Doesn't exist
英語には該当する単語がない

Say Instead:
適切な英語表現:

Connections

Example Sentences:
例文:

He only got that job because he had good *conne*.

He only got that job because he had good ***connections***.

彼は、いいコネがあったからこそいい仕事につけた。

COOL BIZ

Meaning in English:
英語の意味:

Doesn't exist
英語には該当する単語がない

Say Instead:
適切な英語表現:

Lighter/cooler/less formal business clothing to save on energy costs in the office

Example Sentences:
例文:

In the past, most businessmen in Japan wore a suit with a jacket and tie. But now, _cool biz_ is really popular, so a jacket and tie aren't always required anymore.

In the past, most businessmen in Japan wore a suit with a jacket and tie. But now, _**lighter/cooler clothing is popular to save on energy costs**_ in the office, so a jacket and tie aren't always required anymore.

昔は、日本のビジネスマンのほとんどがスーツを着てネクタイをしていた。しかし、今はクールビズが非常に普及しており、ジャケットやネクタイが必ずしも必要ではなくなっている。

FOOD FIGHTER

フードファイター

Meaning in English:
英語の意味:

Doesn't exist, but a *food fight* is when people (usually in a cafeteria-type setting) suddenly start throwing food at each other. This is not a usual situation but can happen occasionally in chaotic school cafeterias or in movies.

英語には存在しないが、
フードファイトとは、人々（通常はカフェテリアのような場所で）が突然食べ物を投げ合うことを指す。これは一般的な状況ではなく、混乱した学校のカフェテリアや映画の中で時折起こることがある。

Say Instead:
適切な英語表現:

Competitive eater

Example Sentences:
例文:

> They had *food fighters* at the festival.

> They had ***competitive eaters*** at the festival.

その祭りでは、フードファイターがいた。

 This sounds like the festival had people who throw food at other people.

お祭りで食べ物を投げつける人たちがいたように聞こえる。

FREE

Meaning in English:
英語の意味:

Without any restrictions or cost
制限や費用が一切ない、または、自由に、無料で

Say Instead:
適切な英語表現:

Freelance

Example Sentences:
例文:

He's a *free* journalist and takes contracts around the world. → He's a ***freelance*** journalist and takes contracts around the world.

彼は、フリージャーナリストで世界中の仕事を請け負っている。

FREE ADDRESS

Meaning in English:
英語の意味:

Doesn't exist
英語には該当する単語がない

Say Instead:
適切な英語表現:

Open desk, Hot desk

Example Sentences:
例文:

Our office is *free address* now. Some people love it; others hate it. → Our office is ***open desk*** now. Some people love it; others hate it.

私たちのオフィスは、今フリーアドレスだ。
それが好きな人もいるけど、嫌いな人もいる。

FREETER

フリーター

Meaning in English:

英語の意味:

Doesn't exist
英語には該当する単語がない

Say Instead:

適切な英語表現:

Doesn't have a full time job *(neutral)*
Works part-time *(neutral)*
Slacker, Unambitious (negative)
Doesn't have a "real job" *(negative)*

Example Sentences:

例文:

I had one date with that coffee shop guy. He was nice but seemed like a *freeter*. He had a good education but zero ambition in life; I prefer someone who has some goals and self-motivation.

I had one date with that coffee shop guy. He was nice but seemed like a ***slacker*** with no goals. He had a good education but zero ambition in life; I prefer someone who has some goals and self-motivation.

あのカフェの店員と一度だけデートしたわ。
彼は優しかったけれど、フリーターのようだったわ。
学歴は良かったけれど、人生に対する野心がまったくなかったの。
私は目標を持って、自分から努力する人のほうが好き。

FREEWRITER

フリーライター

Meaning in English:
英語の意味:

Doesn't exist
英語には該当する単語がない

Say Instead:
適切な英語表現:

Freelance writer

Example Sentences:
例文:

She's a _freewriter_. She's a **_freelance writer_**.

彼女は、フリーライターだ。

GUARD MAN

ガードマン

Meaning in English:
英語の意味:

Doesn't exist
英語には該当する単語がない

Say Instead:
適切な英語表現:

Security guard, Crossing guard

Example Sentences:
例文:

My friend worked as a _guard man_ when he first moved to the USA. My friend worked as a **_security guard_** when he first moved to the USA.

私の友人は、アメリカに引っ越したばかりの頃、ガードマンとして働いていた。

OL

オーエル

Meaning in English:
英語の意味:

Doesn't exist
英語には該当する単語がない

Say Instead:
適切な英語表現:

Business woman, I work for XYZ company

Example Sentences:
例文:

My mom is an _OL_, and my dad is a salaryman for the same company.

My mom and my dad work for the same company as **_general business employees_**.

母はOLで、父は同じ会社のサラリーマンだ。

PART

Meaning in English:
英語の意味:

A piece of a whole or a section or portion of something bigger
全体の中の一部分や大きなものの一部分や断片

Say Instead:
適切な英語表現:

Part-time worker

Example Sentences:
例文:

She is a _part_. → She _**works a part-time job**_.

彼女はパートだ。

This sounds like you forgot to finish your sentence... part of what? ⟨!⟩
文を最後まで言い終わるのを忘れたみたい
に聞こえる。……"part"って何の一部なんだ?

How English Speakers use "part":
英語話者は(part)をどのように使うか:

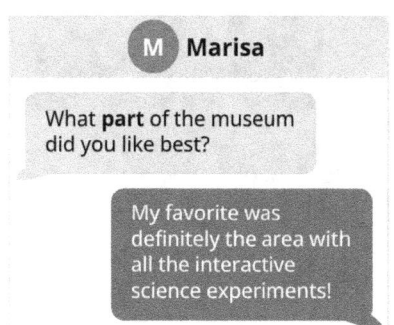

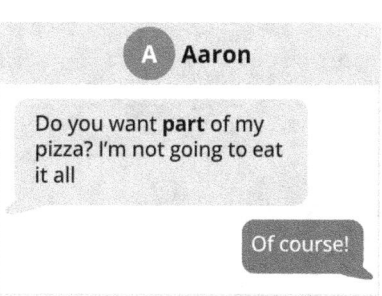

PENSION

ペンション

Meaning in English:
英語の意味:

Money paid by the government or a company after a person has retired or stopped working

退職後に政府や会社から支給されるお金

Say Instead:
適切な英語表現:

Bed and Breakfast

Example Sentences:
例文:

I recommend staying at a _pension_ when you visit Japan.

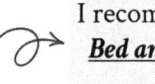

I recommend staying at a _local_ **_Bed and Breakfast_** when you visit Japan.

日本を訪れるときは、ペンションに泊まるのがおすすめだ。

How English Speakers use "pension":
英語話者は（pension）をどのように使うか:

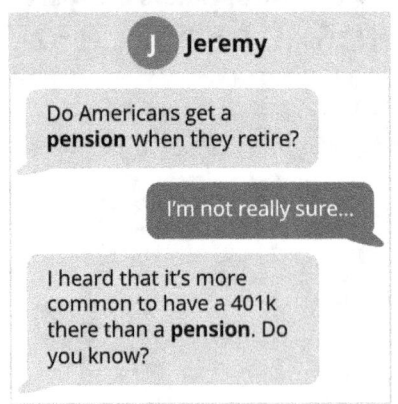

Jeremy

Do Americans get a **pension** when they retire?

I'm not really sure...

I heard that it's more common to have a 401k there than a **pension**. Do you know?

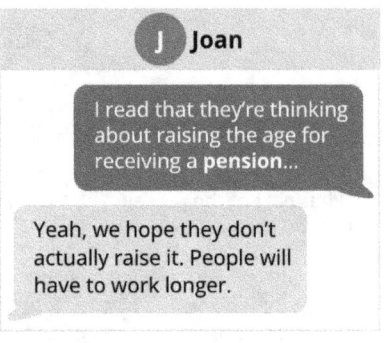

Joan

I read that they're thinking about raising the age for receiving a **pension**...

Yeah, we hope they don't actually raise it. People will have to work longer.

PRESEN

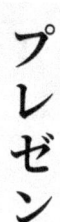

Meaning in English:
英語の意味:

Doesn't exist but sounds like "present"
英語には該当する単語はない
が、"present"に聞こえる

Say Instead:
適切な英語表現:

Presentation

Example Sentences:
例文:

I'm feeling a little nervous because I have to give a big _presen_ tomorrow.

I'm feeling a little nervous because I have to give a big **_presentation_** tomorrow.

明日、大きなプレゼンをしなければならないので、
少し緊張している。

This sounds like maybe you are giving someone a large present tomorrow and feel nervous about it.
明日誰かに大きなプレゼントを渡す予定で、ちょっと緊張
してるみたいに聞こえる。

PRESENTER

プレゼンター

Meaning in English:

英語の意味:

Doesn't exist
英語には該当する単語がない

Say Instead:

適切な英語表現:

TV Announcer, Anchor, Newscaster, Host

Example Sentences:

例文:

He's a really good _presenter_ プレゼンター. He works as a _sports presenter_ 番組の司会 and sometimes gets invited to be the _presenter_ 司会者 at certain sports award ceremonies.

He's a really good **_presenter_**. He works as a sports **_commentator_** and sometimes gets invited to be the **_host_** at certain sports award ceremonies.

彼は本当に優れたプレゼンターだ。
スポーツ番組の司会を務めていて、
時々スポーツの表彰式で司会者として招かれることもある。

PRESENTATOR

プレゼンテイター

Meaning in English:
英語の意味:

Doesn't exist
英語には該当する単語がない

Say Instead:
適切な英語表現:

Presenter, Speaker

Example Sentences:
例文:

I'm feeling a little nervous because I'm the *presentator* tomorrow.

I'm feeling a little nervous because I'm the ***speaker*** tomorrow.

明日、私はプレゼンテイターなので、ちょっと緊張している。

RESC

リスケ

Meaning in English:
英語の意味:

Doesn't exist
英語には該当する単語がない

Say Instead:
適切な英語表現:

Reschedule

Example Sentences:
例文:

We noticed that our Western coworkers *resc* meetings much more often than our Japanese coworkers do.

We noticed that our Western coworkers ***reschedule*** meetings much more often than our Japanese coworkers do.

欧米の同僚は、
日本の同僚に比べて会議をリスケすることがずっと多いと気づいた。

Salaryman

サラリーマン

Meaning in English:
英語の意味:

Doesn't exist
英語には該当する単語がない

Say Instead:
適切な英語表現:

He works at XYZ company.

Example Sentences:
例文:

My dad is a _salaryman_. → My dad **_works for XYZ company_**.

僕のお父さんは、サラリーマンだ。

Salary Up

サラリーアップ

Meaning in English:
英語の意味:

Doesn't exist
英語には該当する単語がない

Say Instead:
適切な英語表現:

Get a raise

Example Sentences:
例文:

I've been waiting a long time for my _salary up_! Hopefully soon! → I've been waiting a long time for a **_raise_**! Hopefully soon!

ずっとサラリーアップを待ってるんだ。今年こそアップするといいな。

SCHEDULE

スケジュール・予定

Meaning in English:
英語の意味:

Your whole schedule or calendar with all your plans in it

すべての予定が記載されたスケジュールやカレンダー全体のこと

Say Instead:
適切な英語表現:

Plans

Example Sentences:
例文:

I can't meet you on Monday. I have a _schedule_. Let me look in my scheduler to see some other options.

I can't meet you on Monday. I have **_plans_**. Let me look at my schedule to see some other options.

月曜は予定があるので会えないんだ。
他の日で都合がつくかスケジュール帳で確認してみるよ。

How English Speakers use "schedule":
英語話者は(schedule)をどのように使うか:

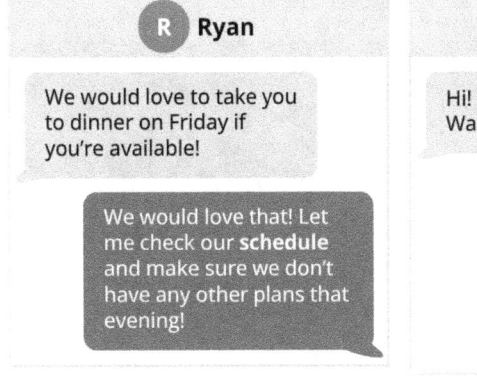

R Ryan

We would love to take you to dinner on Friday if you're available!

We would love that! Let me check our **schedule** and make sure we don't have any other plans that evening!

K Kirk

Hi! You busy tomorrow Want to have lunch?

I'd love to, but unfortunately tomorrow isn't good. I already have some plans, and my **schedule** is pretty full. How about Wednesday?

SIDE BUSINESS

サイドビジネス

Meaning in English:
英語の意味:

A business you own or run that is not your main job in addition to your main job or career

本業とは別に所有・運営している事業（副業）これは、本業やキャリアの傍らで取り組むものである。

Say Instead:
適切な英語表現:

Side job, Second job

Example Sentences:
例文:

> He has a *side business* editing essays for high school students for a local tutoring center.

> He has a *side job* / *second job* editing essays for high school students at a local tutoring center.

彼はサイドビジネスとして、
地元の家庭教師センターで高校生のエッセイを編集している。

How English Speakers use "side business":
英語話者は（side business）をどのように使うか:

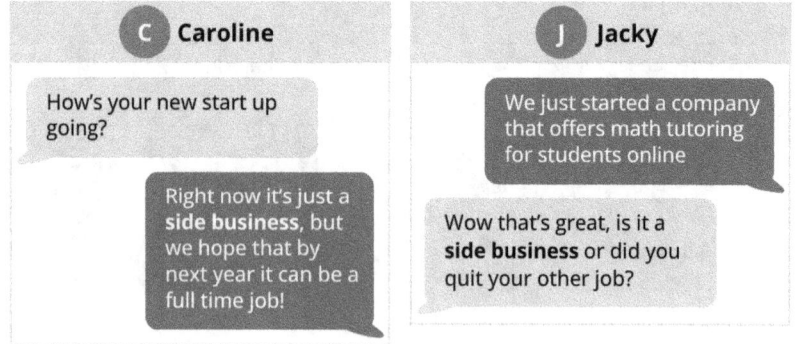

Caroline: How's your new start up going?

Caroline: Right now it's just a **side business**, but we hope that by next year it can be a full time job!

Jacky: We just started a company that offers math tutoring for students online

Jacky: Wow that's great, is it a **side business** or did you quit your other job?

SIGN

Meaning in English:
英語の意味:

1. (Verb) To sign your signature
(動詞)署名する、サインする

2. (Noun) A symbol
(名詞)記号、シンボル

3. (Noun) A billboard or something that gives information (exit sign)
(名詞)標識、案内板(例：出口標識)

4. (Noun) Forewarning or something that points to something else
(名詞)警告や何かが起こることを予示するもの

5. (Noun) Zodiac or astrological sign
(名詞)星座、占星術上のサイン

Say Instead:
適切な英語表現:

Signature, Autograph

Example Sentences:
例文:

| I asked the singer, "Can I have your _sign_ here?" | ↗ | I asked the singer, "Can I have your **_autograph_** here?" |

私は、その歌手に「ここにサインをもらえますか？」とお願いした。

SILVER CENTER

シルバーセンター

Meaning in English:

英語の意味:

Doesn't exist

英語には該当する単語がない

Say Instead:

適切な英語表現:

Job center for senior citizens

Example Sentences:

例文:

My grandpa found an interesting job through a *silver center*. Now he's helping a local gardener prepare and sell some of his flowers.

My grandpa found an interesting job through a ***local job center for senior citizens***. Now he's helping a local gardener prepare and sell some of his flowers.

祖父はシルバーセンターを通じて面白い仕事を見つけた。今は地元の園芸家を手伝いながら、花の世話や販売をしている。

492

STEP UP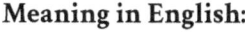

ステップアップ

Meaning in English:
英語の意味:

1. To literally step upwards
文字通り、ステップアップ

2. To rise to a challenge
☞ Example: After the natural disaster, everyone in the community *stepped up* and helped take on responsibilities they didn't normally. Many people spent their free time helping their neighbors rebuild their homes, and others worked overtime so they could help buy food for those who had lost everything.

困難に立ち向かう
例:自然災害の後、地域の人々は力を合わせて、普段は担当していない仕事にも積極的に取り組んだ。多くの人が、自由時間を使って近所の人々の家の再建を手伝い、また、他の人々は残業をして、すべてを失った人々のために食料を買う支援をした。

Say Instead:
適切な英語表現:

Advance your career, Improve your career, Improve your skills,
Move up the career ladder

Example Sentences:
例文:

This course will be helpful for your *step up*.		This course will help you ***improve your skills***.

この講座は、ステップアップに役立ちそうだ。

493

ACKNOWLEDGMENTS

To Tamaki Tiballi, thank you for all your hard work and the hours you put into discussing, consulting, and translating in order to help make this book and its counterpart a reality. Your insights have been invaluable, and this book would not have been possible without your help! Thank you also for your years of hard work at Lauren's Language Lessons as a wonderful Japanese teacher.

To my husband, Kurt Imai, thank you for supporting me throughout this process (again), for believing in me, and reminding me to trust my gut when I doubted myself. Thank you for your extensive help in developing the audio resources for this book, for once again humoring me the many times I leaned over and asked, "Hey, what does this word mean to you?" and for looking through unending piles of variations of layouts, fonts, and photos to give me your thoughtful opinion. I love you and am grateful beyond words to have you on this journey with me.

To my brother, Daniel Green, thank you for your valuable help as audio engineer, for taking the time and effort to clean up all the recorded audio for the audio resources to make it all sound pristine. Thank you also for your and Larissa's valuable input along the way regarding style and design.

To all my Japanese students, past and present, thank you for allowing me to be part of your English-learning experience. Thank you for letting me enter your world, sometimes even your homes and offices, for sharing fresh brewed tea and delicious snacks, and for sharing your culture with me as you learned mine. I am proud of you all for being brave enough to continue learning a new language as adults (or young adults)! It is never easy to learn an additional language, especially English, but don't give up! Remember to never let yourself feel ashamed of your English mistakes. They are essential for your learning and will help you grow if you let them!

To all my friends and students who shared ideas and recommendations of Japanglish words to include in this book, thank you! Your suggestions have made this book better!

To Dr. Steven Turley, thank you for sharing your special expertise in baseball in relation to some of the terminology included in this book and for your general friendship, guidance, and support over the years.

IMAGE CREDITS

The authors and publishers acknowledge the following sources of copyright material and are grateful for the permissions granted. While every effort has been made, it has not always been possible to identify the sources of all the material used, or to trace all copyright holders. If any omissions are brought to our notice, we will be happy to include the appropriate acknowledgments on reprinting and in the next update, as applicable.

Photographs, Images, & Graphis

The following images are from **Adobe Stock Photos**:

Cover (flags): Aroastock; (arrows): wooster; p. 32 (accessories): igishevamaria; p. 33 (suitcase): Coprid; p. 33 (plastic bag): Celeste; p. 38 (hair bands): sasimoto; p. 42 (purse): aneduard; p. 55 (best seller): Suppachok N; p. 72 (bike): thanapun; p. 80 (muffler): sveta; p. 92 (dress): Hein Nouwens; p. 95 (dress): ksena32; pg. 95 (hospital gown): danielabarreto-stock.adobe.com; p. 95 (night gown): vectorikart; p. 98 (uniform): viktorijareut; p. 98 (cables): romiri; p. 101 (swimsuit): Magdalena; p. 147 (fighting): Christos Georghiou; p. 181 (jelly): alter_photo; p. 203 (magician): Ljupco Smokovski; p. 215 (hip): laschi adrian; p. 235 (dryer): BlureArt; p. 236 (flooring): subkontr; p. 249 (veranda): the8monkey; p. 253 (curling iron, crimping iron): GVictoria; p. 270 (consent form): hvostik16; p. 300 (dog): barkhat; p. 302 (ground): Tartila; p. 307 (outside): Stockgiu; p. 310 (sand): New Africa; p. 312 (solar system): sntpzh; p. 313 (summertime): faber14; p. 320 (mail): alestraza; p. 322 (note): sean824; p. 351 (dome): Jemastock; p. 377 (rugby): Redwater Vectors; p. 401 (shipping container): www3d; p. 401 (food container): AlenKadr; p. 401 (storage): Douglas Gingerich; p. 418 (vinyl): hiten666; p. 424 (form): Al Studio; p. 426 (Frankfurt): Serhii; p. 429 (Hamburg): Serhii; p. 433 (suitcase): Pixel-Shot; p. 433 (pencils): Zonda; p. 435 (San Francisco): UVAconcept; p. 468 (punk rocker): Boris Riaposov; p. 474 (bill): Olesia_g; p. 474 (money): あこ; p. 478 (food fight): cartoon resource

The following images are from **Pixabay**:

p. 40 (ruler): ArtsyBeeKids; p. 43 (ribbon): MAKY_OREL; p. 98 (man jumping): OpenClipart-Vectors

The following images are from **Shutterstock**:

p. 20 (plant): Naddya; p. 23 (gym): inspiring.team; p. 27 (minus): G.Rena; p. 32 (phone case): Artem Avetisyan; p. 33 (gift bag): Katerina Maksymenko; p. 33 (duffle bag): gresei; p. 33 (striped bag): AfricaStudio; p. 33 (beach bag): George Dolgikh; p. 36 (earrings): Elnur; p. 39 (bobby pin): ONYXprrj; p. 40 (necklace): Nattika; p. 40 (diamond earrings): Ufuk ZIVANA; p. 40 (leaf earrings): Elnur; p. 44 (shoe cream): inspiring.team; p. 51 (demo): HL12; p. 61 (paper factory): 3D Vector; p. 74 (driver man): Net Vector; p. 74 (golf club): Photoongraphy; p. 86 (rushing): Diki Prayogo; p. 87 (RV): studioworkstock; p. 90 (winking man): Lio putra; p. 90 (sign): infinetsoft; p. 96 (turtleneck): Just Dzine; p. 98 (sweater): Ekaterina Efstathiadi; p. 103 (jeans): nikiteev_konstantin; p. 113 (gym trainer): mentalmind; p. 113 (shoes): Sunny Whale; p. 134 (colosseum): Fourleaflover; p. 141 (viking): YG Studio; p. 148 (goo): WinWin artlab;

p. 154 (mood): mentalmind; p. 168 (cone): nik_nadal; p. 173 (fried potatoes): Mironov Vladimir; p. 174 (punch): Sketched Images; p. 180 (ice): Yeti studio; p. 182 (bay leaves): Natykach Nataliia; p. 183 (left overs): klyaksun; p. 186 (macaroni): Arif_Vector; p. 188 (mushrooms): Andrii Bezvershenko; p. 194 (sweet potato): grey_and; p. 199 (arcade games): klyaksun; p. 218 (liver): WinWinFolly; p. 221 (OB doctor): Fagreia; p. 223 (proportion): kasman vector; p. 226 (sweat): Lio putra; p. 230 (at home): Elena Istomina; p. 239 (my home): Tartila; p. 241 (oven): Inna Kharlamova; p. 245 (stove): Inna Kharlamova; p. 253 (blow): MV stock; p. 253 (hair straightener): Sergiy Kuzmin; p. 258 (lip): Maman Suryaman; p. 260 (makeup): Inna Kharlamova; p. 262 (napkin): mosman.photo; p. 269 (boy): Mashart; p. 271 (crawling baby): tofuneko; p. 273 (ex-lover): Julia Uz; p. 275 (girl): Mashart; p. 283 (sisters): Medivizio by Ann; p. 303 (chick): Veyselcelikdemir; p. 304 (marmot): Eric Isselee; p. 305 (morning): Tenstudio; p. 311 (seal): Elena Istomina; p. 314 (mtn summit): Shirstok; p. 318 (tape): Anton Starikov; p. 319 (mail): Neirfy; p. 323 (printer): nik_nadal; p. 327 (spam): ScottMurph; p. 328 (stamps): Smile_flower; p. 328 (stamp tool): Dodoromeo; p. 338 (coffee kiosk): WinWin artlab; p. 338 (kiosk): Tartila; p. 341 (recycle depository): Lemon Stock; p. 342 (custom made): deepstock; p. 370 (basketball goal): Maxx-Studio; p. 372 (jockey): musicalryo; p. 373 (kickboard): momoforsale; p. 376 (punch): Lio putra; p. 378 (shirt): Nattanopdesign; p. 384 (yacht): Kidung Paripurna; p. 387 (message sign): Sutana4; p. 402 (cooler): nito; p. 405 (jar): Jiri Hera; p. 409 (knives): wordsportrayal; p. 412 (pan): Eivaisla; p. 413 (cooking pot): Jiri Hera; p. 413 (flower pot): Elena Zajchikova; p. 416 (sand bags): pandavector; p. 422 (checkpoint): denisik11; p. 423 (plane departing): ma_Design; p. 424 (house): IGORdeyka; p. 428 (boat): mentalmind; p. 428 (ski gondola): Babka; p. 431 (Kentucky): Ali_A4; p. 434 (cable car): Camac; p. 446 (cameraman): bsd studio; p. 454 (episode): Garno Studio; p. 455 (film): Media Guru; p. 457 (idol): Photo craze; 473 (blank screen): Passatic; p. 485 (presentation): Real Vector; p. 493 (stairs): MAHATHUN

The following images are from **Vecteezy**:

p. 24 (half circle): Hanna Olekseichuk; p. 25 (heading): Muhammad Umar; p. 75 (dumpy car): adem percem; p. 85 (reverse symbol): panom kimsue; p. 88 (shortcut): Saepul Bahri; p. 108 (shorts): Anton Rysak; p. 140 (child measurement): serkan avci; p. 177 (potato hash): Grad Planet; p. 220 (neck): Ivan Ryabokon; p. 222 (pills): HAVID HASANLI; p. 233 (cleaning): gravivector; p. 234 (driveway): The img; p. 238 (mansion): Ashish Biswas; p. 261 (manicure): Dzianis Vasilyeu; p. 267 (toddler car): Idea cena; p. 285 (twins): Millepix Design; p. 312 (solar system): Elena Chernykh; p. 356 (church service): rini astiyah; p. 427 (front): Matt Cole

Other Image Credits:

p. 511 (author photo): Nate Messarra Photography
p. 513 (logo): design by Renee Blodgett

Audio creation: Kurt Imai
Audio engineering: Greenhouse Productions, LLC

BIBLIOGRAPHY

Barton, Erin. "Why Japan celebrates Christmas with KFC," BBC, December 19, 2016. https://www.bbc.com/worklife/article/20161216-why-japan-celebrates-christmas-with-kfc.

"Chilled Coffee Milk Originated in Japan?" J-Simple Recipes, August 23, 2024. https://j-simplerecipes.com/plaza/japanesefoodtips/drink/chilled-coffee-milk-originated-in-japan/#google_vignette.

"CoolBiz オフィス篇 [Office Edition]," 環境省 [Ministry of the Environment], Accessed June 3, 2025. https://ondankataisaku.env.go.jp/decokatsu/coolbiz/office/.

"Frame Type あなたに「似合う」を見つける 骨格スタイル診断 [Find out what suit you with a body style diagnosis]," Pierrot, Accessed May 28, 2025. https://pierrotshop.jp/f/frametype

降矢英成 [Furuya, Hidenari], "ヒステリー(解離性障害) [Hysteria (dissociative disorder)]," みんなのお悩み医学, Last updated March 9, 2022. https://kateinoigaku.jp/disease/200

GaijinPot Blog, "Japanese Apartment Layouts: Terms and Meanings," GaijinPot Blog, July 3, 2024. https://blog.gaijinpot.com/what-do-japanese-apartment-layout-terms-mean/

"キャッシングとは？クレジットカードで現金を借りる方法や注意点などを詳しく解説 [What is cash advance? A detailed explanation of how to borrow cash with a credit card and things to be careful about]," 三井住友カード株式会社 [SMBC], December 11, 2024. https://www.smbc-card.com/nyukai/magazine/knowledge/caching.jsp

"リクルートスーツ(就活スーツ)とは？ビジネススーツとの違い、選び方や着こなし方を解説! [What is a recruit suit (job hunting suit)? We explain the difference between a recruitment suit and a business suit, and how to choose and wear it!]," GINZA Global Style, Last updated June 2, 2025. https://www.global-style.jp/enjoy-order/?p=13237

Hale, Elliot. "Japan's unique tradition of bottle keep, where your drink literally has your name on it," Sora News 24, February 2, 2025. https://soranews24.com/2025/02/02/japans-unique-tradition-of-bottle-keep-where-your-drink-literally-has-your-name-on-it/

山田 ハナ [Hana, Yamada], "あなたはどのタイプ？ ぽっちゃりさん向け骨格診断・似合うファッションスタイリング・髪型(ヘアスタイル) [Which type are you? Bone structure analysis for chubby people, fashion styling, and hairstyles that suit them]," Nissen, Accessed May 28, 2025. https://www.nissen.co.jp/s/smileland/colorear/article/fashion/18122501/

Hirasawa Chen, Namiko. "Royal Milk Tea ロイヤルミルクティー," Just One Cookbook, Updated February 9, 2025. https://www.justonecookbook.com/royal-milk-tea/

金井育子(かない いくこ) [Ikuko, Kanai], "アメリカンコーヒーとは？おいしい作り方・おすすめのコーヒー豆を解説 [What is American coffee? How to make it delicious and recommended coffee beans]," Key Coffee, February 17, 2025. https://www.keycoffee.co.jp/experience/knowledge/detail/american-coffee/#:~:text=アメリカンコーヒーとは、「浅く軽くゴクゴクと飲めます。

いとうみほ[Ito, Miho], "年代別 ギャルの歴史 | 「ギャル」とは何なのか [History of Gyaru by Era | What is a "Gyaru"?]," KLD (Blog), September 8, 2023. https://kld-c.jp/blog/what-is-gal

"クールビズとは？実施期間や服装など社会人が知っておくべき基礎知識 [What is Cool Biz? Basic information that working adults should know, including implementation period and dress code]," Mycard, MUFG, Updated June 3, 2025. https://www.cr.mufg.jp/mycard/beginner/23062/index.html

"クールビズにおける服装の選び方！メンズのおしゃれな着こなしからクールビズに関するマナーを解説 [How to choose your clothes for Cool Biz! We explain the etiquette for Cool Biz from stylish men's fashion]," Orihica, Last updated June 9, 2025. https://www.orihica.com/column/business-casual/cool-biz-male.php?srsltid=AfmBOopQzitnKLMEi7nEsYQV2_Pm_LWUG64fd5syVWuT_BHr6wUVZ-ue

"クールビズはいつからいつまで？期間中の服装やマナーを解説【2025年最新】 [When does Cool Biz start and end? Explaining clothing and etiquette during this period [Updated for 2025]]," Suit Ya, April 27, 2025. https://www.suit-ya.com/column/how-to-dress/when-did-cool-biz-start/?srsltid=AfmBOopxWQijl_-jYo6RePmjheCmO4C_GZPdY2I6TZ-G6xe1seLxelz9

JCB, "Cashing," Accessed June 1, 2025. https://www.jcb.co.jp/cashing/index.html

JP BANK, "キャッシング[Cashing]," Accessed June 1, 2025. https://wwws.jp-bank.japanpost.jp/credit1/cashing/cashing.html

Kaonavi HR Glossary Editorial Department, "シルバー人材センターとは？ 仕事内容、料金、依頼の流れ [What is the Silver Human Resources Center? Job content, fees, and request process]," Kaonavi, Updated June 3, 2025. https://www.kaonavi.jp/dictionary/silver-jinzai-center/#:~:text= 指定は不可-,1. シルバー人材センターとは?,に設置されています。

"ナチュラル・ウェーブ・ストレートからあなたの似合うが見つかる骨格診断によるアクセサリーの選び方 [How to Choose Accessories based on your Bone Structure and find the Hairstyle that suits you best: Natural, Wavy, or Straight]," Novice, March 25, 2022. https://novicetokyo.com/blogs/blog/frametype_accessory#:~:text=What%20is%20skeletal%20diagnosis?,"

工藤 智也 [Kudo, Tomoya], "セミダブルとダブルの違いを比較！ベッドの選び方・サイズ別のおすすめ商品も紹介 [Comparing the differences between semi-double and double beds! How to choose a bed and recommended products by size]," RASIK, Last updated June 7, 2025. https://rasik.style/blogs/bed/47?srsltid=AfmBOookBAyrczZb6Z40jAFK68i1HluO68i58JQZ19DGcJlJoaNr7bxv

熊野 公俊 [Kumano, Kimitoshi], "フリーターとは？ 正社員とのリアルな違いや将来性を徹底解剖 [What is a part-time worker? A thorough analysis of the real differences between part-time workers and full-time employees and their future prospects," The Port, March 19, 2025. https://www.theport.jp/portcareer/article/27505/#:~:text=フリーターは、フリーアルバイター、があるのでしょうか。

"ヒーリングとは？効果やその意味、リラックスに最適な音楽も紹介 [What is healing? Introducing its effects, meaning, and the best music for relaxation]," Mynavi, Last updated January 11, 2024. https://co-medical.mynavi.jp/contents/therapistplus/lifestyle/beauty/130/

"ギャルとは？-由来や特徴- [What is a gal? -Origins and characteristics-]," Galture, Accessed May 29, 2025. https://galture.com/about/about.html

"「スタイルいい」人の特徴や性格的傾向は？ スタイル維持の方法も併せて紹介 [What are the characteristics and personality traits of people with godo style? We also introduce ways to maintain style]," Oggi.jp, May 3, 2024. https://oggi.jp/6786676

"「ヒステリー」とは何なのか、なぜ女性ばかりヒステリーを起こすと思われているのか？ [What is "hysteria" and why is it thought that only women suffer from it?]," Gigazine, October 3, 2024. https://gigazine.net/news/20241003-hysteria-women/

Mok, Charmaine. "Why KFC at Christmas is 'really big' in Japan, as a Michelin-star Tokyo restaurant chef and a cookbook author explain what makes fried chicken great," South China Morning Post, December 22, 2023. https://www.scmp.com/lifestyle/food-drink/article/3245964/why-kfc-christmas-really-big-japan-michelin-star-tokyo-restaurant-chef-and-cookbook-author-explain

"神経症 [Neurosis]," 医療法人 桂川 洛西口 くれたにクリニック [Kuretani Clinic], Accessed on May 30, 2025. https://www.kuretani-clinic-kyoto.com/neurosis/

新田 圭 (ニッタ ケイ) [Nitta, Kei], "フリーターとして働くことのメリット・デメリットとその注意点 [The advantages and disadvantages of working as a part-timer and points to note," Career Research Lab, Mynavi, December 17, 2024. https://career-research.mynavi.jp/column/20241217_89862/

公益社団法人全国シルバー人材センター事業協会 [National Silver Human Resources Center Association], "シルバー人材センターとは [What is the Silver Human Resources Center?]" Accessed June 4, 2025. https://www.zsjc.or.jp/about/about_02.html#:~:text= 全国シルバー人材センター事業協会&text=シルバー人材センター（センター）と、運営をしています。

Orico, "Cashing service," Accessed June 1, 2025. https://www.orico.co.jp/costco/en/contractor/caching.html

ぽんたまん[Pontaman], "【ギャル】を英語で言うと？ギャル文化や語源を紹介！ [How do you say "gal" in English? Learn about gal culture and its origins!]," Native Camp English Conversation Blog, July 3, 2019. https://nativecamp.net/blog/20190703_gal

櫻井 良平 [Sakurai, Ryohei], "ノイローゼになる原因とは？代表的な症状や治し方について解説 [What causes neurosis? Explaining typical symptoms and how to cure them], "こころケア[Kokoro Care], November 15, 2024. https://www.dr-bridge.co.jp/kokorocare/column/neurosis/

"新しいギャル時代の幕開け！「令和ギャル」の定義や特徴とは？ [The dawn of a new era of gals! What are the definitions and characteristics of "Reiwa gals"?]," Galture, Accessed May 29, 2025. https://galture.com/history/reiwa-gal.html

"下着で作る、プロポーションバランス [Creating a balanced proportion]," WACOAL, Accessed May 28, 2025. https://www.wacoal.jp/advice/contents/post-45.html

本田手株 [Toshinobu, Honda], "ネームバリューとは?意味とその効果・高める方法 [What is name value? It's meaning, effects, and ways to increase it]," Kenjans, April 9, 2025. https://kenjins.jp/magazine/company-interview/51955/

"Towel Blanket (Towelket)," Futon Tokyo, Accessed June 1, 2025. https://futontokyo.com/product-category/comforter/towel-blanket/?srsltid=AfmBOoqBFAJn-eqgeqCZwVp1-9RoLRGqHlT54t2WEpIA-k5TRPNU9pK5

"Types of Accommodation," Happy Jappy, Accessed June 2, 2025. https://www.happyjappy.com/travel_tips/types-of-accommodation.html

渡邊 真也(わたなべ しんや) [Watanabe, Shinya], "ヒステリー(転換性障害・解離性障害)[Hysteria (conversion disorder/dissociative disorder)]," 品川メンタルクリニック [Shinagawa Mental Clinic], Accessed May 30, 2025. https://www.shinagawa-mental.com/column/psychosomatic/hysteria/

渡邊　真也（わたなべ　しんや）[Watanabe, Shinya], "ノイローゼ（神経症）とは？うつ病との違いと治療方法 [What is neurosis? How it differes from depression and how to treat it]," 品川メンタルクリニック [Shinagawa Mental Clinic], https://www.shingawa-mental.com/column/psychosomatic/neurose/#:~:text=ノイローゼとは、神経症,説明していきます。

"Which body type are you? We introduce recommended Lolita coordination based on bone structure," Ron Ron, July 6, 2023. https://ronron-lolita.myshopify.com/en/blogs/ronron-column/body-frame-outfit

"夜の社交場「スナック」を英語でなんて説明する？ポイントに分けて説明します!! [How do you explain the nighttime social venue "snack bar" in English? We'll explain it in key points!]," スナック横丁 [Snack Yokocho], Last updated March 10, 2025. https://www.snackyokocho.com/article/8596/

弓削桃代 [Yuge, Momoyo], "コンサバとは？　意味とコーディネートのコツ（イラスト付き解説）[What is conservative? Its meaning and tips for coording it (with illustrations)]," Mynavi Woman, September 15, 2022. https://woman.mynavi.jp/article/200730-5/

ENGLISH INDEX

JAPANESE INDEX

ABOUT THE AUTHOR
創設者・著者について

Lauren is the owner and founder of Lauren's Language Lessons, LLC and has been teaching English for over 15 years. She has a degree in International Studies and certifications in TEFL/TESL/TESOL for teaching English as a Second Language and has taught numerous Japanese students of various ages and levels from a variety of fields and professions.

Lauren is also the author of *Belong with Konglish: A Guide to Understanding Korean-style English and Avoiding Common Miscommunications* and *Wronglish Konglish: A Guide to Avoiding Miscommunications when Speaking English with North Americans*. Lauren is passionate about language and culture and travels every chance she gets. She lives in Houston, Texas with her husband, cat, and dog, and enjoys playing soccer and spending time with friends and family.

　私、Laurenは、Lauren's Language Lessons, LLCの創設者であり、代表を務めています。英語指導歴は15年以上にわたり、国際学の学位と、TEFL/TESL/TESOLの資格を取得しています。これまで、年齢や職業を問わず、さまざまな日本人の学習者の方々に英語を教えてきました。著書には、『Belong with Konglish: A Guide to Understanding Korean-style English and Avoiding Common Miscommunications』や、『Wronglish Konglish: A Guide to Avoiding Miscommunications when Speaking English with North Americans』があります。

　言語と文化への強い情熱を持ち、機会があれば積極的に旅行に出かけています。現在はテキサス州ヒューストンにて、夫・猫・犬とともに暮らしながら、サッカーや家族・友人との時間を大切にしています。

ABOUT THE TRANSLATOR
翻訳者について

Tamaki is a native speaker of Japanese from Japan and currently teaches Japanese as an adjunct college instructor. She holds advanced degrees in language and culture, developmental psychology, and Russian, as well as certifications in teaching Japanese as a second language. She is the author of *Is It Okay that My Child Still Isn't Talking?* a book addressing concerns surrounding children's language development in an accessible and compassionate way. In addition to teaching adult learnings through a college's lifelong learning program, where she offers classes in Japanese language, calligraphy, and Japanese art, she also teaching online private and small group Japanese lessons through Lauren's Language Lessons.

Tamaki lives in Illinois. She enjoys a peaceful life with her husband and two bunnies, cherishing the daily discoveries and joys that come from meeting others and continuing to learn.

　たまき先生は、日本出身の日本語母語話者で、現在、大学で非常勤講師として日本語を教えています。言語と文化、発達心理学、ロシア語の分野で上級学位を取得し、第二言語としての日本語教授法の資格も持っています。また、「うちの子、まだおしゃべりができないのですが大丈夫でしょうか」という本の著者でもあります。現在、大学の生涯教育プログラムで大人向けに日本語、書道、日本美術のクラスを担当するほか、Lauren's Language Lessonsにて、オンラインでのプライベートレッスンや少人数制の日本語レッスンを開講しています。

　たまき先生は、イリノイ州に住んでおり、日々、人との出会いや学びを通じて得られる喜びを大切にしながら、夫と2羽のウサギとともにのどかな暮らしを楽しんでいます。

ABOUT LAUREN'S LANGUAGE LESSONS
ローレンズ・ランゲージ・レッスンズについて

Lauren's Language Lessons is an online language school offering private tutoring and small group English classes as well as lessons in 9 other languages including Japanese, Korean, French, German, Italian, Portuguese, Mandarin, Arabic, and Spanish. Lauren's Language Lessons has taught many students from Japan and has formed both direct and indirect partnerships with several Japanese companies with locations in the United States.

With Lauren's Language Lessons, you can learn English from the beginning, pick up where you left off, or perfect where you are now. All language instructors are native speakers or speak with native level fluency and accent and hold relevant qualifications and teaching experience. Private English lessons are customized to the needs and goals of each student to achieve the best results and can focus on anything including academic English, business English, conversational English, or casual everyday English as well as tailored topics such as accent reduction, pronunciation, reading, writing, listening, speaking, grammar, test prep, cultural fluency, and more. Small group classes on specific topics such as pronunciation and business English are offered periodically throughout the year.

Please visit our website at LaurensLanguageLessons.com or send us an email at LaurensLanguageLessons@gmail.com to learn more!

Lauren's Language Lessons（ローレンズ・ランゲージ・レッスンズ）は、英語をはじめ、日本語、韓国語、フランス語、ドイツ語、イタリア語、ポルトガル語、中国語（標準語）、アラビア語、スペイン語の全10言語に対応したオンライン語学スクールです。プライベートレッスンと少人数制のグループクラスを開講しており、日本からご参加いただいている受講者の方も多くいらっしゃいます。アメリカ国内に拠点を置く日本企業との間では、直接的にも間接的にも語学教育支援や協業を継続的に行っています。

英語レッスンでは、初心者から中級者、上級者まで幅広いレベルに対応しています。講師陣は英語を母語とするネイティブ、またはネイティブ同様の自然な発音で英語を話す言語教育の有資格者で、指導経験も豊富です。プライベートレッスンは、生徒さま一人ひとりの目標に合わせて柔軟にカスタマイズでき、学術英語、ビジネス英語、会話表現、日常英会話のほか、発音矯正、アクセント、リスニング、スピーキング、リーディング、ライティング、文法、試験対策、文化理解などにも対応しています。

また、発音やビジネス英語などをテーマとした少人数制グループクラスも、年間を通じて定期的に開催しています。

詳細については、公式ウェブサイト　LaurensLanguageLessons.com　またはメール LaurensLanguageLessons@gmail.com にてお気軽にお問い合わせください

Other Books by Lauren Green Imai

Hang with Japanglish:
Understanding Wasei-eigo and other Japanese-made English

(For English speakers who are interested in Japanese language and culture)

Belong with Konglish:
A Guide to Understanding Korean-style English and Avoiding Common Miscommunications

(For English speakers who are interested in Korean language and culture)

Wronglish Konglish:
A Guide to Avoiding Miscommunications when Speaking with North Americans

콩글리쉬 잘못됫쉬:
북미사람들과 대화 할 때 자주 할 수 있는 오해를 막아주는 가이드북

(For Korean speakers who want to speak English more like native speakers)

www.ingramcontent.com/pod-product-compliance
Lightning Source LLC
Chambersburg PA
CBHW070902130626
46555CB00001B/6